# Music and the Community

*MUSIC AND THE COMMUNITY*

THE CAMBRIDGESHIRE REPORT
ON THE
TEACHING OF MUSIC

CAMBRIDGE
AT THE UNIVERSITY PRESS
1933

# CAMBRIDGE
## UNIVERSITY PRESS

University Printing House, Cambridge CB2 8BS, United Kingdom

Cambridge University Press is part of the University of Cambridge.

It furthers the University's mission by disseminating knowledge in the pursuit of education, learning and research at the highest international levels of excellence.

www.cambridge.org
Information on this title: www.cambridge.org/9781107445796

© Cambridge University Press 1933

First published 1933
First paperback edition 2014

A catalogue record for this publication is available from the British Library

ISBN 978-1-107-44579-6 Paperback

# CONTENTS

* The nomenclature used is mainly that suggested in "The
Report of the Consultative Committee on the Education of the
Adolescent" (1926). "Senior Classes" means the top part of
elementary schools, and "Modern Schools" means Central
Schools.

# THE COMMITTEE

Opinions expressed in the Report are the personal views
of members. No member belongs to the Committee in a
representative capacity, and consequently no responsibility
for expressions of opinion is accepted by the Board of
Education, the London County Council and other public
bodies because their servants have associated themselves
with this Report.

# LIST

## OF PERSONS WHO HAVE
## SUBMITTED EVIDENCE OR HAVE BEEN
## OTHERWISE CONSULTED

DR R. O. BEACHCROFT, formerly Director of Music at Clifton College.

DR JOHN E. BORLAND, formerly Musical Adviser to the London County Council.

MR JAMES BROWN, B.Mus., Professor at Trinity College of Music.

MR EDGAR T. COOK, B.Mus., Organist of Southwark Cathedral.

MR C. A. ENGLEHEART, B.Mus., Director of Music at Heddon Court School.

MR W. R. FELL, Hon. Secretary of the Liverpool Branch, Music Teachers' Association.

MISS IRENE GASS, L.R.A.M., Assistant Mistress, Preparatory Department of Bristol Grammar School.

DR HARVEY GRACE, Editor of the *Musical Times*.

MR T. MASKELL HARDY, formerly Headmaster of the Bolingbroke Road School, London.

MISS W. HOUGHTON, L.R.A.M., Lecturer in Music at Gipsy Hill Training College, London.

MR H. FAIRFAX JONES, Secretary of the British Federation of Musical Competition Festivals.

MR G. KIRKHAM JONES, M.B.E., Headmaster of the St Andrew's Street School, London.

MR DESMOND MACMAHON, B.Mus., Director of Music at Firth Park Secondary School, Sheffield.

MR A. FORBES MILNE, M.A., B.Mus., Director of Music at Berkhamsted School.

MR P. R. MORRIS, M.A., Assistant Director of Education, Kent.

MR ALEC ROWLEY, A.R.A.M., Representative of the Musical Profession on the Teachers' Registration Council.

MR PERCY A. SCHOLES, Mus.B., formerly Editor of the *Music Teacher*.

MR E. DOUGLAS-SMITH, F.R.C.O., Lecturer in Music at Borough Road Training College, London.

MR C. M. SPURLING, A.R.C.M., Director of Music at Oundle School.

MR H. L. WILLIS, Headmaster of East Lane School, North Wembley.

MR CYRIL WINN, M.A., H.M. Inspector of Schools.

The late MR JAMES BATES and the late MR ERNEST FOWLES also submitted evidence to the Committee.

# PREFACE

The Cambridgeshire Council of Musical Education was formed in 1924, with the encouragement of the Education Authority for that county, to foster the practice and enjoyment of music in Cambridgeshire. From the outset its policy was based on the principle that music cannot take its place as one of the main cultural activities of the community, unless its proper teaching and practice form an important part of the life of every school and of every place of adult education in village and town. In Cambridgeshire the annual Festival of Music has been linked up with the schools and adult education classes for choral and instrumental music, and the Festival has, as a result, shown a progressively rising standard both in technical achievement and in the aesthetic appreciation of music for itself, as well as a marked capacity for corporate artistic effort. But the Council realises that what still remains to be done in their own area—as appears to be the case in other parts of the country—is enormous. The most obvious deficiencies, they are convinced, are due to two main causes—the want of a clearly stated understanding of the true place of music in the education of the community, and the lack of practical and authoritative guidance in the teaching of music in schools and beyond.

With these considerations in mind, the Council decided to invite a fully-representative Committee to prepare a Report. This invitation met with general and emphatic approval, and the Report is now published in the hope that, whatever differences of opinion it may raise, it will be found to be a definite contribution to the cause of national education in music.

The preparation of this Report has occupied several years, and during this period the Committee have observed, with some apprehension, the enormous increase in the *passive* participation of music which has been made possible by the gramophone and broadcasting. The value of these inventions as instruments of musical education cannot be denied, but they carry with them the grave danger that we may become a nation of mere listeners that cannot sing or play an instrument. Neither of these inventions need be feared in a community where by tradition the listeners are themselves also *performers*, in however modest a way. It is the firm conviction of our Committee that *active practical* participation in music, personal and corporate, is absolutely essential to the full understanding and enjoyment of the art, as well as to the part it should play as one of the main elements of a genuine humane education.

The Committee wish to place on record their appreciation of the work carried out by their Secretary, Mr C. Russell Scott, to whose zeal the successful completion of the Report is largely due. The Committee are also indebted to Miss Mabel Chamberlain for her unremitting assistance in the secretarial work; to those contributors, not members of the Committee, who have given valuable help; and to the Carnegie United Kingdom Trust for the generous grant which has covered the full cost of compiling the Report.

E. J. D.

*May, 1933*

*The Committee express their thanks for leave to include in the Report some extracts from articles in* THE SCHOOL MUSIC REVIEW *for May 1930, and in* MUSIC AND LETTERS *for October 1927.*

# INTRODUCTION

To advocate the inclusion of music as an essential subject of education is, at the present day, to beat at an open door. The old barriers of neglect and disdain have fallen and will not be re-erected. Our educational range has grown wider, its aim has grown more liberal and more intelligent; in the general advance music has come to take an acknowledged place, and its progress is welcomed with sympathy and good will.

The door is open; it is for us to enter and explore. To most of us the way is still unfamiliar: we are baffled by technical terms which we have not learned to understand, and by problems of construction to which we do not readily find analogies in experience. The attitude to music of the average listener often oscillates between bewilderment and impatience: a symphonic movement passes over his head as a stream of more or less pleasant sound with occasional islands of recognisable melody which do not endure long enough to afford him safe harbourage. If our music is to hold its place as something more than an amenity or an accomplishment, we must treat it as seriously as we treat literature; and this Report seeks to outline the foundations upon which such study should be laid. Its object is not primarily or chiefly the training of the virtuoso. Some skill, of composer or executant, will probably emerge in the course of school teaching; where it does it can be developed later in specialised colleges or under specialised masters. The principal aim is to establish a general musical culture which all alike, in their several degrees, can turn to account. Music, in short, is treated as a department of humane letters, not restricted to the needs of stage or platform but open to all who can learn to listen and understand.

Such training can obviously begin in early childhood. The love of singing, the susceptibility to simple melody and rhythm, are inherent in almost all children; these should be taken as they come and encouraged and directed to their fullest expression. We hope that particular attention will be given to correct breathing (far more important than is commonly supposed), correct intonation, the use of rhythmic exercises, and above all the choice of the best suitable music for illustration and example. Nothing is more fatal than to "write down" school music to the supposed requirements of young people. The pieces chosen should be short, for a child's attention soon flags; they should be simple, melodious, and easily remembered. But in no case should they fall below a recognised standard of excellence in their kind. They are setting the direction of musical taste in the most plastic years of life, and this cannot be impaired or misled without disaster.

The practice of class singing should begin as early as possible and be continued through the whole course of the school life. To this a daily period might well be assigned: the encroachment on the rest of the curriculum would be abundantly compensated by increased vitality and an improved sense of discipline. The development of the corporate spirit is one of the prime objects of education; it may find one of its most valuable allies in the choral class. A great prima donna once said that "it is impossible to be out of temper while you are singing". If there were nothing else at stake—and there is a good deal—it would in itself be an educational gain.

The age at which children should begin to read music is still a matter of some controversy. Probably the best solution is that, as with other reading, it should be determined in each case by the desire of the child to learn. Both notations should be adopted: the Tonic Sol-fa first, because it is the easier for young singers and because it encourages and strengthens the sense of tonality; the Staff Notation after, and closely overlapping, because it is the current and accepted alphabet of our musical language. At any rate by the end of school life pupils should be able to read music with a facility comparable to that with which they can read a poem or a drama, not only in the sense of playing or singing at sight but of interpreting the text direct from the printed page. This will seem a paradox to those, alone, who continue to regard music as a hieroglyphic mystery, enshrined in sacred symbols which are neither intelligible nor meant to be intelligible outside a narrow circle of experts and initiates. To answer them it is only necessary to translate their view into the terms of any other human pursuit or attainment. Music is a language like English or French or German. Like them, it communicates ideas by means of conventional signs which have to be learned, and when learned can be understood. If we acquire them, and it is no insuperable task, we open for our use a literature of incomparable beauty and value. And if we begin to acquire them in early years, before we have come to exaggerate their difficulty, we have placed in our hands the key of a treasure house which experience will show to be inexhaustible. It may be said that this makes its point by a false analogy: that it speaks of music as a language and assigns significance to its "literature". What does it mean? We are told with at least enough emphasis and frequency that music appeals to the emotions, literature to the intellect; even Burney ("et tu Brute") excuses opera in an unknown tongue on the ground that it is not more irrational than a concert. "It may be asked", he says, "what entertainment there is for the mind in a concerto, sonata or solo? They are mere objects of gratification to the ear, in which, however, imagination may divert itself with the idea that a fine adagio is a tragical story, an andante or grazioso an elegant narrative of some tranquil event, and an allegro a tale of merriment." The answer to all this is a flat denial. Music appeals to the intellect as well as to the emotions, or rather to the whole man as compounded of both. If the eighteenth century really believed that music provided no entertainment for the mind, we need look no further to explain the degradation of its fashionable musical taste. The poetic analogies to which Burney restricts significance are the least important part of the whole matter: they may carry an amusing or picturesque metaphor; they may indicate a point of view or suggest a method of interpretation, but they stop short where the real understanding of the music begins. And if it be asked "What, then, does music mean?" the counter question is "What does this sentence mean?" or even, as the Oxford metaphysicians used to debate, "What is the meaning of meaning?" It cannot be translated into the terms of another medium, any more than, in Professor Tovey's phrase, "you can translate Rheims Cathedral into Greek prose"; its meaning is intrinsic, intimate, determined by the principle of its own structure and the euphony of its own style. In a well-written musical work every part is organically necessary to the whole; we cannot curtail or omit or interrupt without serious loss: and in this matter the analogy with literature is close and exact. The organic principle can be shown in a folk-song as well as a symphony, in a ballad as well as an epic; it is not a question of extent but of inherent vitality. Hence the importance of bringing up young people to the best examples. Their appreciation will at first be passive—almost unconscious—but they will grow to their environment and penetrate more deeply with every enlargement of experience.

The curricula, of which sketches are given in this Report, are suggested rather than prescribed. They form an itinerary of the ground to be covered: they may be modified as occasion serves, provided that they maintain the general principle of organic growth. The course should be graded and consecutive; it should be founded on good voice-production; it should aim at the correlation of eye and ear, partly by musical dictation, as soon as this can be introduced, partly by the progressive study of chosen texts; it should at each stage be easy enough to invite attainment and difficult enough to stimulate interest; it should throughout follow and encourage the natural love of music with which almost all children are endowed. The greatest master of method—the "master of those who know"—has laid it down that if a scheme is well outlined any-one can fill in the details, and that many of these will discover themselves in course of time and experiment. There is a possible danger that some schools may impair progress by impatience, by a desire for short cuts and royal roads: this, at its worst, is better than the old apathy and indifference; it is better still to make sure of each step as it comes and to advance gradually with a definite aim in view.

We of the passing generation have allowed ourselves to be daunted by enormously exaggerating the supposed difficulties of musical study. We are not talking here of genius, which is a rare and unaccountable gift, or of outstanding talent, which involves high aptitude and unremitting attention, but of the ordinary proficiency and intelligence which we take for granted in every other pursuit. If a man professes to be interested in French we assume that, at minimum, he can read it fluently, that he can speak it at least well enough to ask his way to the post office, and that he has, or can acquire, a power of writing it intelligibly. We do not even regard it as a counsel of perfection that he should claim some acquaintance with French history and literature, that he should have heard of the Fronde, and have learned something about the dramatic methods of Racine and Molière. Yet these modest acquirements, which pass without question in the one art, are, in the other, regarded as beyond the capacity of all but practised experts. One eminent man of letters has described as "magic" the gift of noting down a folk-song from the lips of the singer. Another, who is deeply moved by music, has regretted that the printed page of a Beethoven sonata means nothing to him; that his appreciation of it is not imperfect or incomplete but non-existent. Even in public performance there is no certain guarantee. It is not unknown for people to follow a symphony with the wrong score, and one knows more instances than can be recounted of their contentedly missing the first twenty bars without realising that the whole structural significance of the movement is thereby sacrificed.

All this can be remedied, and the surest way of remedying it is to bring up our young people to the familiar practice and understanding of music. Already this is being done: this Report is an attempt to systematise and direct a scheme which is increasingly prevalent throughout the country. The improvement in musical education is having a twofold effect: not only is it good for our music, it permeates and influences every part of our cultivated life. We believe that the older generation will learn from this Report much that is of vital interest and importance; to the younger its value will, we hope, be incalculable.

# PART I

## THE VALUE OF MUSIC TO THE COMMUNITY AND THE PLACE THAT IT SHOULD OCCUPY IN EDUCATION

Music is the greatest of all spiritual forces. Every musician must be firmly convinced of this, even if he has never expressed his conviction in words. The philosophers of antiquity leave no doubt as to their conviction of the spiritual value of the art of music; but later ages, distracted by the complex developments of secular civilisation, allowed the highest aspects of music to become obscured, although the art itself became in the course of centuries ever more skilfully adapted to the fulfilment of its noblest functions. Among primitive peoples—and it is said that there is no race of men, however primitive, which does not make music—the art, whatever technical form it may take, is more intimately and more obviously associated with the intensest of human emotions and feelings. In a state of human society such as is represented by this country to-day music tends only too largely to become a mere matter of business for the professional musician, and for the amateur little more than a pastime, one indeed that receives far less serious attention than many pastimes of little or no artistic interest.

Foreigners have long spoken of us as an utterly unmusical nation. A few generations ago it was true enough that less music was performed in this country than in some other countries. But to-day foreigners are still inclined to pronounce us unmusical, for the very reason that we make too much music. It is indeed difficult to think of music as a vital recreating force when our ears, especially if we live in a big town, can hardly ever escape from some sort of musical sounds, mostly without significance. We have so much useless music in our streets, our churches, our restaurants, and our theatres, to say nothing of the mechanised music which recent years have brought us in ever increasing quantity, that we may well be tempted to regard music as a nuisance from which we are only too thankful to escape. It is perhaps fortunate that most people simply do not listen to the music which they are obliged to hear: that is, they do not listen to it in the way that anyone habituated to good music listens to a masterpiece.

Anyone to whom music is a source of spiritual experience (and such experience, in varying degrees of intensity, is known to many who would lay no claim to be trained musicians) must be shocked at the number of grown-up people in the country who are not ashamed to profess themselves frankly unmusical and indifferent to music. It is a disgrace to our system of education that such people should have lost the chance which every child ought to have, for absolute inability to distinguish one musical sound from another is a very rare form of abnormality in children. "There is no such thing", said the late Sir Charles Stanford,* "as an unmusical ear in normal human nature. Everyone who has a naturally musical ear, or who has had a dormant ear awakened to the appreciation of musical sounds, is capable of attaining the power of hearing music by means of the imagination and the eye." Stanford's ideal, that everyone who is a listener to

* *Music and Letters*, July 1926.

music should acquire the art of reading it silently, may seem beyond the average power of achievement. The contributors to this book point the way to it. Even those who do not succeed in achieving it might at least be taught to listen intelligently, to derive pleasure from music, and if possible something higher than is generally signified by the word pleasure.

The ultimate spiritual experience of music cannot be described in words. The poets have attempted to suggest it, but most of us know that their words, even when they bring us the spiritual experience of great poetry, are but an inadequate translation of the un-translatable. And none of us, however deeply we may think that we have penetrated the meaning of music, can ever know whether we have attained its full significance. It has been said of philosophy that its function is not to provide answers to definite questions, but to enrich our intellectual imagination. It might be said of music that its value lies not so much in the musical works which we accept as masterpieces, nor yet in the acquisition of skill as composers or performers, but rather in an outlook on life which, as we advance in years, we gradually discover to be the result of musical experience.

This musical experience of life is an individual possession; none of us can ever know how far it is shared by any other individual. The same thing is true of all our experiences, when we consider them philosophically; yet none the less it is the desire of most people to help others to enjoy what they themselves have felt to be of spiritual value. The inward life of the professional musician is very far from being an uninterrupted ecstasy; but if he has ever known ecstasy, the thought which upholds him in those moments when music becomes perforce a matter of

professional routine is the remembrance that his experience has given him something valuable which it is
in his power to communicate to others.

Music is something more than an individual possession. If in our own day it has come to be no more
than an individual possession for a large number of
people, it is due partly to the fact that the most popular
instrument is the pianoforte, by means of which one
person can command complete harmony, and partly
to the fact that a great many people are content to
listen to music without taking the trouble to make it
themselves. Such people have cut themselves off from
a larger joy in music, the delight in making music
with others, whether it be in the playing of string
quartets, in membership of an orchestra, or in the
greater community of choral singing. Music made in
co-operation with others gives us not merely the experience of music itself, but the intimate communion
with our fellow-creatures in addition. It is true that
this sense of community may be felt by audiences to
a considerable extent, but the community of an audience is often a mere matter of chance, and in any case
transitory as compared to that of a chorus or orchestra
which rehearses together regularly and feels itself to
be some sort of permanent society.

All over the country we can see musical organisations
of this type, which bring together people of various
ages and different social condition; there is nothing
comparable to a chorus or orchestra for creating a
sense of fellowship among those who in other aspects
of life are unable to achieve it. The contact established
by music is not the mere outward fact of people
meeting in the same room or even of doing the same
thing; the very nature of music and of its technical
details insists upon and achieves an inward contact of

personalities, and a mutual accommodation, a mutual sense of giving rather than of taking, such as no other communal occupation demands in the same degree.

The full experience of music develops along the full experience of life; but as with all the most important aspects of life, musical experience depends largely on early opportunity and training. For that reason alone music may claim its place in every child's education. We must not restrict the training in music to those who show evident signs of unusual musical ability; the same opportunity, and far more patience and trouble, must be given to those who appear to lack that ability, the "dormant ears" which have yet to be awakened.

Teachers have already begun to discover that the study of music is of enormous educational value considered quite apart from its obvious artistic results. Unmusical people hardly realise that the necessary technicalities of music involve the perpetual practice of a number of virtues which it has never occurred to them to connect with the art. The most fanatical disciplinarian could hardly achieve the standards of accuracy, precision, punctuality, and obedience involved in ordinary orchestral playing. Courage, initiative, imagination, sympathy—such things as these are the everyday requirements of the humblest music-maker. It is often alleged that musicians are apt to be narrow-minded and egotistical; it is even suggested that they become intemperate and regardless of moral principle. If it is the fact that musicians are liable to these defects of character, it is due partly to inadequate musical education and largely to the general conditions of social life, for which, in this country, the unmusical people rather than the musicians are responsible. A musician becomes egotistic—he may even become intemperate—for want of understanding and appreciation. He may have his own teachers to blame, if he has learned from them only to handle his instrument for his own private advantage, so that he makes music only for the sake of money or applause; he will certainly have to blame those (and perhaps himself among them) who neglected the opportunity of training others to an understanding of music.

The habit of listening to music is growing rapidly upon us all, the habit of listening to it rather than of making it ourselves. More music is provided than we can adequately listen to, and consequently the habit grows of letting music fall upon our ears without making any effort to hear it accurately and to understand it. It is a good thing that we should listen to music, provided that we bestow our whole attention upon it, and do not allow ourselves ever to regard music as a secondary thing, as a mere background to a meal or a church service. The growing habit of turning on the wireless set or the gramophone as an accompaniment to conversation or on other sociable occasions seems wholly bad: it is bad for the social intercourse, worse for the nervous constitution and worst of all for the musical growth of those present. Real listening demands intense concentration, and considerable mental effort for real understanding. There is much music to which we are of necessity obliged to listen, because we may have neither the opportunity nor the ability to make it ourselves: and indeed, even when we can make the music ourselves, it is a good thing to take the chance of listening to it as well, because we can then perceive aspects of it which we may miss when we are actually playing or singing.

But however deep a pleasure we may derive from

listening, we are losing something which we can only experience from active participation. If we are listeners, we are only receiving, we are creating nothing, we are giving nothing. It may be only to the very few that nature has granted the faculty of real creation in music; most of us have to be content with musical reproduction. But in music, even more perhaps than in drama, every performance, every reproduction, is in itself to some extent a new creation. The printed notes can never represent every detail that was in the composer's mind; even if they could, the audience of Beethoven's day heard his symphonies with a mental background very different from ours, and thus every interpretation of a classic has to be adapted, consciously or unconsciously in the mind of its interpreter, to the particular audience which is hearing it. And so for every one of us who sings in a chorus there is at least some creative opportunity, even in such a well-worn classic as the *Messiah*. We can feel, however dimly, that we are joining in the creation of something, that we are giving something to our fellow-singers and to our listeners, that we are helping others to understand and enjoy that which we know to be the most precious and valuable experience of our own spiritual lives.

It may be only in maturer years that we begin to understand the value of this musical outlook on life; but if we have ever had a glimpse of its value, we are bound to see that the pathway to it is made accessible to the younger generations. If we wish them to face life with better opportunities than we have enjoyed ourselves, we must begin at the earliest possible age to develop their musical faculties. The musical training must not only be suitable to the age of the pupils, but it must be continuous. There must be no risk of a child's abandoning music for other  tudies at a period when the interruption may hamper his musical faculty for life. And in all musical training the ultimate value of music to humanity must be steadfastly borne in mind—that music is to be regarded not as a mere means of earning a livelihood, nor yet as a mere distraction for spare time, but as a guiding principle to regulate and illumine all the activities of our existence.

# PART II

## SPECIMEN SCHEMES OF MUSICAL TRAINING FOR CHILDREN AND ADULTS

### INTRODUCTORY

This Part gives a number of typical schemes of work showing a bird's-eye view of the ground that may be covered in musical education—practicable schemes for nearly every variety of educational institution. In a few cases, however, in which the conditions are especially variable, we have only discussed the contribution which may be made generally to musical education.

It may be objected that what follows savours too much of a series of "model" syllabuses; and that even schemes of work whose lines are broad and bold are of little value to teachers, since, if a teacher does not prefer a scheme of his own invention, he is unlikely to follow someone else's intelligently. As regards the first objection, nothing has been further from our minds than the production of model syllabuses; these are possible and desirable only when uniformity of practice is inevitable, and no subject would suffer more from it than music. Concerning the second point, we hope that all teachers will find suggestive the order of introduction, and the balance of the different branches of training, and many of the special ideas in individual schemes.

The admitted increase of interest in musical education has not been accompanied by a proportionate amount of clear thinking, and the consequent developments have resulted in a general lack of coherence: this position might be held to demand an exhaustive critical survey. We feel, however, that the space available in a Report of this kind can better be devoted to constructive suggestions for schemes of work than to elaborate criticisms of the present position. If this Part affords teachers a fresh point of view from which to overhaul their own schemes of work, time will not have been wasted in its preparation. Furthermore, we believe the schemes to have two added merits. They should help, first, to give head teachers a standard by which to measure the success of the music in their own school or institution. In some cases, even, where the music is particularly undeveloped, the schemes may serve to show the place which music can take in the curriculum, the age at which a particular branch of musical training might be started, and the standard which could be attained at a given age. Secondly, the schemes should help Local Education Authorities, and other authorities concerned, to see that continuity of instruction in various kinds of schools is necessary and how it can be achieved. In this connection it will be noted that schemes do not begin in every case exactly where their predecessors end. The Committee look forward to the day when such neat dovetailing will be possible, but they realise that in present circumstances the ground in the earlier stage will not always have been effectively covered. Account has been taken of this probability, and while the forward view has been kept, provision has been made in the earlier stages of each successive type of school for a certain amount of recapitulation.

The variety of practice due to differences among individual teachers, differences of staffing, in the size of schools and classes, and in equipment, will inevitably lead many teachers to find much of the detail of the schemes unsuited to their own conditions; at the same time the schemes do embody certain broad principles which the Committee would like to see generally applied. On these principles there is indeed an increasing agreement. They may be summarised as follows: Pleasure in music should be the basis of all teaching in the subject, and the environment and experience of the pupils should be taken into account. Since all music is based on singing, singing should be the starting-point of all musical education, and the practice of singing (due care being taken of voices during the period of change) should be continued uninterruptedly throughout the whole of education. It need not be excluded even from instrumental or theoretical teaching.

The best way to get on intimate terms with music is to make it oneself, and singing is the one form of music in which every person is, or ought to be, able to join. Everybody, instrumentalists included, ought to be taught to sing at sight.

Courses in music should be graded and continuous. The foundation of all musical training should be laid in the Infants' School and Kindergarten. The Tonic Sol-fa should be used as an introduction to Staff Notation, but all pupils ought eventually to be able to sing from Staff and learn to do so as soon as possible (see footnote, p. 173, Part V). At the same time Tonic Sol-fa should not be forgotten, for it can be a valuable help even to trained professional musicians.

It is desirable that courses should be so co-ordinated that a pupil leaving one school for another can go on with music at the point where he left off. Since the transition from primary to post-primary education is a vital step in education, it is particularly important that the type of teaching in the post-primary school should be distinctive, though related to the work in the Junior School. The Junior School course (outlined on pp. 24–29 of Part II) should always be completed by the age of about eleven years.

In all musical training the sound should be taught before the notation, and theory should follow practice and be taught not as a separate thing but as the explanation of practical work. It is important that ear-training should be taught by examples drawn from real music.

Children should receive an all-round musical education rather than concentrate on one branch to the exclusion of others. The chief aim of music teaching should be to develop the capacity for fullest enjoyment of music in maturer life, not to ensure the passing of examinations. The teacher should beware of imposing his own taste rigidly on his pupils; varied types of music should be presented, both for practice and for listening. The child should be encouraged to form his own taste, and not to be ashamed of changing it as he grows older. Listening to music is, therefore, of great importance.

These are the principles upon which we hope for general, or at least considerable agreement: we repeat that, except in so far as they incorporate these principles, we put forward the schemes themselves only as specimens—specimens of courses of work that are practicable and at one time or another have been substantially carried out. We do not intend to convey the idea that the work should be done *only* in the way suggested, but rather that each scheme is one of a number of possible good ways.

## 1. *PRIMARY EDUCATION*

### (i) INFANT SCHOOLS

In the following outline scheme, it is assumed that the normal period available is about three years, from the beginning of the pupil's fourth year to the end of the sixth. Where children enter school at three years of age, simple and short lessons can be begun at once, with proportionately more variety and organised movement. A later start at school often implies better previous home training, and it should then be possible to cover the prescribed work in a shorter period. All pupils should, if possible, reach the stage indicated at the conclusion of this section by the end of their sixth year.

#### SCHEME OF WORK

*First Year.* Age about four years.

##### VOICE

(*a*) Some attention to breathing, vocal tone, and enunciation, but no formal vocal exercises. E′ to D a safe compass.

(*b*) The singing of a number of traditional nursery rhymes and other easy songs (see Appendix A, 1).

##### EAR

Review of previously heard sounds in nature and everyday life: development of sense of pace—counting 2's and 3's to music: ear-tests (presented rhythmically), including, as taught, notes of *doh*-chord, in association with words—i.e. *doh soh* to the words "*jump up*", and the crotchet: recognition of difference between single sounds and sound-combinations (melody and harmony): walking and running to music: appreciation of difference between quick and slow, and soft and loud: rhythmic interpretation of very simple songs, and suitable musical compositions for which the gramophone may be used.

### EYE

Staff Notation approached by Tonic Sol-fa Notation (see Part III, 1): *doh, me, soh* on lines: *doh, me, soh* in spaces: the crotchet (*taa*).

*Second Year.* Age about five years.

### VOICE

(*a*) Cultivation of easy, noiseless breathing: gentle development of vocal tone, and natural enunciation of words: a few very simple vocal exercises, principally within the compass of $E\flat'$ to D, and to syllables such as *loo, law,* or *lah.*

(*b*) Singing of further traditional rhymes, and other simple songs (see Appendix A, 1).

### EAR

Memorising a given sound, C′ is suitable (fixed pitch): counting 4's to music: ear-tests (presented rhythmically), including, as taught, *doh′, soh,,* the remaining notes of the *soh*-chord—*te* and *ray,* and the minim: singing upper of two sounds: tripping to music: appreciation of increase and decrease of tone and pace: rhythmic interpretation of simple songs, pianoforte pieces (see Appendix D), and other suitable musical compositions for which the gramophone may be used.

### EYE

Staff Notation approached by Tonic Sol-fa Notation (see Part III, 1): addition of *doh′* with *doh* in several positions: addition of remaining notes of *soh*-chord, *te* and *ray*, and of *te*, and *ray′*: the minim (*taa-aa*): time-signatures (without technical explanation), $\frac{2}{4}$, $\frac{3}{4}$, $\frac{4}{4}$.

*Third Year.* Age about six years.

### VOICE

(*a*) Cultivation of easy, noiseless breathing: further gentle development of tone, and natural enunciation of words: simple voice exercises, descending scales, descending and ascending arpeggios and descending sequences, within compass of F′ to D, to syllables such as *m-oo*, *m-aw*, *m-ah*.

(*b*) Singing of more traditional rhymes and other simple songs (see Appendix A, 1).

### EAR

Further practice in memorising C′: listening for melody in treble and bass: counting 6's to music: ear-tests (presented rhythmically), including, as taught, the remaining notes of the *fah*-chord, *fah* and *lah*, and the quaver: singing upper of two-part music by ear: recognising a note within an octave played with key-note (first lessons in intervals): simple introduction to four families of orchestra and acquaintance with sound of one instrument from each group: phrasing simple nursery rhymes: simple melody making—singing answering phrases (see Part III, 9): smooth and "lightly touched" music (legato, staccato): simple ways in which ideas are expressed in music (by rhythm, as for instance the galloping of a horse in *Wilder Reiter* (*The Wild Rider*) by Schumann, and by *melody*, as for instance the running up and down of the mouse in *Dickory Dock*): rhythmic interpretation of simple songs, pianoforte pieces (see Appendix D), and other suitable musical compositions for which the gramophone may be used.

EYE

Staff Notation approached by Tonic Sol-fa Notation (see Part III, 1): addition of remaining notes of *fah*-chord—*fah* and *lah*: *doh* in as many positions as possible: the quaver (*taatai* or *taté*): time-signature $\frac{6}{4}$ (without technical explanation): introduction to the notation of a few suitable and familiar nursery rhymes.

## (ii) JUNIOR SCHOOLS

Children on completing their primary education should be musically alert, and ready for the further training that post-primary education has to offer. To gain the greatest good from this more advanced work, pupils should be able, by the time they leave the Junior School, to use their voices with reasonably pleasant tone and correct pitch, they should be actively aware of the beauty and variety in music, and be keen to learn more about it; and they should have sufficient acquaintance with notation to enable them to read simple melodies and to understand general references to music script. Then, after a preliminary period of testing, the post-primary school will be able to provide for its pupils, according to its facilities, the particular kind of musical training for which they appear to be most fitted.

In choosing vocal and instrumental music for the Junior School, the teacher should prefer music that will be useful later. Thus, the simplest song by Schubert, or pianoforte piece by Schumann, will be an interesting introduction to the study of these composers' works in subsequent years.

Rhythmic movements should find a regular place in the music scheme, for some children find them the simplest approach to music, and all obtain closer understanding of rhythm through bodily response to music. Boys who do this work with girls in the Infants' School and then drop it would also benefit by continuing such devices as stepping and beating to music.

The extemporisation of melodies should be a feature of the music course. In schools where classes are small the writing of music can be developed from this. Hints upon this subject are given under "Extemporisation and melody writing" in Part III, 9 of the Report, and under "Ear-training in melody and harmony" in Part III, 4.

Periodical grouping of the whole school (or as much of it as possible) for combined singing should form a regular part of the Junior music course, for its influence upon the corporate life of the school cannot be exaggerated; this theme is more fully developed in Part IV, 1, "Music and the corporate life of the school".

The inauguration of class instrumental teaching (see Part III, 10) can be considered in the last two years of the Junior School, but again the general scheme should not be neglected for it. Children should have acquired some musicianship before taking up an instrument, so that the mind may be more free to deal with the problems of instrumental technique.

### SCHEME OF WORK

*Fourth Year.* Age seven to eight years.

#### VOICE

(a) Cultivation of easy, noiseless breathing: further gentle development of tone, and natural enunciation of words: simple voice exercises, descending scales, descending and ascending arpeggios and descending sequences, within compass of F′ to D to syllables such as *m-oo*, *m-oh*, *m-ah*, *m-ai*, *m-ee*, and consonants as they need attention (see Part III, 2).

(*b*) Periodical revision of traditional nursery rhymes: learning of some simple and suitable folk, national, classical and modern unison songs: also rounds (see Appendix A).

### EAR

Further practice in memorising C′: memorising pace—60 metronome—in association with suitable and familiar music: ear-tests (presented rhythmically), including, as taught, the new exercises set under "Eye" in the next paragraph: singing by ear, lower part of two-part music: numbering from *doh* intervals heard within octave: further acquaintance with orchestral instruments (one more from each group): stepping or clapping of time-patterns of simple tunes: melody-making (as third year): simple form—two- and three-part (binary and ternary): difference in sound of major and minor: marks of expression learnt as met in music: rhythmic interpretation, or appreciation without movement, of simple songs, pianoforte pieces (see Appendix D), and other suitable musical compositions for which the gramophone may be used.

### EYE

Staff Notation approached by Tonic Sol-fa Notation (see Part III, 1): all the notes of the major scale, stepwise and with easy skips: *doh* in as many positions as possible: quavers as half-beats (*taatai* or *taté*) in $\frac{2}{4}, \frac{3}{4}, \frac{4}{4}$ music: dotted minim (*taa-aa-aa*) and semibreve (*taa-aa-aa-aa*).

*Fifth Year.* Age eight to nine years.

### VOICE

(*a*) As in fourth year, with additions under (*a*) of vowel practice of long and short vowels associated with words, and some consonants (see Part III, 2).

(*b*) Periodical revision of songs previously learnt, further suitable folk, national, classical and modern unison songs: also rounds and canons (see Appendix A).

### EAR

Periodical revision of C′: memorising pace—120 metronome—in association with suitable and familiar music: singing of simple sequences to practise scale relationships: time-patterns: identifying tapped rhythms of well-known tunes: ear-tests (presented rhythmically), including, as taught, the new exercises set under "Eye" in the next paragraph: numbering intervals within octave from Tonic: singing lowest sounds of chords: two-part ear-tests: further acquaintance with orchestral instruments: melody-making: simple form—combined two- and three-part (binary and ternary): simple introduction to woven melodies (contrapuntal music): marks of expression learnt as met in music: rhythmic interpretation, or appreciation without movement, of simple songs, pianoforte pieces (see Appendix D), and other suitable compositions for which the gramophone may be used.

### EYE

Staff Notation approached by Tonic Sol-fa Notation (see Part III, 1): keys with simple explanation and introducing the sharpened fourth (*fe*): semibreve, minim and crotchet rests.

*Sixth Year.* Age nine to ten years.

### VOICE

(*a*) As in fifth year, with addition of diphthongs and further consonants, and careful increase of compass to include G′ and C (see Part III, 2).

(*b*) As in fifth year with addition of descants (see Appendix A).

### EAR

Periodical revision of C′: memorising pace—132 metronome—in association with suitable and familiar music: further simple sequences for the practice of scale relationships: further time-patterns: identifying tapped rhythms of well-known tunes: ear-tests (presented rhythmically), including, as taught, the new exercises set under "Eye" in the next paragraph: naming intervals from Tonic: singing lowest sounds of chords: two-part ear-tests: further acquaintance with orchestral instruments and combinations thereof: melody-making: simple form—air and variations: marks of expression learnt as met in music: rhythmic interpretation, or appreciation without movement, of simple songs, pianoforte pieces (see Appendix D), and other suitable compositions for which the gramophone may be used.

### EYE

Staff Notation approached by Tonic Sol-fa Notation (see Part III, 1): keys with simple explanation and introducing the flattened seventh (*ta*): dotted crotchet followed by quaver as one-and-a-half-beat and half-beat notes (*taa-aatai* or *taa-até*): time signature $\frac{6}{8}$ (counting two to the bar): dotted minim rest.

*Seventh Year.* Age ten to eleven years.

### VOICE

As in sixth year, with special revision of the song repertory (see Appendix A).

### EAR

Periodical revision of C' and pitching other notes from it: memorising pace—88 metronome—in association with suitable and familiar music: further sequences for the practice of scale relationships: further time-patterns: identifying tapped rhythms of well-known tunes: simple rhythmic canons: ear-tests (presented rhythmically), including, as taught, the new exercises set under "Eye" in the next paragraph: naming minor intervals: singing middle sound of 3-note chord: two-part ear-tests: further acquaintance with instrumental combinations: melody-making: simple form—rondo: marks of expression learnt as met in music: rhythmic interpretation, or appreciation without movement, of songs, pianoforte pieces (see Appendix D), and other suitable compositions for which the gramophone may be used.

### EYE

Staff Notation approached by Tonic Sol-fa Notation (see Part III, 1): simple explanation of clefs by means of the Great Stave and of scale construction:* revision of major keys with sharpened fourth (*fe*) and flattened seventh (*ta*) approached by easy leap: the minor scale (tonic—*lah*)† first without inflections (Aeolian Mode), then with sharpened seventh (*se*): half-beat rest.

* In schools where many of the pupils learn the pianoforte this explanation could be given in the fourth, fifth, or sixth year as considered convenient.

† Some teachers may prefer to use *doh* as the key-note, naming

## (iii) PREPARATORY SCHOOLS (BOYS)

In Preparatory Schools it is too seldom realised that all boys are potentially musical, and the study of music is too often limited to those who on entry already show a marked aptitude for it. This attitude, which has lingered here longer than elsewhere, is to be deplored. Every effort should be made to develop the musical

the notes of the minor scale as follows: *d r ma f s la t d'*. There are three advantages in this: (1) The tonic, or key-note, is still the "firm" note, or note of "repose". In other words, the *mental effect of the key-note*, which is the basis of the Sol-fa system, is not upset. In the *lah* minor the tonic, or key-note, is the "sad" note. (2) The singer is aware of a modulation to the relative major, whereas in using the *lah* minor this is unlikely, as the *doh* remains the same throughout. (3) The *doh* minor helps in more advanced transposition.

To these three points those who prefer the *lah* minor method would reply that: (1) Mental effects are relative, not absolute; in the Aeolian Mode *lah* becomes firm, and in the Dorian Mode *ray* becomes firm. *Doh* is not the only firm note. (2) The Sol-fa singer is fully aware of the modulation to the relative major because of the relation of the notes and the mental effects. (3) Experience in the use of the *lah* minor does not suggest that it is less helpful than the *doh* minor in advanced transposition.

Advocates of the *lah* minor method also see the following objections to the *doh* minor: (*a*) It is not historic. The minor scale did not evolve from the major. (*b*) It is derived from a purely keyboard attitude towards music. It may be an easy method of teaching harmonic minor scales on the piano to tell students to flatten the third and sixth, but that is a mechanical operation and not a musical. The approach to music should always be by the ear. (*c*) Many complications are introduced: for instance, chromatic notes are used as diatonic, and the number of accidentals is greatly increased (compare *l, t, d r m f s l* with *d r ma f s la ta d'* and *r m f s l t d' r'* with *d r ma f s l ta d'*). (*d*) Tonic Sol-fa principles are falsified, and John Curwen's reasoning with regard to the *lah* minor has not been proved faulty. (*e*) *Lah* minor is much easier to teach. (*f*) Difficult music in the minor and such works as modal polyphonic motets and madrigals are simple when read by means of the *lah* minor, but difficult with the other.

faculty in those whose home education has failed to recognise it.

The study of music is an essential part of a sound curriculum. All Preparatory School boys should have the chance of following a broadly drawn scheme of musical education. There is no satisfactory reason why the earlier part of the musical training of many boys should be denied them.

On the whole the function of the Preparatory School, so far as music is concerned, is that of the Junior School and the Senior School to about the age of fourteen, allowing for the differences in organisation which result from there being no change at the age of 11 plus.

Teachers in Preparatory Schools would be well advised to study the schemes outlined for these types of school and to adapt them as far as it is practicable to the conditions of Preparatory School work.

As in other schools, singing should be the basis of all musical training, and all boys should be expected to learn to sing at sight. Preparatory Schools should bear in mind that the musical activities of the Public Schools are limited by the standards they achieve. Despite the immense progress made within recent years in musical education, the tendency is not yet extinct in Preparatory Schools to regard music as something eccentric and hardly normal. The result is that in many Preparatory Schools music is regarded as an "extra", and "music" generally means pianoforte lessons. Preparatory School teaching should aim at sowing the seeds of lifelong enthusiasm for music.

It is urgent that some form of music teaching, such as ear-training and sight-singing, should be part of the ordinary work for the whole school. This training is also valuable, if not indispensable, for boys who are allowed to learn the pianoforte or any other instrument, and it is the only defence which the school has against the parent who is unwilling or unable to afford private music lessons for his son. Where pianoforte lessons are taken, music masters should be warned that boys may become technically proficient as performers without developing any grasp of essentials in music. It is most important to safeguard against this; singing and playing at sight are valuable correctives if taught musically in such a way that the implications of the notes separately, and as a whole, are grasped. This point is more fully discussed in Part III, 6 and 7.

Generally speaking, the Preparatory School should aim at reaching at least the standard indicated by the following syllabus:

### (1) VOCAL

#### (For all Pupils)

(*a*)  Sing isolated notes played or sung within the compass of an octave.

(*b*)  Reproduce from dictation (or sing at dictation) a simple diatonic phrase of four to six notes.

(*c*)  Use the voice confidently and properly.

(*d*)  Sing at sight a simple hymn tune or folk-song tune, and understand the rudiments of music that it embodies.

### (2) HISTORICAL

#### (For all Pupils)

Know something about the most important classical composers, such as J. S. Bach, Handel, and Beethoven, their music and its significance. Only a broad view of these composers' music is needed at this stage; but the ground should be prepared for more intimate study later.

### (3) INSTRUMENTAL

(For those learning instruments)

(*a*) Show adequate technical training. (Scales should be left alone by young pianists and beginners generally.)

(*b*) Read fluently a short piece at sight (from bass and treble with both hands together in the case of pianists) of an easier grade than the last piece learnt.

(*c*) Know simple rudiments necessary for the understanding of the music learnt and its form and modulations.

It cannot be too strongly urged that generally speaking the difficulty of music attempted should be within the child's intellectual or imaginative grasp.

## 2. *POST-PRIMARY EDUCATION*

### (i) SENIOR CLASSES AND MODERN SCHOOLS

The general organisation of Senior Classes and Modern Schools allows for three- or four-year courses, and the scheme of work for music should be planned accordingly. In the larger schools there will be more than one class doing each year's work, in which case there will be parallel courses, say, slow and fast, or slow, medium and fast.

We do not propose to give three different schemes for three possible parallel groupings, as these groupings would be made on educational grounds not concerned with music; but some modification would have to be made in the music scheme to suit the requirements of whatever parallel classes there may be.

In the general work of the school, the slow and

medium courses will probably include a greater proportion of practical work, and the faster course will be more literary. Children taking the former courses may go less far in the study of the theory and literature of music than those taking the latter course, and they would then have more singing, dancing, and listening to music. This merely indicates one direction in which parallel courses can differ. To make the modification possible, classes doing the same year's work must be taken separately.

The voice, ear and eye-training of the Junior School should be continued in the Senior School (see Part III, various sections), but it will now be possible to do the work as part of a wider scheme that will include appreciation and history. The scheme given below could be used to supply the *subject foundation* of each lesson, and so implant that historical and appreciative interest in music which is most likely to last beyond the child's school life. It must never be forgotten, however, as we stress elsewhere in the Report (see Part I, p. 15) that the only satisfactory approach to an ultimate understanding of music is by learning to make it in one way or another. A scheme such as this ensures that the children know they are following a definite line of work covering the whole ground of music; thus the weakness of many otherwise admirable schemes, that they give the children no sense of continuity, is avoided. The practical work is given as much attention as ever, but it is fused here with the historical, and there is no danger that the work will follow haphazard lines. An idea of the method can be gathered from the following particulars of the work for a typical set of lessons, to which perhaps a month could be devoted. The whole of the scheme is meant to be conducted on these lines.

## LESSONS ON THE GERMAN CHORAL
### *See First Year's Course*

(These lessons should be correlated with history and literature.)

The choral arose from the desire of Luther and his adherents that the congregation should take a more active part in church service than was customary in the Mediaeval Church, which largely depended upon the clergy and choir for its music.

The Lutheran Gospel became popular because it was sung in the vernacular, and because the tunes used were either already popular or were composed in a popular vein.

Among the tunes so used,* which can be sung by the class, were:

(*a*) Carols and songs from Mystery plays:

*Good Christian Men, Rejoice* (the well-known tune); *Who is He, in yonder stall?* (612); *A great and mighty wonder* (19); *What star is this?* (44).

(*b*) Familiar Latin hymns, translated into German and their plain-chant adapted to the rhythm of the translation:

*Come, Holy Ghost* (153) plain-song and metrical version.

(*c*) Folk-tunes and traditional melodies:

*The duteous day now closeth* (278), once *O world, I must forsake thee*, but originally a journeyman's song *Innsbruck, I must forsake thee*, the tune being ascribed to Izaak. For an English parallel see *Soul of Jesus* (89),

* To show how easy of access the material for lessons can be, we shall draw upon one book only, *The English Hymnal*, for our illustrations. The numbers in brackets refer to hymns in that collection. Other hymn books might serve equally well.

an adaptation of a sixteenth-century Morris, now sung as *The Maypole*.

(*d*) Original tunes composed in the spirit of the changing times:

*A safe stronghold* (362); *Sing praise to God* (478); *Great God, what do I see and hear!* (4). It is said that Luther composed these tunes himself. Among later additions to German choral song are the beautiful chorals: *Wake, O wake!* (12) by Nicolai; *O sacred head* (102) by Hassler —now called the Passion Choral, although in its original metre it was a love ditty; *Now thank we all our God* (533) and *Ah, holy Jesu* (70), both by Cruger; *O Lord of hosts* (458) by Neumark.

Pupils should notice that the choral has the metrical rhythm of such simple poetry as was being shaped in Germany during the Middle Ages. The melodies were at first given to the tenor part when they were harmonised. Afterwards, in order to be more audible, and in accordance with a growing practice in connection with secular song, the tunes were placed in the treble. For English contemporary examples showing this procedure see hymns 267 and 3 by Tallis. Note also hymn 365, Dowland's version of the *Old Hundredth*, a French tune originally used for Beza's metrical translation of Psalm 134 for the Genevan Psalter, but later sung in England to *All people that on earth do dwell*, the hundredth Psalm. Both arrangements of each tune are given. All the chorals learnt at various times for these lessons are in common use to-day, and most of them will be required for subsequent lessons. It can be shown from the hymn-book versions that Bach harmonised the chorals in a contrapuntal manner now considered especially effective for this type of hymn

Great care should be taken that the lessons do not become lectures. The pupils should sing the musical examples themselves, and this will keep up practice in sight-reading and in proper voice-production. The examples can also be used to furnish exercises in ear-training, and to illustrate the principles of form and harmony in so far as it is thought desirable to teach them.

As a sequel to the lessons, the children can be shown the use by later composers of some of the chorals we have mentioned; by Bach in his choral preludes, his cantatas, especially *Wake, O wake* and *A safe stronghold*, his *Christmas Oratorio*, and his *St Matthew Passion* and *St John Passion*; by Mendelssohn in *St Paul* and the two *Hymns of Praise*. It should be pointed out that Luther's *A safe stronghold* is introduced in Mendelssohn's *Reformation* Symphony and in Meyerbeer's *The Huguenots* as an historical allusion.

Examples illustrating this use of the choral should be played, and the attention of the pupils should be drawn to the regular performance of several of these works by the British Broadcasting Corporation.

### SCHEME OF WORK

We outline a "medium" course of instruction which can be modified on fast or slow lines. We assume that, at least, the equivalent of two half-hour periods each week will be devoted to actual music teaching in every class, and that there will be additional opportunities for listening to music.

So far as possible, the musical illustrations to every lesson should be sung. Even orchestral and other concerted works, to which the pupils must inevitably listen, will be found to contain themes best remembered by being sung. Appendix E gives lists of books which can be studied in connection with the scheme.

## First Year: Song and Song Writers

A background of knowledge upon which modern music relies for its interpretation and understanding. Primitive Song—Music of the Ancient Nations—The Rise of Plain-song—Early Folk-Music and Carols—The Minstrelsy of the Middle Ages—The German Choral—The Story of Song Accompaniments—The Art Song.

## Second Year: Oratorio Music and Musicians

Early Ceremonial Music—The Mediaeval Dramas on Sacred Subjects—The Invention of Recitative—The First Oratorio—The Italian School—The Rise of the German School and Use of the Choral—Sacred Music and Instrumentation—Modern Oratorio.*

## Third Year: Opera and its Composers

Early Dramatic Entertainments with Music—The Invention of Recitative—The First Opera—The Development of Italian Opera, *seria* and *buffa*—The Rise of French Opera—The Masque and English Opera—The Growth of Abuses; the Introduction of Reforms—German Opera—Modern Opera.†

* As a class-room lesson, an oratorio can be presented by interspersing an account of the story with solos and choral numbers. Gramophone records may be used, but solos and other items within the competence of the pupils should be learnt and sung. When an oratorio is being taken, teachers might prepare booklets from which the children could sing the themes of the choruses and instrumental movements, if there are any suitable for this treatment.

† For class-room purposes, an opera can be presented in the same way as an oratorio. The story, told dramatically, should link up the extracts which have been learnt. A more elaborate performance can include contributions by individual members of the class. In the case of *Tannhäuser*, for instance, an instructive class-room performance can be extemporised by the use of the following: Hymn to Venus, Wolfram's welcome to Tannhäuser,

*Fourth Year: Instrumental Music and its Development*

Primitive Instruments and their Use—Early Dance Music—The Ancient Suite—The Development of Chamber Music—The Growth of the Orchestra—Modern Instrumental Music, the Suite, Sonata, Quartet, etc., Symphony and Tone Poem.

Besides working to a syllabus, Senior Classes and Modern Schools should practise music in many less formal ways.

Schools might have a piece of music sung or played every morning at the opening of the session. With class-room doors thrown open a whole school could combine without being dependent upon a hall. In schools where a full assembly is held daily there will be many opportunities for mass singing and mass listening, and there will be scope for a school choir and orchestra (see Part III, 15 and 16, and Part IV, 1).

Schools adopting the House System can form Singing Guilds, Gramophone Clubs, etc., and arrange inter-House activities similar to those mentioned in the syllabuses for Secondary Schools and Public Schools (Part II, 2 (ii) and (iii)).

Concerts and musical plays given by school choirs can be valuable extensions of the music scheme. They do much to interest parents and the general public in educational matters. These functions can range from simple displays of folk-music and folk-dancing to staged performances of classical ballets and operas. They are most commendable when they are the natural outcome of work actually done in the class-

Pilgrims' Chorus, the March, items from the Tournament of Song, Elizabeth's Prayer, O Star of Eve, Tannhäuser's song relating his failure at Rome, and a gramophone reproduction of the Overture. The characters can act their parts even if the "Pilgrims" go to Rome only by walking down the corridor.

rooms. Money raised by concerts and staged plays should be used to improve their quality and not for other purposes.

Every interest likely to further musical training should be developed, and the syllabuses given in this Report for other types of school will provide teachers with suggestions which can be adapted in Modern Schools. Attention is also directed to *Concerts for Children* (Part IV, 2) and *Musical Festivals and Competitions* (Part IV, 6).

## (ii) SECONDARY SCHOOLS

The musical activities of the school fall roughly into two groups, (1) *lessons* in which a definite sequence of work is taken, and (2) *general activities*, some of which will naturally be voluntary.

(1) (*a*) Among the courses of *lessons* an important place should be given to aural training, which includes sight-singing, musical dictation, counterpoint, harmony, extemporising, analysis, etc. (30–40 minutes a week).

(*b*) The *Choral Work* has as its starting-point the *Song* classes (20–30 minutes a week), where in the early stages folk and national songs are taken. Later on the work should include classical songs and a certain amount of modern music. Unison songs should be the rule for the younger pupils, but two- and three-part songs should be taken later. In these classes the aim is a general knowledge of song literature rather than a detailed knowledge of a restricted group of songs.

Simple exercises in *Voice-Production* should be given at the beginning of each lesson (see Part III, 2). It is important to avoid strain on the voice when it is "changing" (see Part III, 3).

The more musically gifted pupils will probably form a special *Choir*, which will lead the hymn singing at prayers and add "descants" from time to time to the better known tunes.

The whole school should occasionally take part in *Community Singing*.

(c) *History of music*: this is discussed in Part III, 8. It may be mentioned that the Music Club referred to later (p. 42) provides an occasion for additional work of this sort.

(d) A certain amount of *correlation* is possible between the history and literature lessons of the general school course and musical history and musical literature. The pupils will have a new view of the lives and works of the great musicians when they hear of them in some of their other lessons (see Part III, 13).

(e) The work done in the ear-training classes should be supplemented, for pupils in the School Certificate classes, by further instruction in harmony, counterpoint, musical form and the history of music. This course would be partly dependent on the current examination syllabuses.

(f) The *Instrumental* work may begin with class lessons for small groups of pupils. From the beginning stress should be laid on the importance of *Sight-Reading*, the foundation for which will have been assured by the work done in the ear-training classes. Each teacher of an instrument should be responsible for the application of this work to the needs of the instruments. There should be a Sight-Reading Library, containing sets of graded books of examples. A small subscription of 3*d*. or 4*d*. a term from each pupil who learns an instrument will be enough to keep the library well stocked and up to date. For suitable graded Sight-Readers for the Pianoforte, see Appendix D, section xi.

(*g*) The school *Orchestra* should take an important part in school functions, and every pupil who learns a suitable instrument should be encouraged to join the orchestra, in however humble a capacity

(*h*) In some schools it is possible to arrange classes in *Dalcroze Eurhythmics*, which are very useful in the musical development of a pupil, especially if such development tends to be slow.

(2) We now come to the *general musical activities* of the school.

(*a*) From time to time recitals of vocal and instrumental music should be given by the pupils. It is a good plan to arrange these so that the *average* pupil has an opportunity to add something to the general enjoyment. Some schools are tempted to reserve this privilege for the better performers, with the result that a valuable stimulus and a useful piece of training are lost for the others.

(*b*) A short *Demonstration* of aural work is welcomed with keen interest by the pupils, provided the standard of the work shown is not too high. Children may feel nervous at the idea of singing melodies at sight, or doing dictation and improvising in public. But if they know beforehand that the examples chosen will be of the easier types which they have been studying they will rise to the occasion.

(*c*) Simple *Incidental* music for school plays can be composed by the more ambitious pupils: it should be carefully corrected by the teacher before it is performed in public, or a false standard will be created in the minds of the young hearers.

(*d*) The *Music Club* can be of the greatest possible use in stimulating a general interest in music. A member of the school staff provides a short "popular" lecture on a great musician. Illustrations of his work are then given by the pupils, including a performance by the school orchestra.

(*e*)  *Competitions* are a useful adjunct to the musical life, provided the preparation does not interfere with the ordinary work of the school. Care should be taken that too much effort does not fall on individual pupils through their having to compete too often.

(*f*)  *An occasional lecture or recital by outside musicians* will be warmly appreciated by the whole school, including the staff. A "new voice" produces a special impression and leaves a definite memory in the minds of the hearers.

(*g*)  The possibility of *Visits to outside Concerts, Operas, Lectures, etc.*, will vary according to locality. In large towns there are many opportunities for school parties to go to musical "treats".

### Scheme of Work

The courses referred to by *Stages* in this scheme of work are fully described under "Ear-training in melody and harmony" (Part III, 4), and "Extemporisation and melody-writing" (Part III, 9).

*First Year.*  Age eleven to twelve years.

#### SIGHT-SINGING

As the major keys should have been thoroughly dealt with in the Junior School the chief part of the work will now be the minor keys. Before the end of the year two-part singing will be begun.

#### DICTATION

Stage III of the course given in Part III, 4 belongs to this grade of work, i.e. the dictation of four-bar phrases in minor keys and simple two-part dictation. Later on, the three-part chord is taken. All this work is taken on a vocal basis (Par. 2 of Stage I in Part III, 4).

### EXTEMPORISATION AND COMPOSITION

If the pupils have had plenty of practice in the vocal extemporisation of 16-bar phrases, with primary modulations, they will now be ready for Stage II of the course given in Part III, 9. Stage III may also be taken during the year. The work will thus include simple pianoforte accompaniments to vocal melodies. At the same time the "wild flowers" of extemporisation will gradually develop into the "garden flowers" of composition.

*Second Year.* Age twelve to thirteen years.

### SIGHT-SINGING

Part-singing in two or three parts, with occasional practice in more difficult unison exercises.

### DICTATION

Stage IV (Part III, 4) is taken, i.e. four-part chords, with revision of previous work.

### EXTEMPORISATION AND COMPOSITION

Stage IV (Part III, 9), i.e. the Classical Dance Suite, together with free improvising. The greater part of the work is still vocal, with pianoforte accompaniment. Simple compositions are written, chiefly founded on the suite form.

*Third Year.* Age thirteen to fourteen years.

### SIGHT-SINGING

More advanced examples of the work for pupils aged twelve to thirteen.

### DICTATION

Stage V (Part III, 4), i.e. dictation of "mixed" phrases. Deduction of chords from a given note outside the chord.

### EXTEMPORISATION AND COMPOSITION

Stage V (Part III, 9), i.e. work in irregular rhythms, both in extemporisation and composition. Extemporising on a given theme.

*Fourth Year.* Age fourteen to fifteen years.

### SIGHT-SINGING

More advanced work of the type above.

### DICTATION

Stage VI (Part III, 4), i.e. phrases similar to those found in the Classical Dance Suites.

### EXTEMPORISATION AND COMPOSITION

Stage VI (Part III, 9), i.e. simple pianoforte or string extemporisation. Vocal extemporisation above or below a given *canto fermo*.

*Fifth and subsequent years.* Age over fifteen years.

A solid basis of elementary musicianship has now been laid. Beyond this stage all that is needed is further practice in different varieties of the work sketched above.

## (iii) PUBLIC SCHOOLS

### Scheme of Work

#### (1) INSTRUMENTAL TEACHING.

Facilities should be provided for the teaching of pianoforte, organ, all stringed and wind instruments and solo singing in an adequately equipped Music School. Not less than two lessons a week, each of twenty minutes, should be given. Under modern conditions the time available for practice is necessarily limited, but speaking generally very few boys should finish their Public School musical career without sufficient enthusiasm and technical equipment to continue the study of their instrument with advantage when they leave. It should be possible to allot two school periods a week for music. Half of each period would be spent at the lesson and half at practice. Apart from this allowance all lessons and practice would take place in a boy's spare time.

The general standard of attainment in the school instrumental training would be brought to the notice of the school each year in the Inter-House Competitions.

#### (2) CLASSES.

(a) The lower forms, at least, should be allotted two school periods a week for music. Sight-singing, voice-production, and the learning of unison and part-songs should form part of this scheme, and the opportunity should be taken to impart as much general knowledge as possible, using the class as a training ground for good listeners and critics as well as for proficient choral singers.

(b) A voluntary singing class for broken voices once a week, to learn the main principles of voice-production. If the average age of this class is sixteen, it will serve as a nursery for recruits for chapel choir and choral society, and discover exceptional voices; these should have individual training.

(3) SOCIETIES.

(*a*) *Chapel Choir* should be specially selected for vocal quality and musicianship. Sectional practices for trebles and altos, and tenors and basses, and at least one full practice each week.

(*b*) *Choral Society*: the chapel choir would form the nucleus of this society, to which may be added practically any boy who is keen to practise part-singing, provided a suitable balance of parts is kept. Not less than one hour a week to be devoted to some choral work or works with a view to end-of-term performances before the school.

(*c*) *School Glee Party*: a very small and carefully selected group of singers who can be easily assembled at odd times for the practice of glees and part-songs to supplement concert programmes. A party of whom a really high standard of performance would be expected.

(*d*) *Orchestra*: boys who have attained a certain proficiency in the playing of stringed and wind instruments should be admitted as vacancies occur. Not less than one hour a week to be devoted to orchestral music with a view to end-of-term performances.

(*e*) *String and Wood-wind Ensembles*: weekly practices for the more efficient performers.

(4) COMPETITIONS.

These may be instrumental and choral, and should be annual Inter-House events. They serve chiefly to increase activity in practice, to stimulate initiative in the training of vocal parties without professional help, and to indicate to the whole school the work and progress of the music school.

## (5) GENERAL.

The general musical education of the whole school can be fostered in various ways by an active and ingenious music master. The following are the most usual and practicable methods:

(*a*) *Gramophone Club*: which affords limitless opportunity for hearing the best music under informal conditions, when explanations can be given.

(*b*) *Sing-songs*: another informal affair in which the whole school may share in choruses or complete songs, with opportunities for instrumental items between the songs.

(*c*) *Professional Concerts*: three or four a term according to the funds available. A full orchestral concert at least once a year for which some special preparation would be made by lecture.

(*d*) Other informal concerts as talent and opportunity are available.

(*e*) Regular musical lectures with illustrations.

Music masters at Public Schools should keep a very careful watch over the one or two individual boys who show an exceptional talent for music, and may eventually proceed to a musical degree at the University with a view to making music their life's work. Parents are not always sympathetic to such ambitions. Yet the history of music provides many examples of great composers who took up music against the wishes of their parents, and the recent history of English music shows that several musicians of high distinction have come from the Public Schools.

## 3. *SMALL SCHOOLS*

COVERING *PRIMARY*: (i) INFANT SCHOOLS,
(ii) JUNIOR SCHOOLS; AND *POST-PRIMARY*:
SENIOR CLASSES

The class of wide age-range, common in small schools, calls for special planning. Class singing is the easiest branch of music in the circumstances, and can be the continuous and connecting part of the music course. Care must be taken that the younger pupils do not sing too loudly in an endeavour to equal the older ones. The most convenient arrangement of the class is to have the several groups massed together, from back to front of the room, the juniors on the left, the intermediate group in the middle, and the seniors to the right. Variety can be secured if the different groups perform specially allocated verses. For rounds and canons, the class is better divided from side to side, so that in each part there are some singers from each group; the quality of tone is then more equal. If part-songs are sung, the youngest children are best placed in the treble group. Hints on the choice of songs are given in Part III, 15.

In the other branches of music, the successful working of a progressive course is extremely difficult, if not impossible; either some pupils are obliged to take a section of the syllabus several times, or others must omit it altogether. Since progressive grading is essential for subjects like ear-training and sight-singing, some different procedure must be adopted.

The plan of working short courses in sequence is one worth considering. This allows a subject to be taken progressively, though there will be lapses of time between the end of one section and the beginning of the next. Briefly, the plan is to choose as many courses as there are age groups in the class. For example, the whole school is divided into three classes, respectively (1) the Infants' School (ages 3–6 years), (2) the Junior School (ages 7–10 years), and (3) the Senior School (ages 11–14 years). The school life is divided into ten years, of which three are spent in the Infants' class, four in the Junior class, and three in the Senior class. Ignoring for the moment the extra year in the Junior school, there will be three periods of three years. Three courses can therefore be arranged:

COURSE (1).

*Ear and Eye-training* (rhythm and melody only): divided into three graded periods: (*a*) to be taken in the *Infants' class*, (*b*) in the *Junior class*, (*c*) in the *Senior class*. Reference can be made to Part II, 1 (i) and (ii) of the Report, from which the items bearing upon rhythm and melody should be taken. The ground covered will vary, but an effort should be made to reach at least the end of the Junior School course.

COURSE (2).

*Musical Appreciation*: (*a*) *Infants' class*: through rhythmic movements; (*b*) *Junior class*: through history (see Appendix E, 11) and some rhythmic movements. (*c*) *Senior class*: through either the course *Oratorio Music and Musicians* or *Opera and its Composers*, or a short review of the two (Part II, 2 (i)).

COURSE (3).

*Miscellaneous*: (*a*) *Infants' class*: first section of ear-training (Harmony and Instruments of the Orchestra) and rhythmic movements; (*b*) *Junior class*: second section of ear-training (Harmony and Instruments of the Orchestra) and rhythmic movements; (*c*) *Senior class*: Instrumental Music and its Development (Part II, 2 (i)), or The Development of Instrumental Music from the Dance (Part II, 5 (i)), illustrated by dancing where possible.

For (*a*) and (*b*) the portions from Part II, 1 (i) and (ii) which deal with Harmony and Instruments of the Orchestra can be taken.

The extra year in the Junior School could be used for repeating with different illustrations any one of the three Junior School courses, at the discretion of the teacher or by the vote of the children; *or* for the construction and playing of primitive musical instruments (see Appendix E, 2).

The arrangement of the scheme may be seen by following a child through the school. His courses could be as follows: *First Year*: Course (1) (*a*) (see tables above); *Second Year*: Course (2) (*a*); *Third Year*: Course (3) (*a*); *Fourth Year*: Course (1) (*b*); *Fifth Year*: Course (2) (*b*); *Sixth Year*: Course (3) (*b*); *Seventh Year*: Repeated Course, or Making and Playing Instruments: *Eighth Year*: Course (1) (*c*); *Ninth Year*: Course (2) (*c*); *Tenth Year*: Course (3) (*c*). All children would receive the same total training, but the order of the courses would vary from group to group of pupils. Nevertheless, in the case of the ear and eye-training courses, which must be progressive, the successive steps fall correctly for every child. Parallel with this training would be a continuous course of voice training and song singing.

There are disadvantages in this scheme, such as the fact that the courses are not all continuous. But, in our opinion, they are less serious than those which would result from giving a *graded* course to a class whose composition changed two or three times between the entry and exit of a particular group of pupils.

## 4. *TRAINING COLLEGES*

### THE TWO-YEAR COURSE

Students taking music as a subject in a two-year training course might reasonably be expected to cover the following scheme of work:

(*a*) *Practical Music:*

(i)   Ear-training, including simple dictation.

(ii)   Sight-singing from Staff Notation (through the Tonic Sol-fa Notation).

(iii)   Choir singing of representative unison and part-songs (classical and modern).

(*b*)   *Theoretical Music:*

Enough of the elements of musical theory to understand any music required in school teaching.

(*c*)   *Study of Teaching Methods:*

(i)   Teaching of a graded ear-training course, including appreciation of music by rhythmic movements.

(ii)   Teaching of reading from Staff Notation by means of the Tonic Sol-fa Notation.

(iii)   Training of children's voices with special consideration of the curing of faults.

(iv)   Conducting of choirs and orchestras.

(v)   The selection of suitable music, text-books and apparatus.

Students who have special musical gifts should take a more advanced course, to include the following additional items:

(vi)   Simple harmony (first at the keyboard, then written), musical form, and musical history.

(vii)   One solo subject: singing or playing an instrument.

(viii) Simple pianoforte playing for accompanying and illustrating lessons.

(ix) Special study of a particular branch of music teaching.

College classes should be small enough for individual exercises in ear-training and sight-singing (heading (a) of the scheme). It is impossible to gauge individual progress with massed response, and singing alone, necessary to the giving of a successful music lesson, cannot be practised. The effort of singing "in public" is usually a real difficulty to the young teacher and should be faced and overcome.

The importance of the work under heading (c) (the Study of Teaching Methods) cannot be over-emphasised. Students should have many chances to watch model lessons, either in schools or given to school children in college. Some lessons might be taken by students in the presence of the music lecturer and other students, and subsequently discussed. Where possible, these lessons should be arranged as a progressive course, to show the importance of continuity in teaching. Also it is of the greatest moment that students should be made familiar with all possible devices for varying the exercises in sight-reading and ear-training so as to avoid the monotony which so often characterises this work. Good teaching can make the singing lesson one of the most enjoyable of all. These devices should be put to the test in the periods of school practice.

Students should be informed of those provisions of the Copyright Act which concern the copying of music and words in which rights are reserved.

The development of initiative can be encouraged by:

(a) The formation of small groups to specialise in chosen branches of school music, each group visiting suitable schools; the working out of practical schemes,

which should be tested on the group and during school
practice; the writing of a combined thesis on the
schemes. When the work has justified it, special mention should be made on the student's testimonial.

(b) The formation of a Music Society or Club,
managed mainly by the students. There should be
regular meetings, including any of the following: song
and instrumental recitals by students; stories (read or
told) of operas, with musical illustrations; gramophone
or player-piano recitals with commentary; community
singing; and House music competitions (vocal and
instrumental). The Music Society can foster a spirit of
social service by giving concerts to people who have
little opportunity of hearing music.

Musical experiences outside regular lecture hours
should be as varied as possible. Visits to concerts,
operas, etc. should be encouraged, and occasionally
outside performers should visit the college. Two neighbouring colleges can sometimes combine to afford a
higher fee.

The collecting and classifying of reference matter
should be begun in college. Material gathered during
the course will be most valuable later if carefully
indexed.

## THE THIRD-YEAR COURSE

Third-year courses are encouraged by the Board of
Education and are available at many colleges. In
music they are best taken at centres where training is
available at a neighbouring music school. In London,
for instance, training can be taken at the Royal
Academy of Music, the Royal College of Music, and
Trinity College of Music; a Teachers' Certificate,
and perhaps some training as a solo performer, would
be the main objectives. A similar plan is in operation

in Scotland, and students may attend the Scottish National Academy of Music for third-year studies. Supervised teaching practice and certain lectures have to be taken concurrently at the Training College. The third-year course is best suited to students who have covered an advanced course in music during the previous two years in college. Occasionally the third year may be deferred, the experience proving very fruitful after some years in school.

### REFRESHER COURSES

The practice of arranging Refresher Courses for former students is to be strongly commended. Local Education Authorities frequently help teachers to attend a one- or two-week course of this type. The course should include lectures in up-to-date methods by the college staff, and visits to schools. Two other most valuable forms of Refresher Course in which music takes a place, are those arranged by Local Education Authorities and Educational Associations at Vacation Schools, and in special week-end and weekly classes.

## 5. PART-TIME FURTHER EDUCATION (ADULT EDUCATION)

### (1) FIRST APPROACHES

It is not always understood that progress in adult education depends upon securing a real interest in the early stages. We strongly recommend that if the members of a new class have little knowledge of music the first approaches should be simple, and the meetings social rather than educational.

The music actually performed or heard should provide the text for early study: in this way, ear-training, including recognition of pitch, rhythm and time, tonality, tone qualities, formal structure, and reading can be introduced, and a desire for more knowledge created.

Full use should be made of every possible performer who has attained a reasonable standard. Highly trained singers and players, while of value in setting standards, are not essential. They should be brought in occasionally to illustrate music already known by the class as an incentive to reach a higher level.

The use of the gramophone is important at this early stage because it introduces music that would not otherwise be available and permits the student to listen to it in his own home. Wireless music is useful, but to a more limited extent.

A session of, say, six months should be spent in this way, nurturing a general interest in and giving familiarity with the things that matter in music. Study becomes a gradual development of experience rather than a recurring plunge into the unknown. One must remember that interest may fade because of a wrong beginning. A course of study in the historical development of vocal music, for instance, may result in a gradual waning of enthusiasm; although the songs are beautiful in themselves, the idiom is strange and unconnected with modern music as known to the student.

As an example of an interesting approach for those with little previous knowledge of music, we give the following outline of a course on the development of instrumental music from the dance.

(a) The word "dance" arrests attention. A simple talk on dance music would therefore command interest—Waltzes (not forgetting those by Mozart, Beethoven, and Schubert), Jigs, Reels, Mazurkas, Polonaises, Gavottes, Minuets, and so on.

(b) This could lead to ballet dances and the linking of the dance to a story: and so to the Suite, a linked group of dance or other tunes, (i) sometimes with a story—as in the Casse Noisette and Peer Gynt Suites—(ii) without a story.

(c) By means of (b) (ii), a return could be made to the time of Bach and Handel and there the knowledge of the class may be widened by the introduction of some of the old dances, omitted from the earlier lesson until the class should be prepared for them.

(d) This would lead to the keyboard music of Purcell, Bull, Byrd, and Giles Farnaby, and the dance tunes and songs of early times.

In this way a point of contact has been established with the beginnings of an organised course; the students have a bird's-eye view of the subject, their interest has been led from the familiar to the unfamiliar, and a more ambitious course can safely be undertaken in the orthodox way. Landmarks, too, have been set up which will be useful in further studies.

The work is sufficiently general in character to bring it within the activities of any social or educational group and can be organised by voluntary associations such as The Workers' Educational Association, Women's Institutes, Adult Schools, Settlements, and Social Clubs. Music societies such as the British Music Society, and the Local Festival Committees, should regard it as a missionary activity, and help it by providing leaders who would form and take charge of the classes. It is suggested also that Local Education Authorities should compile a list of teachers for this or more actively educational work in their various districts.

The maintenance of the classes involves a very small outlay, but at present the cost would not normally be admissible under the Board of Education's Regulations for Further Education; we make a recommendation on this point in Part V, 18 (p. 184).

## (2) THE ORGANISED COURSE

When these informal meetings have once aroused interest, work more definitely educational in character becomes possible. The most satisfactory basis (except in the case of study circles, with which we deal later) from both the financial and educational standpoints is to hold the courses under the regulations of the Board of Education. Courses in music conducted by the Local Education Authority are recognised by the Board under the Regulations for Further Education, provided that definitely educational work is undertaken; whilst Voluntary Associations can earn grants for similar courses under the Board's Adult Education Regulations. Three kinds of course are possible: a Choral Class, an Orchestral Class, and a Course of Lectures.

### (a) THE CHORAL CLASS

Of these, the Choral Class is the most widespread and we give below a typical scheme of work for one. Usually some fifteen to twenty meetings of one-and-a-half or two hours each would be held during the season.

The scheme can be used to cover the work for a number of years; the times represent what might be spent *on an average* on each branch of work in a class of one-and-a-half hours and would be varied from meeting to meeting and according to the standard of the class. The more elementary classes should work only on the simpler parts of the scheme and technicalities should be avoided. The songs sung by the class (heading (iv) of the scheme) should always be used to provide the material for the first two headings.

(i) *Theory of Music* (10 minutes), sufficient to enable students to practise reading music at sight. Tonic Sol-fa Notation (for the early stages); Staff Notation, including clefs, major and minor scales and key-signatures; pitch; the time values of notes and rests; bars and time-signatures; musical terms. Occasional short talks on composers, the history of music, musical form and so on may be given, and the more advanced classes should attempt melody writing.

(ii) *Ear-Training and Sight-Reading* (15 minutes). Exercises to cultivate aural recognition and correct reproduction of scale notes with reference to a given tonic, intervals, time-patterns, and rhythm. For more advanced classes, written music from dictation.

Students should learn to read music at sight with ease. The importance of constant practice in sight-reading cannot be over-estimated, and the aim of every class should be to read music with as little difficulty as the written word. The memorising of tunes by mere imitation is to be avoided.

(iii) *Voice-Production* (10 minutes). The compass of the voice; breathing, with exercises based on scales and common chords; enunciation; articulation; attack, phrasing and flexibility.

(iv) *Learning of Choral Works* (55 minutes). Beginners to start with unison songs, folk-songs and shanties (the gaining of confidence from the outset is important); if the song has a chorus, individuals should be given turns at singing the verses. Part-singing should be introduced by rounds, catches, canons, and descants. Elizabethan madrigals should be sung, both for their own sake, and as examples of finished contrapuntal writing. At least one major choral work should be studied by the more advanced classes each year.

Such a course is only valuable, however, if, as each new step is taken, it is at once linked up with actual music as illustration and for practice. Mere bookwork and exercises on these lines would be valueless. We give in Part III, 17 suggestions for the training of adult choirs.

### (b) THE ORCHESTRAL CLASS

The nature of the Orchestral Class depends upon its standard. In elementary classes, consisting largely of learners, instruction would be given mainly in the technique of playing particular instruments, in elementary musical theory and in the playing of easy orchestral pieces. What is said in Part III, 10 on "Learning Instruments in Class" will be found helpful to those engaged in training beginners. More advanced classes would extend their knowledge of the elements of music, would play more advanced works, and might devote time to listening to and studying orchestral works played by gramophone and wireless. Suggestions for the training of adult orchestras are given in Part III, 18.

### (c) THE LECTURE COURSE

The Lecture Course may be shorter than the above courses, since the Board of Education approve special Short Courses in this case. The lectures should be illustrated if possible by members of the class. There is, of course, a very wide field from which to choose subjects; the following are a few suggestions: the Lives and Works of Great Composers; the History of Music; Opera; English Music; the Appreciation of Music, including analysis and the reading of scores.

### (3) STUDY CIRCLES

In forming small groups or study circles for the study of definite branches of music, historical, biographical, theoretical, chamber or orchestral, it is important that they should be communal in character, that all the members should contribute, and that they should not develop into a series of lectures with examination papers. The circle should not be a solitary ripple, but the first of an expanding series, and from each circle should emerge local leaders qualified to form and lead other circles: to accomplish this aim, each member of the circle should be invited in turn to give a brief lesson on a phase of the same subject at the next meeting. The advantages over the examination paper system are obvious. All the members share in the results; each effort is under the immediate direction of the leader and the benefit of his remarks or criticisms reaches each individual. Discussion is provoked, and this discloses personality. Briefly the method is—a lesson, and practice in giving that lesson, at alternate meetings.

The gramophone is a valuable adjunct, especially with such a comprehensive series of records as those issued by the International Education Society. Wireless will be even more helpful here than in most other branches of musical education.

What has previously been said about organisation and maintenance under "First Approaches" applies equally to Study Circles.

### (4) More Advanced Work

For adults who wish to take up the more advanced study of music the University Extra-Mural Class seems the most suitable agency. We consider it essential that members of such a class should first have had experience in the practice of vocal or instrumental music either at school or in one of the organised adult education courses mentioned above.

The following is a specimen of what is possible in a four-year tutorial class, of twenty-four meetings to each session, in "Appreciation of Music".

### FIRST SESSION

*Development of Musical Forms*: (i) Construction of simple melodies—Analysis of simple folk tunes—Binary form—Ternary form. (ii) Suite: (*a*) as a whole, (*b*) dances in detail—Allemande, Courante, Sarabande, Gigue; examples analysed—Bach's Suites; decay of the Suite. (iii) Development of the Sonata—First Movement Form—Modified Sonata Form—Slow Movement—Final Movement, Rondo or similar Form—Examples analysed—Beethoven's Sonatas. (iv) History of Sonata (from seventeenth century to modern times). (v) Chamber Music. (vi) Symphony. (vii) Concerto. (viii) Overture. (ix) Fugue: examples from Bach's *Preludes and Fugues* analysed. (x) Variations.

### SECOND SESSION

Details may be altered as the needs of the class dictate. In all cases the dates given are approximate:

| Meeting | Dates of period | Subject |
|---|---|---|
| 1. | 1650 | Instruments in Use |
| 2. | ,, | General Conditions |
| 3, 4. | 1650–1750 | Clavier Music |
| 5. | ,, | Organ Music |
| 6. | ,, | Violin and Orchestral Music |
| 7. | ,, | Cantata and Passion |
| 8, 9. | ,, | Oratorio |
| 10. | ,, | Opera |
| 11, 12, 13. | 1750–1820 | Clavier Music |
| 14. | ,, | Chamber Music |
| 15, 16. | ,, | Symphony |
| 17. | ,, | Song |
| 18. | ,, | Mass, Oratorio, etc. |
| 19, 20 | ,, | Opera |
| 21. | 1820–1850 | General Conditions |
| 22. | ,, | Pianoforte Music |
| 23. | ,, | Chamber Music |
| 24. | ,, | Orchestral Music |

## THIRD SESSION

| Meeting | Dates of period | Subject |
|---|---|---|
| 1. | 1820–1850 | *Song.* Schubert, Schumann, Loewe, Franz |
| 2. | ,, | *Cantata and Oratorio.* Spohr, Mendelssohn, Berlioz |
| 3, 4, 5, 6. | 1840–1890 | *Opera*: France, Italy, Germany |
| 7. | Liszt: Pianoforte works and songs. Influence on virtuosity | |
| 8. | ,, Orchestral work, impulses in new direction | |
| 9. | Classical School *versus* Liszt and Wagner | |
| 10. | Brahms: Orchestral Music | |
| 11. | ,, Chamber Music, Pianoforte Music, Songs | |
| 12. | Modern Germany, Wolf, Strauss, Reger, Schönberg | |
| 13. | The Rise of Russia. The Nationalists | |
| 14. | ,, ,, Succeeding writers | |
| 15. | Modern France. The School of César Franck | |
| 16. | ,, ,, The Impressionists and others | |
| 17. | English Music: Tudor Period. Instrumental | |
| 18. | ,, ,, ,, ,, Vocal | |
| 19. | ,, ,, Commonwealth and Restoration | |
| 20. | ,, ,, Henry Purcell | |
| 21. | ,, ,, Eighteenth century | |
| 22. | ,, ,, First half of nineteenth century | |
| 23, 24. | ,, ,, Modern England | |

## FOURTH SESSION

Analysis of the following works: *Exsurge Domine* (Byrd); *Stay Corydon* (Wilbye); *Cease sorrows now* (Weelkes); *What is our life?* (Gibbons); Motet, *Jesu, Joy and Treasure* (Bach); String Quartet, the *Emperor* (Haydn); Symphony, the *Jupiter* (Mozart); String Quartet, Op. 135 and Pianoforte Concerto No. 4 (Beethoven); Overture, *The Mastersingers* (Wagner); *Enigma* Variations (Elgar); *Till Eulenspiegel* (Strauss).

## 6. *THE CONTRIBUTION OF THE UNIVERSITIES*

The universities serve the cause of musical education in two ways: (1) by training composers and teachers of music, (2) by creating a body of keen amateurs who will later encourage musical education, either in schools where they are teaching other subjects, or in boys' and girls' clubs and musical societies for adults. Whether university training in music be intended for professionals or amateurs, its fundamental principles are to inculcate an intellectual attitude towards music and the sense of leadership which should make every student feel that he has a mission to do all he can to develop music in others.

The course for a degree in music, which will be taken by those who intend to make music their profession, generally (and rightly) includes acoustics, counterpoint, harmony, composition in various forms (including fugue) and the history of music. In addition to this, professional life requires a fairly high standard of proficiency in singing, instrumental playing and conducting. Although these things may not form part of the degree examination, university life ought to afford opportunities for their study and practice. Conditions are bound to vary in different universities, and though Oxford and Cambridge may set the highest examples, each university will have to organise its resources in its own way.

If the work of the university is to be effective, its musical life must be as rich as possible. Musical organisations which do not form part of official studies should be encouraged and if possible co-ordinated so as to avoid overlapping and the useless dispersal of

musical energy. Students should seize every opportunity to make music themselves as well as to listen
to it. In some foreign universities this music-making
(*Collegium musicum*) is organised by the university and
placed under the supervision of university lecturers;
but our own national temperament generally prefers
that such activities should be less formal. They can
often be organised admirably by students themselves,
and the mere organisation of them is an excellent
training for musicians. Professors and lecturers ought
to be willing to co-operate in these activities on unofficial terms, and such co-operation can promote very
valuable personal relations. The university authorities
ought to give some sort of recognition to such groups
and societies and if possible provide accommodation
for them. The ideal arrangement would be to have a
special building with a concert hall, library, lecture
and practice rooms and even club rooms, in which all
the music of the university can have its focus, so that
it would be the headquarters not only of the official
music department but also of such essential institutions
as the choral and orchestral society, the operatic
society and the chamber music club.

Everything that is of value to the amateur is of
necessity valuable to the prospective professional. The
professional student of music will learn much from
helping the amateur and from the organisation and
conducting of small groups such as instrumental ensembles got up for particular occasions, madrigal
ensembles and choirs of chapels. Such activities often
afford useful training to the amateur as well; many
who never attended a lecture course have done yeoman
service with their village choral society or local festival
on the practical experience gained in a college or
university musical society. This is not to say that they

would not have done better if they had taken a course.

Besides those who take a strictly professional course in music there will be students who expect to do a certain amount of music teaching in conjunction with other subjects; at present it is not generally possible to take music amongst the subjects for an Arts degree; nor does music take an adequate place in the post-graduate teachers' training course (see also Part V, 23 p. 185).

The system of including music as one of the subjects for an Arts degree, if adequate teaching for it is given, is found to be of great practical value, owing to the help which it gives to small schools which cannot afford a full-time music master. In such cases a visiting professional musician may give the instrumental lessons, but a university-trained resident assistant master who has a sound amateur knowledge of music will have a far greater power and opportunity of making the school genuinely musical, and he can sometimes give theoretical instruction which is beyond the abilities of the humbler professional instrumentalist.

The study of opera has recently made considerable progress at the universities. It has at present little bearing on the professional operatic stage, and its aim should not be primarily to prepare students for an operatic career. But the practical study of opera by amateurs has a great educational value. All schools are now recognising the importance of acting plays and operas, and any schoolmaster may be called upon to help in a school production. Even if it is only a play, it will probably require incidental music, and here a sound knowledge of musical history and some experience of operatic work will be of the greatest assistance.

An all-important need, for a university, is a well-stocked library of music and books on music. It should have a reading room where scores may be studied in silence; if possible there should be also a room with a pianoforte where readers may play the music through, subject to suitable safeguards against disturbing other students. It should also be possible for students to take books out of the library, and certain books and collections which are useful for class work should be available in a large number of copies.

Lastly it should not be forgotten that scientific research in music, as in other subjects, is a proper function of a university. Much valuable work of this type has been done in England, and by university graduates; but it has seldom been done under official recognition and with official assistance. To discuss it fully would be beyond the scope of this Report; but it ought not to be ignored. The present widespread practical interest in old English music is due in the first instance to the labour of those whose patient research discovered its existence and made it accessible to the public. There is always a further need for trained scholars of this type.

# PART III

## SUGGESTIONS ON TEACHING METHODS

A large proportion of the recent contributions to the study of teaching methods has been concerned more with the teaching of the individual than the class. The concern of this Report is, in the main, with class work, and the hints on teaching methods that follow furnish a summary of what we believe to be the best practice of the day.

The hints cover a wide field, and one of the objects of this Part is to discuss, as briefly as possible, the chief problems which face the teacher in every branch of class music. Those who wish to obtain more detailed information should refer to books mentioned in the Appendices.

The suggestions may also be regarded as a supplement to the schemes of the preceding Part. The various aspects of training have had to be treated separately here; they should not be taken as subjects for separate study in school, for even if one is singled out for special attention, there will always be others which have a simultaneous bearing on what is being done.

### 1. INFANTS' INTRODUCTION TO MUSIC IN SCHOOL

We feel that the importance of laying a sound foundation in the Infants' School cannot be too strongly emphasised, for upon that the whole educational structure has to be built.

All music lessons must be made enjoyable. The

normal reaction to music for most people should be one of pleasure—physical, emotional, and intellectual, in varying proportions. If the music lesson is not one of the best liked in the curriculum by the majority of the class, it is a sure sign that the teacher needs to overhaul methods.

During the first seven years of life the imitative and rhythmic faculties are more amenable to training than at any other time. Therefore a beginning should be made as early as possible in all essential branches of music study. If the learning of the spoken language be taken as an analogy, music should be presented in the following order: Song-Singing and Voice-Training, Ear-Training, and Eye-Training: that is, the training of the vocal mechanism to produce tuneful and intelligent sounds, the cultivating of the aural sense to appreciate musical idiom, and the exercising of the visual sense to relate those sounds to the notational symbols. In language training, there is a fourth branch, that of writing. In music, however, this study is usually better left until later in the course, though small children enjoy writing large-type music notation, which they think of as music pictures.

In reviewing the whole course, one or two outstanding features need special emphasis. In the early years of training there should be a spirit of play in the lessons in order to make a happy introduction to music. This does not imply that the teaching should be aimless. On the contrary. The skilled teacher will see that there is a useful purpose behind every section of the lesson. Indeed, in view of the increased musical demands which are now made upon young people in post-primary schools, it is essential that the Infants' School should take a larger share than formerly in the school music course.

In view of the youthfulness of the pupils and of their natural desire for movement, early lessons should be short (about 20 minutes) and frequent and contain plenty of activity. Stepping, clapping, and other bodily movements usefully directed will afford this physical outlet and, with an occasional song, can be used at any time to let off steam or to stimulate flagging spirits. There should, however, be periodical times for rest when tranquillising music can be played.

Attention may be called to the following points in the specific branches of training:

### (1) SONG-SINGING AND VOICE-TRAINING

Much if not all of the vocal training in the first two years of school must be developed by imitation of patterns (usually songs and brief phrases accompanied by suitable words) given by the teacher, if possible, or by members of the class whose production is naturally good. Simple directions on the shape of the lips are often a help (for instance, a trumpet shape to produce a forward tone). Breathing exercises may be disguised by an appeal to the imagination, as by pretending to smell flowers. In all these play exercises noisy breathing should be discouraged. Loudly filling paper bags with air may be good fun, but does not encourage the ideal of natural inaudible breathing. An emission of breath too gentle to disturb a feather is a more suitable illustration.

For songs, little children should be taught as many traditional nursery rhymes and singing games as possible. They are a musical heritage to which they have a right, and should be part of everybody's stock of musical knowledge. The melodies of the rhymes are often good models, and can be quoted later in the music course. When they are known, more modern settings can be taught, as well as many other appropriate songs (see Appendix A, 1). Care must be taken that the compass (E′ to D is a safe limit) is suitable. The early songs should have a melody support in the accompaniment.

Children of this age are usually un-self-conscious, and the attitude of mind should be sustained throughout the school period: to this end, solo performances of songs and exercises should be interspersed among the class items.

## (2) EAR-TRAINING

The lessons in ear-training should include a large proportion of exercises demanding physical movement. Of rhythm, melody, and harmony, *rhythm* is the easiest for children to appreciate, and rhythmic movements in the form of marching, running, and tripping should be used from the first: but the ease of this part of musical training must not tempt teachers to concentrate too much upon it, when the children could pass on to more difficult work (see also Part III, 5, for hints on dancing). Percussion bands are particularly liable to over-use. Whilst fully approving the training in rhythm (and also to some extent in design and colour), and the spirit of co-operation which the bands encourage, we consider that there is a tendency to devote more than a wise proportion of the music period to them. Normally they should be regarded as an introductory device, and be superseded gradually as children are able to undertake more advanced work. In schools with a thorough music scheme the children themselves come to regard the percussion band as an outgrown amusement. *Melody* needs patient and graded teaching with constant reference to the ear. In a comprehensive course, with careful attention to singing and the correct shaping of the vocal organs, the so-called "drones" will become fewer and may even disappear. The percentage of little children who, under proper training, are unable to make correct sounds, because of slowness of ear or of muscular response in the larynx, is extremely small, and can be further reduced by individual tuition. Elementary ideas of *harmony* can be introduced in simple exercises tending to make the ear more acute.

### (3) EYE-TRAINING

As soon as sounds have been taught, their symbols may be introduced. It is undesirable to bury the notation under fanciful descriptions and elaborate pictures such as notes dwelling in houses, or fairies and birds sitting on fences and telegraph wires; small children prefer normal treatment. Whilst some illustration is acceptable, it should be used with moderation.

The teaching of the first approaches to the reading of music must aim at preparing the way for the ultimate use of the Staff Notation. Reviewing the various teaching methods in use, we consider that the employment of a fixed *doh*, which depends upon a sense of absolute pitch, is difficult and unsuitable for all save the specially gifted. A second method makes a direct approach to the stave, using the Sol-fa syllable for pitch. Very good results appear to be obtained by this method. A third method introduces the Staff Notation by means of the Tonic Sol-fa Notation, and this we feel is the *easiest* approach, particularly for average and below average pupils. The reasons appear to be the use which the Tonic Sol-fa Notation makes of easily read letter names for relative pitch, and its regularly spaced stress-marks. The letter names are particularly helpful when scale relationships are being learnt, and the stress-marks in impressing the idea of "rhythmic swing", so vital to music. With scale relationship and rhythmic sense firmly established by means of Tonic Sol-fa Notation, Staff Notation can be approached with the mind free to wrestle with the problems peculiar to the notation. The simplest plan is to teach the two notations, side by side. In the early stages the time spent on the two notations would be about equal. As the course proceeds, the amount of time spent on the Tonic Sol-fa Notation would decrease until, in the post-primary school, it would be used only to explain any new topic in Staff Notation.*

## 2. TRAINING OF CHILDREN'S VOICES

A detailed method of voice-training cannot be given here, and therefore we confine our discussion to a few broad principles and the main dangers of incorrect teaching.

The chief aims of voice-training lessons should be (1) easy and supple use of the voice, (2) the cultivation of vowel sounds of true quality, (3) the development of flexibility of voice.

Easy use of the voice depends partly upon good habits of breathing, and exercises to this end should be simple. The most usual defect in children is the taking of insufficient breath through failure to expand the lower parts of the lungs. An all-round expansion at the level of the lower ribs will produce an ample supply of breath; indeed this will be afforded by the

* It must never be forgotten that Tonic Sol-fa is not merely a matter of naming or notation. It is a complete teaching method and its logical nature can make class-singing as enjoyable as any other lesson. Teachers who "pick up" Sol-fa and try to teach it in class without a proper knowledge of the method are courting failure and are likely to do an injustice to their pupils and to music.

expansion of the ribs at each side. The expansion of
the lower chest should, in fact, become an automatic
action, and children should at first be given an appre-
ciable time in which to concentrate upon the effort
of expansion until the movement is easily controlled.

The teacher should watch to discover those who
unduly raise the upper chest and, perhaps, shoulders,
and neglect the lower expansion. He should give them
individual help. He may be able, by reforming their
habits of breathing, to improve greatly the health of
some children.

When the right kind of inhalation has been learnt,
practice will be needed to make it automatic and to
increase its rapidity. Exercises for this purpose should
be continued for a considerable time.

The acquisition of good tone by classes of children
is so vitally a matter of pattern and imitation that the
teacher's voice should be sufficiently cultivated to give
patterns of artistic tone and well-controlled, pure
vowels. Imitation is a most important factor in the
training of children's voices, for the right quality of
tone can be learnt only by example; no descriptions
of tone quality can bear a meaning except through
practical example, just as the word "acid" can only be
understood through the taste. Liking for a particular
quality of tone on the part of the teacher may be misleading and result in harmful habits. Many teachers
prefer and teach a tone which is too sombre and causes
too constricted a use of the vocal muscles. An element
of brightness, which characterises what is commonly
called "forward" tone, is essential. The teacher should
be thoroughly familiar with the score or so of vowel
sounds and diphthongs of the English language and
be able to identify them in their varied modes of re-
presentation; there are, for example, more than twenty

different ways of representing the sound *a* as in "make".
He should know that each of the main vowels tends to
develop a characteristic quality when sung, for instance,
intensity but thinness of tone through the use of *ee*,
roundness through *oh*. The most natural vowels, that
is, those produced by the most balanced poise of the
resonator muscles, are *ah* and *oh*. Practice of scales,
arpeggios and sequences should therefore be upon
these vowels when they are once properly produced.
The extreme vowels, whether of openness and depth,
as *aw* or short *o* (loll), or of closure and thinness, as *ee*,
are obtained by a particularly contracted condition
of certain muscles and should therefore never be used
for any length of time in training children. Indeed it
may be said that the three last-mentioned vowels
should hardly be given to children except to teach
their correct use in words.

Exercises on sustained tones may be used for the
study of true vowels and tone quality, but they tend
to loss of suppleness in muscular adjustments, and
therefore should be frequently alternated with exercises
in flexibility (scales, arpeggios and sequences) which
should make up the bulk of voice exercises.

A great number of exercises are not necessary for
children. A few of the most suitable should be
memorised so that the whole attention can be focused
upon the *aim* of the practice. These may consist of:

(*a*) Single notes for perfecting individual vowels.

(*b*) Slow-scale passages of three, four, five and eight
notes, particularly in descending order, for fixing a
perfect quality of tone, or "placing" voices.

(*c*) More rapidly performed scales, arpeggios and
sequences to cultivate flexibility, freedom and other
qualities.

The difficulty of adapting exercises to the varied

compass of members of a class is easily surmounted if the teacher examines a number of his pupils' voices and generally keeps the compass of his exercises within the average. If the exercises of more extended range consist chiefly of arpeggios such as

or, more advanced,

and pupils are told not to strain after notes they cannot reach, there should be no danger of strain or injury. A vigilant eye should be kept upon the best and most enthusiastic pupils who are the most likely to work to excess.

With regard to ENUNCIATION, a teacher should have a perfect knowledge of the various classes of consonants as well as of the vowels, so that he can *analyse* defects in the articulation of his classes. If he can show just what is needed to correct defects such as a voiced consonant which is not voiced, an inaudible breath consonant, or a hummed consonant too briefly sustained, he will find that his children's choirs will enunciate perfectly. This power of analysis is one of the most important assets of a teacher of voice-production, and skill can only be acquired by careful personal training. In all vocal practice, not the form of the exercise, but the manner of its performance, is all-important. It is easy to set exercises and have them performed in a perfunctory way with no definite aim and, consequently, little or no improvement.

In manuals on voice-training for children "Downward Training" is often prescribed; the exercises are to be sung on descending notes. Many inexperienced teachers interpret this instruction too literally and confine their practice to descending scales. The advice is given to prevent the upward "forcing of the register" of the voice, a grave fault which may lead to great difficulties later if serious voice-training is pursued. But ascending passages have to be sung often in songs and should not be neglected in exercises.

It must be remembered that the dangers of using girls' voices over-strenuously, or through too wide a compass, may be even greater than with boys. The practice of treating the compass of a girl's voice as mature and using music written for adults is pernicious. It is also harmful to assign the temporarily deeper voices permanently to an alto part. To aim at a full mature tone is fraught with serious possibilities, and it is lamentable to see girls' choirs in adult competitions, where they have to vie in power with their elder sisters.

Teachers of music should realise that upon them rests a serious responsibility for the well-being of their pupils' voices. In too many cases, voices are treated with no sense of responsibility whatever. But if a teacher is at all qualified for the work and can recognise a properly produced, artistic tone; if he avoids the mistake of working for power, there should be little danger of forcing voices during school singing.

Voice-training shares in the general musical neglect in many boys' schools, especially Preparatory and Public Schools, but boys are, nevertheless, made to sing in the school choir and on occasions such as

Speech Days and concerts. Many boys' voices suffer through wrong production and excessive use, especially during the period of the "breaking" of the voice. Girls' voices also should have special treatment during adolescence, and the next heading is on this subject.

## 3. TREATMENT OF ADOLESCENT VOICES

There can be no actual "training" of adolescent voices. The period, with both sexes, is one in which there can be little or no vocal development; the voice should now be used as a means of preserving and quickening musical instinct, and its future usefulness is infinitely more important than the immediate vocal results.

*Boys.* A sharp division of opinion exists here. One school forbids singing altogether on the ground that any use of the changing vocal apparatus is harmful. The other allows singing and points to the fact that some of the greatest vocalists did not desist during the unsettled period. The danger of acting according to the first opinion is that for those years in which the intellect and emotions are developing most rapidly, the youth is denied one of the most potent influences in their growth, while the growth of other interests may cause the appeal of music to weaken and die. The danger of following the second is that the adult voice may be damaged by excess. It is clear that solo work is out of the question, but the value of concerted singing is so great that opinion generally is swinging towards the second school. There are two difficulties. First, the boy's delight in his new-found deep voice and increased power tempts him to exploit his lower notes. In his ambition to be a *basso profundo* he produces his voice in a heavy manner and has difficulty in his upper range as a result. Many potential tenors are lost in this way. Voice tests among large numbers of young men of eighteen encourages the belief that there is a greater proportion of tenors than is generally assumed. Secondly, the voice is so much out of control to begin with, that it skips about from man's to boy's and back again, and produces a self-consciousness which makes the youth ashamed to sing. The chief remedies are restriction of compass to the middle part of the voice; preservation of the upper tones, however feeble or poor in quality, by bringing their quality down well over the break; and insistence upon soft, sweet singing. With care, dangers may be avoided. In classes of boys in which some voices have not broken, sight-reading exercises and songs of a compass not going above C′ may be used beneficially, if all sing in unison, and instructions are given to the broken voices to refrain from any troublesome upper notes.

*Girls.* Individual tests reveal the fact that voices may change frequently from time to time, sometimes showing an upward trend, sometimes a downward. There is very often also a tendency to breathiness, possibly due to inability to approximate the vocal chords adequately. The dangers of forced singing or too wide a compass mentioned above ("Training of Children's Voices") are even greater at the change of voice. Solo-singing becomes a serious danger unless great care is taken to avoid concert songs and an adult style of singing. *Development* of voice should never be aimed at—there is plenty of time for that in after life. A moderate compass, rarely using and never exceeding the upper reaches of the treble stave, abstention from songs which demand much articulation of words in the higher part of the voice, pleasant, sweet quality, particularly on upper and lower notes, and not too long periods of singing, are imperative. It is infinitely better to err on the side of reticence. Vocal strain, easily perceptible in individual work, is often lost in the massed sound of a class, and irreparable damage may be done before the teacher is aware. This does not imply a negation of musical results, but rather working within a scale suitable to the vocal material. *Fortissimo* is really a relative term; proportion is the most important factor in effects produced by musical dynamics.

## 4. EAR-TRAINING IN MELODY AND HARMONY

It is wise to use the *voice* as well as the *ear* in all early work in ear-training. Children should hum a note before trying to realise its position in the scale, and when this habit is once formed it will be of far-reaching benefit later, especially when listening to inner parts of a harmonised melody.

By the age of seven, if the pupil has had regular instruction in aural work, he will be familiar with the relations of the different notes of the scale to the key-note. The course can also include the dictation of simple groups of notes.

If a pupil has not been through this preparatory course, he will take it before attempting the stages of work which we now suggest.

### STAGE I

Some teachers think that when the principle of the "movable *doh*" has been once established the pupil can practise singing at sight and do dictation in *any key*. Other people feel that at this stage it is best to restrict children for a time to the three keys C, G and F major, in order that the eye may not become confused by constant changes in the position of *doh*.

Ear-tests should now be written in Staff Notation, two bars at a time. The key should be stated, the test is then played three times, the pupils listening and memorising; they then sing it to *lah*, and write it down. $\frac{2}{4}$, $\frac{3}{4}$, and $\frac{4}{4}$ time is taken.

A useful exercise is the singing of a well-known melody to the Sol-fa names.

### STAGE II

Pupils taught on the second plan of the two mentioned under Stage I will now begin to write *four-bar tests*, the procedure being as before. The sharpened fourth and fifth, and the flattened seventh can be introduced (*fe, se, ta*).

### STAGE III

Dictation of four bars in *minor* keys can now be given, and $\frac{6}{8}$ time is introduced. After steady work at this the pupils can begin two-part *dictation*. It is good practice for them to hum the lower notes before writing them down. Passing notes should be introduced between the chords. The *three-part chord* is then taken, the pupils singing all chords in arpeggio before writing them down. Root positions should be accurately recognised before inversions are attempted.

This stage of work ends with the chord of the dominant seventh and its inversions and resolutions.

### STAGE IV

Work in *four-part chords* should now begin. At first the pupils can only attempt to *recognise* the chords, without writing them down. The three primary chords (tonic, dominant, subdominant) are taken first, played in cadences, and varying the upper notes. This work is so fundamental that it should not be hurried, or a firm foundation will not be laid for future work. Root positions only should be taken at first. The other chords follow, and phrases including modulations to the dominant, subdominant, relative minor and major can be added later.

### STAGE V

An interesting piece of work can now be started—the dictation of four-bar phrases containing two-, three-, or four-part chords. Very simple phrases are necessary at first, or the pupils become discouraged. Chords should occasionally be *deduced*, from a given note struck on the pianoforte, and sung in arpeggio, e.g. the first inversion of the chord of B♭ major as deduced from middle C. This is an excellent test of sound work, as *guessing* can be detected immediately.

### STAGE VI

The pupils now need practice in more difficult tests of the type suggested in Stage V. It is useful to give phrases similar to those found in the Classical Dance Suite Forms.

If the above stages of work have been taken seriously, the pupils would have no difficulty with the aural tests in the examinations held by the Associated Board and set in the Matriculation examinations of the Universities.

In some schools attendance at classes for ear-training is voluntary after the age of fifteen. But by this time a firm foundation should have been laid, and all that is necessary for the average pupil will have become part of his musical equipment.

## 5. TRAINING IN RHYTHM AND MUSICAL DICTATION

A sense of *Rhythm* is one of the most fundamental assets in a musical education, and it should be trained from more than one point of view.

*Beating* and *clapping* in time to music, *conducting* and *tapping* in imitation of rhythmic patterns can be taken from the earliest stages.

*Physical exercises* of various kinds, with or without music, are means to the same end. The simpler exercises, evolved by Dalcroze for his courses of *Rhythmic Gymnastics*, are excellent.

There is a peculiar value in *Dancing* for the development of the rhythmic sense, which may be further developed by singing or humming the tune. This vocal accompaniment is recommended as a good substitute in default of an instrument, but teachers should be warned against the strain of singing and dancing at the same time. It is usually best to make one section of the class sing while the others dance.

In any case, Folk Dances would be taken first, and the various movements of the Classical Dance Suite would follow (Minuet, Gavotte, Sarabande, etc.). A fuller insight into the *form* of the latter dances is given in Part II, 5 (1) and Part III, 13.

As soon as the pupil begins to study the *time values* of musical notes, there is no method so helpful as the French system of time names, adopted by most teachers who work along the ordinary Sol-fa lines. The results are out of all proportion to the small amount of time necessary for the work (see also Part III, 6, *Time*).

Opinions vary as to the exact stage of ear-training in rhythm which corresponds to any given stage of ear-training in melody. Some teachers believe in accustoming the ear to recognise the *time values* of quite complicated groups of notes before introducing the pupil to the simplest intervals in melody. Others think that ear-training in melody and rhythm should be linked together as much as possible. In the long run, they attain the same end, and we believe that there is little to choose between the two methods.

Teachers of the latter persuasion would limit the pupil at Stage I in the ear-training in melody (see Part III, 4) to the use of the following notes and combinations:

as used in $\frac{2}{4}$, $\frac{3}{4}$, $\frac{4}{4}$ time.

At Stage II they would sanction the teaching of:

At Stage III the pupil would work at corresponding groups of notes in $\frac{6}{8}$ time.

After this stage, any combination of notes of any value, in any time-signature, is possible.

## 6. VOCAL SIGHT-READING

Vocal sight-reading can be taught accurately and scientifically by minutely graded steps, with every difficulty prepared for and circumvented by specific devices. The fact that some people who are more or less musically gifted can read fairly well without special training has nothing to do with the matter. It must be realised that the foundation of all fluency in reading, vocal or instrumental, depends upon the cultivation of a feeling for phrase-length and balance. Accuracy in pitch and time can readily be obtained by the steps mentioned above; but without the impelling force of rhythmic conviction, significant reading will not be secured. The teacher's appreciation of the fact that sight-reading can be taught is generally blunted by the varied standard of musical attainment of the average class, particularly in post-primary schools of secondary type. Children enter the school in various stages of musical training, some well taught, others ill, and many not at all. Even among those who have been taught sight-reading there has been a diversity of method. Add to this the considerations that no two children have the same innate musical capacity; that classes are grouped only according to capacity for other school subjects; that time can rarely be spared to teach sight-singing thoroughly; and that it is frequently interfered with by other musical demands; and one has a chaotic condition which exists in no other department of school life. Frequently the teacher despairs of finding a common denominator and is perforce content with a superficial attempt to teach the rudiments of reading. Moreover, specialist teachers are often prevented from appreciating the difficulties of the child by their own specialisation and intensive training, and by their familiarity with instrumental rather than with vocal music. Yet in spite of these adverse conditions it *is* possible to formulate schemes and teach on a definite basis. Common faults in teaching are (1) assumption that a knowledge of notation implies ability to convert it into sound, (2) presentation of the essential facts in a non-educational manner, (3) absence of real grading, (4) hurrying from one difficulty to another before the first has been thoroughly mastered, (5) ignorance of the causes of faults and their method of cure, and (6) a lack of variety in the actual practice of the material in hand.

Pitch and time should be presented separately.

*Pitch.* The best order in teaching new pitch sounds is (1) the sound, by vocal pattern from the teacher, (2) its Sol-fa name, the class imitating suitable phrases sung by the teacher and given on the modulator, (3) its position on the stave, with use in tunes pointed on a Staff modulator, (4) examples of combined time and tune, introducing leaps to the new sound in long notes only at first, thus allowing time for thought and preventing guess-work, (5) presentation of the sound approached and quitted in various melodic and rhythmic ways.

*Time.* Certain time divisions are best taught by (1) sound, with French time names, (2) name, (3) sign. With others, where the aid of the eye facilitates understanding, it is better to proceed by (1) the modification of a known sign into an unknown (e.g. ♩ ♫♩ ♩ into ♩ ♫♩ ♩ = ♩. ♪ ♪), (2) time names, (3) sound on a monotone to a syllable (*doh* or *lah*).

*Time and Tune.* An important rule when new material is introduced into melody tests is that where the time is difficult the tune should be made easy (scalewise at first), and where the tune is difficult the time should be easy.

No more *theory* should be taught than is absolutely essential. The teacher should talk little, and make the children sing much. Their ear must be appealed to continually. Ear-training and sight-singing should go hand-in-hand, the one helping the other. Opinions differ as to the best order of teaching new notes and leaps, but the following may serve as a basis upon which to work: (1) notes of the tonic chord and the major scale stepwise, with leaps to notes of the tonic chord, *doh'* to *me* being treated last; (2) the simplest leaps in the dominant chord; (3) the simplest leaps in the subdominant chord; (4) the more difficult leaps of the three primary chords; (5) leaps of sevenths; (6) *fe* treated stepwise; (7) *ta* treated stepwise; (8) easy leaps to and from *fe* and *ta*; (9) the minor scale (beginning on *lah**) with *soh* as the seventh note; so much modal folk-song is now used, and so many modern school songs have modal characteristics, that this step is advisable; (10) *se* approached stepwise; (11) the easiest leaps in the major dominant chord of the minor key; (12) the subdominant chord of the minor key; (13) more difficult leaps in the dominant chord; (14) the melodic minor scale; (15) the remaining chromatic notes approached and quitted stepwise. Modulation may be introduced after (6), or may be delayed. It is enough to say that in the teaching of *time values* the more intricate divisions should not be used in combined time and tune reading until an advanced stage is reached.

We would emphasise the point that there is no need for conflict between the *Sol-fa* and *Staff* Notations. The fact that all should learn to read Staff is the very reason why Sol-fa should be used. Sol-fa provides the easiest method of approach to the problems of Staff. Well taught, it ensures the most thorough mental training; it is so simple that musically weak children can progress steadily. Its terminology is infinitely more simple than that of its sister notation. Quick and accurate response of brain and voice to visual impression and the habit of looking ahead, which constitute fluency in reading, is much more surely

* See footnote, pp. 29–30.

cultivated by learning at first from Sol-fa Notation than from Staff. There is no waste of time in teaching and using both notations, because the Sol-fa system is so simple that it is readily grasped and singing from Sol-fa makes singing from Staff easier and more accurate in the long run. Both notations should be used at every step, Sol-fa first as a preparation for Staff. Even in the latest stages it is useful to refer to the letter notation, although it may not be used regularly.* There is no need to use time divisions in Sol-fa beyond quarter beats. Sol-faing from the Staff *appears* difficult, and reading to *laa*, although often more fluent, is mostly guess-work and the class is led by its more musical members. As a factor in *early training*, reading to *laa* is well-nigh useless. The Sol-fa syllables help to store the mind with melodic progressions; the names fix them in the memory, to be called up at will. It is essential that children should have much practice in applying Sol-fa names readily to Staff notes. Failure to achieve this is the chief cause of indifferent singing and time spent over it is never wasted. This is where grading of difficulties is so important. The plan of beginning in Staff notation with key C and proceeding through more complicated signatures emanates from the key-board, a piece of mechanism which has little con-nection with a melodic outline mentally conceived. In singing, all positions of the tonic on the stave should be used from the beginning: results at first may not appear good, but final results are infinitely better. It is unnecessary to explain key-signatures for the first years, i.e. before the introduction of *fe*, *ta*, or *se*. The indication of the position of *doh* or *lah* supplies the necessary information.

No teacher of sight-singing can afford to neglect the

* See also Part III, 1, pp. 73–4.

works of John Curwen (see Appendix E, 1). Even though his musicianship was not advanced, and many of his ideas are now out of date, there will be found in his writings the soundest musical-psychological truths and the most profound insight into teaching problems.

## 7. INSTRUMENTAL SIGHT-READING

### (a) PIANOFORTE

There is no real compensation for inability to read at least simple music at the pianoforte. Both string players and singers are greatly helped by being able to read their own pianoforte accompaniments. For the pianist, however, there can be no alternative. His reading must advance with his hearing and playing.

It is often not realised that increase of performing power is not necessarily accompanied by progress in reading or thinking. A familiar analogy may be found in those who speak a language, but lack the power to read it, or to express in it the highest quality of thought.

In the first place, reading demands a thorough grasp of the rudiments of time and pitch: (a) knowledge of what the symbols stand for; (b) quickness of mental reaction in translating the symbols. Formerly, *theory classes* dealt with this part of the subject. We should not wish to restore the *theory class*—in its old form, at least; but it would appear that nothing constructive has been put in its place. It is well to state emphatically that there can be no intelligent progress in reading without a proper knowledge of the symbols of notation.

The second need is to acquire the power to correlate the written symbols. This is derived, not from a continual and imperfect playing of passages at the keyboard, but from an experimental knowledge of how

the passages become clear unities of idea and effect.
The first two bars of Beethoven's First Pianoforte
Sonata will explain the point at issue. We will imagine
a student already able to read the actual signs of the
notation. What is his next step? Clearly, to discover
the force which links every note within the two bars in
question—a force somewhat analogous to that which
unites the grammatical units of a sentence. Until this
has been discovered, the student's reading of the
passage may be faultless in point of accuracy, but he will
not have reached the idea represented by the notes.
As soon, however, as he visualises the whole as formed
upon a single chord, his difficulties vanish and he re-
produces the passage as an organic whole. Some form
of elementary instruction in harmony is therefore
essential to intelligent reading. How far that instruction should be pursued is a matter for the individual
teacher.

The two foregoing steps are necessary preliminaries
to the third, namely, the rhythmic reproduction of
music at sight. In a book recently published, it is
pointed out that the effect of the spoken delivery of a
sentence is that of pure rhythmic momentum. From
that it is deduced that the momentum depends ante-
cedently upon: (*a*) a complete knowledge of the letters
and of their make-up in the form of words; (*b*) the
power to unite the words in a grammatical group.
When these two elements of language have been
grasped, the mind is set free to say the sentence
with rhythmic freedom. The parallel is obvious. To
read music rhythmically one must learn by the clear
and intelligible stages outlined above. The empirical
method, which consisted of reading a few bars daily
with no result beyond a superficial reproduction of the
actual notes, has had its day; the empirical and con-

ventional must now be supplanted by the logical and educational.

The power to read is an essential part of even moderate musicianship; and further, the better the method on which one has learnt, the sounder one's musicianship.

## (b) STRINGS

During the first six years, say from three to nine, the child's musical progress towards instrumental playing should move along the lines of unlearned tradition or folk-music: he should begin by "picking up" and making up tunes and rhythms and playing them "by ear". He should "play with" a miniature percussion set, in order to exercise his sense of timbre, pulsation and time patterns, and with a flageolet, for tune. School toy bands may well supplement, but cannot replace, this early experience, which makes him already an instrumental musician of long standing and some skill, by the time he is ready to tackle the bowing and fingering difficulties of a stringed instrument. Reading, to such a child, will turn out to be a fairly easy proposition (subject to certain conditions to be mentioned later). A word of caution is necessary at this point. The introduction of reading should *not* be the signal for the abandonment of ear-training. Indeed, the latter should continue and develop concurrently with the "literate" education.

Playing at sight, or reading, may be defined as the correct and ready performance of certain pre-determined actions in obedience to signs. It *also* means the deliberate inhibition for the time being of all the inherited "folk" faculties—guessing, improvising, playing imitatively and from memory. This definition, and especially the second half of it, must be clearly understood by the pupil.

*Reading practice.* A sure way to become a good reader is to give *five minutes daily* to reading only. Passages chosen for reading practice need not be "unseen".

*Pitch and Duration.* Since each note indicates (1) a pitch, and (2) a time value, and since pupils tend to read the pitch and to disregard the time value (especially of rests), pitch and duration should be separated during reading practice; attend, one day, to pitch only, and next day to time only. This plan saves many hours of labour. In order to facilitate, and to check, pitch reading and time reading, a most effective method is to "recite" the pitches and the durations.

*Grading.* Reading practice should be carefully graded. A player should never be asked to read any sign of which he does not know the meaning. The difficulty of reading tests should be increased only at a rate which will always permit correct playing. The reading should be exhaustive, and not a single sign on the page should be allowed to escape the reader. After about five years of this kind of training, with five minutes' daily practice, good reading of a tolerably crowded and complicated page may be expected.

*Musical understanding.* Meanwhile there is need for "reading between the lines". Throughout the course, such things as metrical values, time spotting, the rise and fall of phrases, harmonic significance, bowing style, mood, and tone colour, should have regular attention as an integral part of the reading work. Reading has no value whatever if it lacks interpretation.

*Ensemble.* Facility in reading can also be developed by means of ensemble playing. In every school or centre there should be graded String Orchestras, preferably under a good *string* player. Students should be encouraged to play duets, trios, and quartets together.

*Repertory.* At every stage of the work, both individually and in groups, pupils should constantly be given new music to play, with something fresh to read at each lesson or rehearsal.

## 8. TEACHING THE HISTORY OF MUSIC

Considered historically, music can be looked at in two different ways: it can be studied as a connected whole, or it can be regarded as a part of general history. There is very little likelihood that any time will be available in school for taking the history of music as an independent study, so provision should be made for treating it as an incidental feature of the music syllabus. If it can be incidental to the teaching of general and social history, so much the better. Every age of history will become more vivid to children if they are told that people in those days made music, and that much of it can be reproduced by themselves. The battle of Agincourt will become a far more real thing to a class which sings the historic "Agincourt Song". The personalities of the Tudors will be more intimately understood if something is known of the music which they enjoyed; Henry VIII was a composer, Mary and Elizabeth played the virginals. Indeed it is impossible to form a just conception of the life of the Elizabethans if it is forgotten that they were passionately devoted to music. Cavaliers and Roundheads had each their own tunes; the difficult history of the later seventeenth century can be brightened by the political songs and catches of the time. It is easier to remember a tune than to recall a picture or a building, and there are tunes which have made history.

Every child knows *Hush-a-bye, Baby*; how many teachers of history know it is the famous tune of *Lilliburlero*?

Old English music should be as familiar as old English poetry. Pupils ought to be told that the works of Shakespeare, Herrick, Milton and other poets were set to music by composers who were their personal friends; they should hear the poetry and the music together. A number of poets have described music; their poems would be better understood if the actual music of which the poet was thinking could be heard (see also "Correlation of Music with other Studies", Part III, 13).

To turn to the consideration of musical history as viewed from the musician's angle: the average child music-lover of to-day hears music belonging to all sorts of periods and countries, not only in school, but probably also in the cinema, in the street, or in church. The study of music in school may become more interesting if he is told who were the people who first heard the song which he is singing. Often the lives of famous composers provide material of interest. It can be pointed out how certain types of music (choosing examples from the ordinary repertory) are closely associated with the general life of their period, how their style is determined by the size of the rooms in which people lived then, by the instruments they had, or even by the sort of clothes they wore. The history of scales, pitch, instruments, bands and orchestras, of music as a way of occupying leisure, and of music in ceremonials, can be taught in the same light.

For more advanced pupils the historical view of music is as important as the historical view of language. Musical phrases and chords change their meanings in the course of time just as words do; as in literature, so in music, old-fashioned phrases remain imbedded in the language. All musical compositions have their place in musical history; some gain meaning from their ancestry—they are in a tradition; some are significant because of their posterity—they were originating types; others are of interest as daring experiments, though they may appear to have had no progeny. The important thing to remember is that the history of music can be learned only from the music itself. Teachers will naturally want the help of books (see Appendix E, 11) to provide them with an outline, but books without music—and the music must be actually heard, or better, performed—are useless. It is not a matter of vital importance to know the exact dates of Handel's birth and death; it is of some importance to know that he was a German by birth, studied in Italy and eventually settled in England. It is more important to connect him in our minds with Queen Anne and the first two Georges; but far more important to know enough of his music by heart to be able to recognise the Handelian style at once when we hear an unfamiliar work of his.

It is possible to lecture systematically on musical history and musical appreciation without any useful result; it might be far better that music should be taught as music, that is, as music which pupils sing and play themselves, and that the teacher should let no opportunity slip of throwing in an appropriate historical explanation or illustration. The teacher who is competent to do this adequately will be equally competent to teach the history of music as a separate subject, but the opportunities for that will be rare, and in any case it is probable that an historical approach to normal music teaching is, for most children, more helpful than a separation of practice from theory (see Part II, 2 (i), Scheme of Work for Senior Classes and Modern Schools, p. 33).

## 9. EXTEMPORISATION AND MELODY-WRITING

Children should be encouraged, when quite young, to sing improvised melodies. They enjoy doing this, and the experience serves as a basis for later musical training.

The study of harmony is a dreary task for pupils who have had no practice in making simple tunes for themselves. Vocal improvisation is a natural first step to the composition of tunes.

If the pupil is taken through the following stages of work he will have enough facility to begin formal melody-writing, which can be corrected by the teacher more thoroughly than is possible with exercises in *vocal* extemporisation.

### STAGE I

(*a*) The teacher plays or sings the first half of a four-bar phrase, which is then completed by different pupils in turn.

(*b*) The pupils can now take it in turn to improvise the first half of the phrase, which is finished by somebody else.

(*c*) The same thing is then done with an eight-bar phrase, which is divided into two four-bar sections. Modulations can be introduced when the work of the class in sight-singing has made them familiar with the functions of the notes known as *fe*, *ta*, and *se*.

(*d*) The sixteen-bar phrase is taken next. It is a good plan to divide the phrase among different pupils, each of whom is responsible for a section. More than one modulation can be introduced. Sometimes the teacher will decide the nature and place of the modulation. At other times this will be left to the discretion of the pupils. It will be noticed that children express themselves almost invariably in the idiom of the music with which they are most familiar.

## STAGE II

The simple extemporisation of chords can now be started, easy accompaniments being added by pupils in turn on the pianoforte; only the three primary chords, which will be familiar from the aural training class, should be used until the players are quite at their ease. Sometimes the pianist should be tied down to a fixed *pattern* of chords, to which he must improvise and sing a melody. Now and then he should be allowed to *sing and play* freely. When the pattern of chords has been decided on, different pupils can add other vocal parts to the melody. Occasionally the whole class can join in.

## STAGE III

Other chords can then be used in the accompaniments, and modulations introduced.

## STAGE IV

At this point the class is ready to study the Classical Dance forms. They are shown what is meant by a Minuet, Gavotte, Sarabande, etc., and their improvisations will include specimens of these. Opportunity must be given for *free* improvisations of their own choice.

## STAGE V

At this juncture stress is laid on *irregular* rhythms of more than one kind. Pupils will experiment with short melodies in $\frac{5}{4}$ time, adding accompaniments. They will realise the interest of four sets of three-bar phrases and of five-bar phrases, and will unconsciously acquire some knowledge of various kinds of musical *balance*.

STAGE VI

A certain amount of simple pianoforte extemporisation can now be taken. The stages of work will correspond roughly to those suggested for vocal work. Progress will naturally be influenced by instrumental technique. From time to time vocal improvisation above or below a given *canto fermo* is useful. If done without a pianoforte accompaniment this is not as simple as it may appear, but it is an excellent test of knowledge.

## 10. LEARNING INSTRUMENTS IN CLASS

### (a) PIANOFORTE

All the early work in learning the pianoforte can be done in classes. Any number of pupils up to twelve is practicable, and power to supervise that number is quickly secured. The aims should be (1) reading; (2) familiarity with the keyboard; (3) transposition; (4) making harmony. All these can be taught in class in a stimulating way.

The advantages of pianoforte classes are:

(i) Reduced cost of lessons without any reduction in the teacher's fee.

(ii) Economy in the teacher's time.

(iii) The prevention of heavy expenditure until results prove that it will be worth while.

(iv) Communal instead of individual work.

(v) Increase in the number of private pupils owing to a diffusion of interest.

A room of moderate size, say, 20 ft. by 16 ft., with small tables or desks about the height of a pianoforte keyboard (inexpensive folding card-tables are admirable), a blackboard, and a pianoforte are necessary. Inexpensive and portable model keyboards are also required. As a result of experiments over a period of three years a method (with apparatus) was published towards the end of 1928 (see Appendix E, 15). The folding model keyboard is made of cardboard and has a range of four octaves. The method is based on ear-training, and on the *mental* realisation of sounds when looking at the written signs or when using the keyboard. The idea of sound is fostered by singing or humming the melodic phrases played: that of touch by a slight finger or hand pressure as if overcoming the weight resistance of the key, but always with insistence upon continual relaxation of the muscles. In everything played, each member of the class in turn plays on the pianoforte while the remainder continue at their models, or listen and learn to criticise the sounds, the tone, and the touch produced by the player. Familiarity with the keyboard—seeing through the finger ends—can be acquired as easily on the model as on the pianoforte. First steps in transposition and the formation of scales are taken at the first lesson and are simplified by the use of a transposer card, an adaptation of the modulator, which also simplifies the learning of intervals and harmony.

Classes, consisting of children in primary and post-primary schools and of adults, are working in several parts of the country with increasingly satisfactory results. It is found that the model keyboard can be practised in homes where there is no pianoforte, although quicker progress is made where there is access to an instrument. As in the case of most educational innovations, the classes when organised by schools are voluntary and held out of school hours: but it is no idle conjecture that class teaching brings much nearer the possibility of instrumental lessons in the school curriculum.

### (b) STRINGS

Beginners on violins, violas, and 'cellos may be taught in one class, and many string classes of this kind up and down the country have developed into successful orchestras and chamber music combinations. The underlying principle of the work is *one thing at a time*, e.g. violin and bow are not brought together until each has been studied separately; when they are used together everything should be learnt on the principle of first learning to do, and then, when it can be done, of reading the signs which express the doing.

The practice of regarding a good ear as necessary in order to learn a stringed instrument is too often made a stumbling-block for would-be players. The aural sense can be improved by training, and this is a part of the class work as important as the training in technical agility (see Appendix E, 15).

### (c) WIND

There is no reason why classes for wind instruments should not take their place with other instrumental work. In America they are common and the result is that an enormous number of schools have their own complete bands (see Appendix E, 15).

In class work it is essential to keep the members busy and to give equal attention to all.

## 11. LISTENING TO MUSIC

Most people who hear music do not really listen to it at all; they let it fall upon their ears as a pleasant succession of sounds, making no effort to understand it and taking their chance of being soothed or stirred by it. At the same time many people have heard so much music, of one kind or another, that they have subconsciously developed the rudiments of under-standing; they can recognise a piece of music which they have heard before, at any rate after they have heard it several times, and they are often conscious that a piece of music gives them more pleasure as it becomes more familiar to them. But for such people their gradual acquaintance with certain music is a matter of mere chance—or rather, there is every chance that the music which they will hear most often is music of a trivial and vulgar type such as is played in places of popular resort. This type of music thus becomes for them the standard type by which all other music is judged.

The full appreciation and enjoyment of the best music involves concentrated attention on the part of the listener. The ideal listener should be not only willing but able to make the intellectual effort of following every note and grasping its relation to the whole. But we have to admit that in certain cases this process is one of extreme difficulty even to the most highly trained professional musician; yet at the same time it is perfectly possible for quite young people of average musical ability to follow clearly the structure of a simple harmonised melody such as a hymn tune. It is therefore important that the art of intelligent listening should be cultivated at an early age so that it may become natural and habitual.

Some educational writers talk much about the "formation of taste", but it is much more important that the individual should be in a position to form his own taste and to develop and change that taste as often as he may find it necessary in the course of his life, than that his musical appreciation should be permanently cramped by the extraneous imposition of a "good taste" which he has not discovered for himself.

We naturally cannot expect from young people, let alone from small children, the standards of musical attention which ought to be the ideal for mature and experienced listeners. The child must be taught step by step, and only such difficulties placed before him as he may be reasonably expected to overcome. With small children the first thing is to encourage the idea that music is a delightful thing. But as the whole object of education is to train human beings to face difficulties and overcome them, we must avoid any system which pretends that music is nothing more than an agreeable game. Listening to music has difficulties which must be faced; the child must be taught to recognise them and take a pride in conquering them one by one.

It is obvious that strongly marked rhythms at once appeal to children at an early age. This is generally recognised in the process of teaching children to make music themselves, but we are here concerned with the training of children in listening to the performance of music by others. At a very early stage it is useful to encourage children to beat time or to make movements in time to the music which is being played, but by the time a child is old enough to sit still the appeal of music to the imagination and intellect should be the main objective. The habit of listening in a spirit of anticipation should be acquired, so that at any moment the mind is looking forward to what is coming. The pupil should learn when to expect the arrival of such elementary things as tonic and dominant cadences, to realise that discords require resolution and to anticipate that resolution mentally. But the teacher should avoid burdening the young mind with too many technical terms; it is no use knowing the names of chords if the sound of them is not automatically recalled, and it is much more important to be familiar with these different sounds than to remember their technical names.

The imagination may be deeply stirred by music which is not completely understood intellectually, and young people should be encouraged to listen to music imaginatively even when it is of a type supposed to be beyond their years. It is well known that children are often deeply stirred by passages of Shakespeare and other great poets which they are as yet incapable of understanding completely. The same applies to music. The association of music with some sort of picture or story has often been condemned, but there is no doubt that for the young it is often a great help. In teaching, many details can be indicated in two ways, technically or descriptively, and it is common knowledge that the descriptive method is often the most practical because the imagination—even with professional musicians in an orchestra—often acts more quickly than the intellect. It is certainly a mistake to suppose that every piece of music must tell a story, but a story will often prepare the way more agreeably for formal analysis. It will prepare the way better if the teacher can supply varied illustrations and does not let pupils associate certain pieces invariably with the same picture. The idea of moonlight may for a moment help the appreciation of the "Moonlight" Sonata, but it will go only a very little way to even the emotional enjoyment of the work. One of Mendelssohn's *Songs without Words* is sometimes called "Spinning Song" and sometimes "The Bee's Wedding"; either picture will do, according to the pupil's greater familiarity with bees or spinning-wheels. The "Story" or "Picture" in a piece of music is in fact much the same as the childish names by which various people or objects are known in early years. Childish delight in the "puff-puff" may eventually encourage the boy to become an engineer; but a grown-up person should not be expected to remain for ever in the "puff-puff" stage, although he can enjoy a modern poet's allusion to "the softly panting train".

A valuable factor in the art of listening is the development of the historic sense in music. It is doubtful whether any but exceptionally musical children derive much benefit from being taught how the symphony grew from Haydn to Elgar; but it is certainly a contribution to general culture if music can be associated with other facts of general history. Elizabethan music helps the understanding of Shakespeare and his contemporaries, Purcell illustrates the reigns of Charles II and of William and Mary, Handel the age of Queen Anne and the Hanoverians. The pupil should be made to realise that music, so far from being "timeless", as ecstatic critics have sometimes said, is very much of its period. Not only will music illustrate general history, but history must illustrate music.

It is obvious that in these days much listening will be done to music which is mechanically reproduced. This is inevitable, and the advantages of mechanical reproduction must be recognised by all. But we must not forget that all music suffers in quality by mechanical reproduction, and that a large part of the spiritual value of music depends on the establishment of personal contacts. The teacher who can play or sing to his pupils with some real artistic power of interpretation will obtain a much more vital hold on their imaginations and affections than one who does no more than wind up a gramophone, and his teaching will be more effective in consequence.

Listening to music, as distinct from learning to sing or play it, is important in musical education. It gives the pupil's imaginative and intellectual faculties free play; in learning to sing and still more in learning an instrument so much brain power is occupied in reading the notes and finding the right places for the fingers that very little is left for musical understanding. The irksomeness of practising in some cases leads the pupil to regard the particular work studied, if not indeed all music, with positive hatred and disgust.

### PRACTICAL POINTS ON LISTENING TO MUSIC

Exercises in listening should be related to music of lasting value, chosen so that children will hear in that music the particular features which the teacher wishes to illustrate. An attempt should also be made to justify the composer's use of those features.

Thus, a diatonic scale passage, though sung as an exercise, can often be listened to in music of Handel's style as the customary way of indicating running water, the surging of the sea, and the wind. The chromatic scale can be recognised as the stock method of suggesting both the soughing wind and the raging storm. The Prologue to *The Golden Legend* and the Overture to *William Tell* supply examples which come readily to mind; but many of the simplest songs, besides those like Schubert's *Erl King*, have scale passages in their accompaniments, which may be recognised as describing the elements.

The ancient modes, the various pentatonic scales, the modern major and minor scales, should be sung from and heard in actual music, so that their differences in character can be noticed. A composer who deliberately uses those scales with their restraints for his effects, is assuming that his listeners are trained to appreciate his procedure.

The understanding of music depends largely on the

storing up of certain auditory patterns in the mind. It is a function of the teacher to point out the most obvious patterns which recur frequently in music, such as the resolution of discords, the progression of cadences and the principle of sequence. Listening to music proves pleasurable when a state of tension is followed by an anticipated state of repose. Composers have always relied on consistent reactions to familiar musical patterns. For instance, Wagner often portrays unsatisfied desires by postponing cadences and so denies to the listener the points of repose which his knowledge of earlier music leads him to expect. But those who have not been trained to anticipate these things lose the excitement of frustrated anticipation, and may thus find Wagner's music tedious.

Points such as these arise in a general way. When dealing with any given composition, training in listening must be specific. The first task is to break down, as quickly and effectively as possible, the barrier of unfamiliarity. This can be done more easily with a short piece of music than with a long one, and short pieces should be the rule. The power to listen to extended compositions can be developed by taking sections of the works as separate pieces. Young children will listen intelligently to a *Minuet*. They will enjoy a beautiful *Adagio*. Eventually they will appreciate at one sitting a whole *Suite* or *Sonata* when they have become thoroughly familiar with each movement separately; but not before.

The right frame of mind may be induced in young and inexperienced listeners by suggesting a picturesque title, but the habit of translating all music into pictures should not be continued beyond the early stages. For this reason it is not advisable to ask pupils to suggest titles for a piece which they have heard. Many familiar titles (not always given by the composers) such as "the Saints in Glory" for Bach's Fugue in E major, are misleading. But the titles of dance forms are helpful, and before a dance is played, the class should be told about its steps and movements, as well as the dress and manners of the period to which it belongs.

More complicated forms, such as the Fugue, may well be explained by graphical methods. In the following diagram, which illustrates the beginning of a four-part Fugue, the order of entry of subject and answer (indicated by whole lines), and the relative position of the counter-subject (indicated by broken lines), are given pictorially, and listeners can *see* what the composer wanted them to notice:

Treble _____

Alto _____ _____

Tenor_____ _____

Bass _____ _____

The construction of the Stretto can be made clear by a similar diagram, as the lines can be made to overlap as the entries overlap in the actual Fugue.

Such musical devices as the inversion of melodies, and the expansion or contraction of melodies, can be shown quite effectively by graphical methods. At (*a*) is given a melody, and underneath it a sketch of its contour. At (*b*) is its inversion also with contour below.

Beethoven, Pianoforte Sonata, Op. 110 (Fuga).

(Both examples are given in the same key for the sake of clearness.)

(*a*) Subject

(*b*) Inversion

It should be borne in mind that when Beethoven *does* invert a melody in working out musical ideas, he wishes the inversion to be heard as an inversion, and not as a new tune unrelated to what has gone before. That justifies the teaching. On the other hand, in suggesting the use of graphs to illustrate music, we do not mean that music lessons should be used to give practice in co-ordinate geometry; nor are we opening out fresh vistas for those who compile psychological tests. We merely suggest the simplest graphical aids to listening, and nothing more.

Whether music is being listened to with or without a score, a teacher should not fail to call attention to every important effect the composer plainly wishes to be noticed. When scores are available, means should be devised to identify readily points of entry, the position in the score of themes and instruments, the beginnings of sections, and the lay-out generally. Whilst music is in progress, this should be done as unobtrusively as possible, so as not to interfere with the listening, while preventing the music from being unintelligible.

It should always be remembered that music can be thoroughly understood and yet make but little appeal, owing to personal predilections. The music should be varied, therefore, so that each listener has something to his own taste.

It may seem superfluous to say that no teacher should face his class without having prepared the lesson. Still, teachers often take lessons of all kinds unprepared, and an experienced teacher may be able to deal adequately with such a task as an unprepared piece of Latin. But it is more difficult in the case of music, because the understanding of music depends on its rhythmic continuity. A teacher who hesitates and stumbles while reading a piece of music at sight on the pianoforte will not give his class a satisfactory impression of it. The gramophone will save him the embarrassment of his own mistakes, but he will be unable himself to follow the music mentally with sufficient clearness unless he has a score in front of him at the same time, so that he can read ahead of the record and see what requires explaining to the class. In fact it may be said that a lesson which uses the gramophone requires very much more careful preparation on the part of the teacher than one which is illustrated by the pianoforte or the voice.

Modern reproductive mechanism makes it possible for children to hear music by modern pioneer composers as well as that of the classical and romantic schools. Musical education should be based firmly on a knowledge of the classics, but teachers should not exclude modern music, even if they are not attracted by it. Young people often have an intuitive enjoyment of modern music which older people find difficult to understand at all. The tendencies of modern music are so various and complicated that it is impossible to suggest methods of analytical teaching; but it is certainly desirable that young people should become accustomed to the sounds of modern music, and if examples are chosen with care, and repeated, their structure will gradually become clear.

## 12. THE USE OF MECHANICALLY REPRODUCED MUSIC

The value of this method of providing music for "listening" lessons is generally acknowledged and will not be discussed. It is not so widely known, however, that the gramophone (with care) and the player-piano (quite easily) can be used for accompanying songs and hymns, and a school violin class, and that this allows one to use music with difficult accompaniments which is yet suitable for school use in other respects. The gramophone and the player-piano are so easy to work that it is soon possible to train pupils to use them efficiently; the teacher can then concentrate on the class work of teaching, conducting, and directing. This applies also to the accompaniment of physical and rhythmic exercises and folk dances.

There appears to be no limitation to the general usefulness of a player-piano: it does all the school pianoforte can do and more, and the specially prepared rolls (see Appendix I, 3) which are now available are model lessons in appreciation, singing, and rhythmic work. Where new instruments are being supplied to schools we feel that there is a very strong case for spending the few extra pounds necessary to instal a player-piano instead of the ordinary pianoforte.

A gramophone, too, is a necessary part of the musical equipment of a school. In addition to the wide range of music which it makes available, it provides interpretations by eminent executants for study and comparison (see also Part III, 11—Practical Points on Listening to Music). The player-piano also does this for pianoforte music.

A large number of gramophone records have been specially prepared for educational activities, including musical history, marching, folk dancing, rhythmic movements, and voice-training, as well as a series of illustrated lectures by distinguished musicians. (For further particulars see Appendix I.)

In the early days of school broadcasting many teachers were discouraged, usually on account of the shortcomings of the receiving set, from giving the wireless any prolonged trial in the music class. This reaction against the use of broadcast lessons has meant that the improved standard of reception and the better broadcasting arrangements are not now getting worthy recognition from teachers. The weekly music lessons broadcast to schools in England are arranged by the Music Committee of the Central Council for School Broadcasting. The course is planned on a one-year basis; provision is made for two grades of pupils, elementary and advanced, in order to meet the needs both of schools which have never listened before and those which have listened to past courses.

The chief aims of the broadcast lesson are to arouse a love of rhythmic melody, to accustom children to melody as a natural language, to help them in sight-reading and to teach them to write tunes. What may be called the principle of rhythmic contagion underlies the work. A broadcast rhythm quickly infects the listening teams, and if they are invited to join in, the response seems invariably ready. Tune writing has become a leading feature in the broadcast music lessons. The principle of binary and ternary form is taught by analysing folk-tunes and showing how they are built phrase by phrase. The four-phrase tune which falls into the combined binary and ternary scheme known as A, A, B, A catches on quickly, and children will easily respond to tunes in this pattern.

Thirty lessons in each course, junior and senior, are

provided through the school broadcasting year, each lesson lasting half an hour. The lessons are arranged under the following headings: (1) lesson on the subject of the week; (2) reading practice and work on the song of the week; (3) short concert; (4) playing of tunes written by the children. The junior lesson deals with first principles, for example, with musical intervals and phrases and the building of simple rhythms. The senior course includes an advanced study of similar subjects, but gives more attention to design in the music of the great masters.

The subjects and main themes of the works studied are reproduced in the pupil's manual issued by the British Broadcasting Corporation, a copy of which should be in the hands of each listener. The manual also contains songs and tunes (some of them written by children), verses to be set, and musical phrases illustrating the lesson of the week. These phrases, called "echo" phrases, have proved helpful in reading at sight and in helping team phrasing and team thinking. The "echoes" have been made up in many cases of famous phrases from classical works. The long tune from the Finale of the C minor Symphony by Brahms, the exquisite example of repartee in the Rondo of Beethoven's Fourth Piano Concerto and the choral melody from Beethoven's Ninth Symphony are typical examples of phrases from the classics used as "echoes".

In addition to the weekly music lessons, three-quarters of an hour at the end of each Friday afternoon is devoted to concerts for schools. The first concert is in the form of a concert lesson; each item in the programme is discussed at the microphone. The following Friday the same pieces are broadcast without further comment. From time to time, various individual instruments of the orchestra are broadcast. Listening strain is relieved during each concert by the singing of two or more chorus songs; the verses are sung from the studio and the listening children are invited to join in the choruses. Teaching notes are supplied for each concert at least a week before the programme is broadcast. This, shortly, is what the B.B.C. provides for schools.

The wireless must be used judiciously as a supplement to the ordinary school course, not as a substitute for it. It is found that the periodical broadcast lesson stimulates the teacher and class by bringing into the school a new "voice" on the subject, and teachers whose musical skill is limited benefit from hearing a specialist teach. To help the children to get the greatest good from the wireless lesson the teacher needs to co-operate with those who are broadcasting. It is not enough to leave the class in the hands of the B.B.C. The manual should be studied carefully to see if the listeners need preparation. If they do, it is best to use different musical examples so that the broadcast lesson is not robbed of its freshness. The teacher should sit at the back of the room during the lesson, and make notes. From these, the work can be revised if necessary and points driven home. In revising it is best to use the broadcast examples.

In Scotland various series of broadcast lessons and concerts are arranged by the Music Sub-Committee of the Scottish Council for School Broadcasting. The schemes of work are adapted specially for Scottish schools.

Careful organisation is necessary if the wireless lesson is to yield its fullest help. The time-table should be arranged so that the music period allows time immediately before or after the broadcast lesson for the teacher's co-operative work. A quiet room and adequate wireless reception are essential. Where conditions are favourable the broadcast lesson is enjoyed by the children and their musical progress is marked.

The wireless provides courses of lectures and concerts which are most valuable for Study Circles (see Part II, 5). The effect of broadcast music on the general taste must also be mentioned: there can be little doubt that it is markedly raising musical standards, thanks to the enlightened policy of the British Broadcasting Corporation. In music the bad currency does not drive out the good: the jazz tune or sentimental ballad is a thing of the passing moment, whereas good music gives more to the listener each time it is heard.

## 13. CORRELATION OF MUSIC WITH OTHER STUDIES

Lack of correlation in teaching is responsible for the habit of regarding each subject as an isolated unit in knowledge rather than as a contribution to the whole. In reality, all knowledge is so interwoven that to deal with any subject in isolation is educationally unsound; the multiplication of evidence impresses knowledge far more firmly on the child's mind. Music, as much as any other social activity, touches life on all sides, and in most cases musical works can be given full meaning only through these contacts. It is therefore of primary importance that the interests with which music is allied in life should be allied with music in school, and this correlation of music with life is best made through the correlation of music with other subjects. "Music time", too, is saved by this means, for other teachers contribute to the music syllabus out of the time allotted to their own subjects. Their good will is very important: sympathy and unanimity of aim are needed. If they have the wrong attitude, they will do more harm than good.

The detail of correlation will depend upon the rest of the school scheme, but a few suggestions, indicating how different subjects are linked with music, may be helpful to head teachers.

RELIGION and music are indissolubly united. Psalms can be chanted and special attention paid to their pointing, hymns can include chorals and plain-song. Scriptural studies can take in their stride most of the stories chosen for oratorios, cantatas, and operas based on sacred subjects. Something of the history of hymns can be taught.

HISTORY may be linked up with music in two ways. An historical period or event can be linked with the actual music of composers who lived at the time—*contemporary correlation*; or the linking can be effected by taking musical settings of something connected with the historical teaching, although the composers may belong to a different age—*associative correlation*. Each form of correlation can supplement the other. With ancient and early history, however, contemporary music will not be available, and only the second form of correlation can be used. Handel's works alone include Julius Caesar, Tamerlane, Judas Maccabaeus, Xerxes and other historical characters. In fact, all historical periods are well represented in musical works of lasting value.

LITERATURE, in its several forms, has always been a fruitful source of musical inspiration. The lyric, the narrative poem, the epic, religious literature, comedy and drama have all been drawn upon by composers— and the music teacher, too, should be able to draw upon the work of the literature teacher in these spheres.

An examination of the names of poets and dramatists

who wrote the libretti of musical works will amaze anyone who has not given the subject much thought. Poetry and prose gain from a good setting: Schubert has added something to *Who is Sylvia?* and *The Erl King*, and Parry to *Blest Pair of Sirens*.

Then instrumental music based on literary "programmes" must not be overlooked. Overtures to plays (the *Coriolan* and *Egmont* of Beethoven), incidental music (Grieg's *Peer Gynt*, Mendelssohn's *Midsummer Night's Dream*), ballets (Rimsky-Korsakov's *Scheherazade*, Vincent d'Indy's *Istar*) and symphonic works (Strauss's *Zarathustra, Don Juan, Till Eulenspiegel, Macbeth,* and *Don Quixote*) with which a first acquaintance should be made in school, are all useful; if the net is thrown wide, examples like those given will correlate music, through literature, with other subjects such as history, legend and myth, and the dance. Literature, especially poetry with its form, rhythm and poetical feeling, has much in common with music, and a sympathetic teacher of literature can help to give children the right attitude to music.

The association of music with the DANCE should begin with the first steps in rhythmic work. Since music was given definite shape through the dance, school dances should be used to show how the shaping developed.

Rhythmic tapping with the feet, clapping of hands, percussion, and so on, can be employed to show how accent and metre were given to music. By grouping these taps in characteristic ways, children can learn how music came to have little rhythmic figures like those which distinguish one dance tune from another. They can then be shown how a set of these rhythmic steps would make a mould for the complete dance "movement".

Singing and dancing grew up together. This is made clear when children notice that early folk-songs are often folk dance-songs. Maypole, Morris, and other country dances might well be performed to the songs with which they are commonly identified.

By dancing the Minuet, followed by the Trio which *doubles* it, and by playing ring-games like the Rondo, in which a chorus dance is repeated after each solo performance, children can be made to understand how the larger structures in music arose out of the repetition and expansion of the single dance.

The changes introduced into music which is composed in the style of dance music, though not meant for dancing, can be detected easily if attempts are made to use such works for a regular set of dance steps.

Children should be allowed to do a number of different dances in sequence, and find by experiment the order which proves to be most satisfying. Translated into music, these experiments will represent the procedure which led to the accepted sequence of dance rhythms in the classical Suite, and which ultimately determined the sequence of movements in the Sonata and Symphony.

A simple history of the dance up to modern times, with musical illustrations, can be made to throw interesting light on the customs as well as the music of different periods of history.

SCIENCE is correlated with music directly by the study of acoustics. All musicians ought to have some elementary practical knowledge of acoustics, so that they understand the mechanical means by which music is produced by the voice and by various instruments. They should know how instruments are tuned and how music is recorded on the disc of the gramophone. The universal interest in wireless reproduction should easily stimulate a desire to understand the elementary acoustical and electrical principles underlying it. The fact ought to be made clear to students that music furnishes many interesting problems of physics which can be approached with a scientific mind.

The nationality of a composer and the national characteristics of a musical work cannot be mentioned without reference to GEOGRAPHY. Folk-music of different countries, and the music of their leading composers, can be taken profitably when the corresponding geographical studies are in progress. If compositions definitely bearing on geography are available, all the better. For example, in Russian music there is Borodin's *On the Steppes of Central Asia*; Rimsky-Korsakov's *Sadko* not only combines music with legendary lore but, with its Merchant, Viking, Hindoo, and Venetian songs, emphasises the historical importance of Novgorod as a great commercial town on the highway from the north to the middle east. *The London Symphony*, *The Hebrides Overture*, *Finlandia*, *The New World Symphony* and the like, have varying values for association with their place names. Gramophone records of all kinds of genuine Oriental and African music exist and might be used with advantage in the teaching of Geography.

ARTS AND CRAFTS may be brought into practical correlation with music when pupils produce any musical play or opera requiring scenery, dresses and properties which can be made in school. The making of musical instruments (See Appendix E, 2), even if only of a primitive kind, is also of interest. In teaching the history of the arts attention may be drawn to the numerous sculptures and pictures of all periods representing musical subjects—sometimes with singular accuracy of detail—and such works of art can sometimes be illustrated in the music class or by the gramophone. If a famous picture is shown in which musicians are represented, the question naturally arises, "What is the music that they are playing?" Let the class hear it, or at any rate hear music that would be appropriate to the period of the painter and the circumstances depicted. It is sometimes interesting too to hear modern compositions which have been suggested by pictures or other works of art, e.g. Respighi's Suite on three pictures by Botticelli.

The correlation of music with the practical crafts could have a vocational interest for children who show special aptitude. If sufficiently attracted to the music trades, they might find it possible to take up the making and testing of musical instruments, type-setting, engraving, lithography, process work or sales-manship.

The interplay of music and most subjects of the curriculum has now been surveyed, and we believe that through correlation of the kind suggested the music teaching can considerably enrich the rest of school work.

## 14. MUSICAL EDUCATION OF DIFFICULT AND RETARDED TYPES

The interesting task of giving musical training to children with retarded mentalities is of so experimental and varied a character that we have not felt able to prepare a specimen scheme of work. Certain funda-mental principles have been established, however, as primarily important in this type of training, and a brief survey, with hints upon their application, will help those who need to adapt the ordinary schemes in Part II for use with sub-normal children.

There is little doubt that music and pre-eminently *rhythm* has a striking and subtle power to quicken slow intelligence. Where instruction has been built upon rhythm, nervous energies have been co-ordinated, stammering has decreased and articulation improved beyond recognition. Even an elementary feeling for numbers has been developed. In fact, the effect of rhythm is so powerful that it seems to open a reservoir from which the physical and mental systems draw energy. It is desirable, therefore, to set the vital currents flowing by means of suitable rhythmic exercises before lessons of all kinds. Indeed music should not be allocated to one or two specific periods a week, but should permeate the whole curriculum. Since children of this type can only concentrate for very short periods, the value of rhythmic stimulus at frequent intervals cannot be exaggerated. The following suggestions indicate a number of ways in which rhythm may be used:

(1) *Rhythmic Breathing.* Breathing exercises with musical accompaniment at a suitable rate to secure balance and control of breath.

(2) *Rhythmic Movements.* Marching, stepping, hand-beating, arm-beating, and other movements appropriate to the character of the music which is being played: exercises in recognition of phrase-endings, either by change of direction in marching or by varied movements (these are particularly valuable as they aid the sense of balance so often lacking in sub-normal children): exercises in quick response to develop co-ordination, concentration and memory: rhythmic games such as "Horses and Driver".

(3) *Song-Singing.* Singing of songs specially selected for their strong rhythmic lilt, sung and accompanied with a well-marked stress.

(4) *Percussion Bands.* Playing of percussion instruments, in rhythmic swing with the music: individual conducting with a stick or by the playing of a percussion instrument.

(5) *Figure Stepping and Dancing.* Stepping in response to music to form simple figures and patterns, at first in imitation of the teacher, and then from memory.

(6) *Verse Speaking.* The whole class speaking together with marked rhythm, and, where suitable, with instrumental accompaniment.

We have suggested already that music can be used to advantage at other times as well as in the music lesson; for instance, as a stimulus to fresh activities. It fulfils a useful purpose also when used as a background in lessons involving manual work. Here the effect is to increase output and relieve monotony. Music can be used to rouse or to soothe children as occasion demands. Indeed, a particular composition, such as the first movement of the Op. 27, No. 2 Pianoforte Sonata by Beethoven, may be used to indicate immediate quiet in the room. Instructions can sometimes be given musically instead of verbally. Orders such as *Stand up*, *Sit down*, can be associated with a rising and a falling musical cadence.

A few comments on the teaching of the different branches of music will show how each may be made to benefit retarded children. Schemes of work will be found under the appropriate headings in Part II.

*Voice-Training.* All exercises should be presented rhythmically, very simply, and briefly. Loud, raucous singing, so characteristic of children with limited mentality, must be gently but firmly checked; superfluous or uncontrolled energy should be directed into other channels such as physical movements.

*Song-Singing.* The rhythmic element can be reinforced by suitable and expressive movements. Songs should be verbally simple yet sensible. The teacher should carefully note preferences and avoid forcing unwelcome songs upon the children. For a list of suitable songs see Appendix A.

*Ear-Training.* Development of aural acuteness is usually accompanied by improved mentality, and ear-training is, therefore, an important branch of music. Plenty of imitatory practice should be given to stimulate weak memories. Ear-tests should be associated with descriptive words, and an appeal be made to the imagination whenever possible. Exercises should be short and varied, and rhythmic movement be resorted to frequently.

*Musical Appreciation.* Backward children are extremely "fond" of music, but it is unwise to dogmatise on the true nature and extent of their appreciation. Music which has colour and dramatic intensity, especially when associated with miming and scenic effects, makes a firm appeal. A promising field for experimental work is indicated by the fact that backward children of tender years have been noticed to sit in rapt attention through a whole opera, and to go to considerable trouble to repeat the experience.

*Sight-Singing.* In beginning to teach the children to sing from notation, the first essential is to establish firmly the mental effect of each note of the scale in relation to its key-note. The notes of the *doh*-chord should be thoroughly learnt first, with any suitable aid, pictorial or imaginative (see Appendix E, 10).

Children should also sing first in imitation and then from memory simple well-known phrases, using the words and Sol-fa names alternately. Hand-signs, and the two modulators, displayed on the blackboard, can be used in turn to promote variety. This association of music with the corresponding Sol-fa names needs frequent practice, but should be limited to small doses, and other musical activities be used for relief. All work in sight-singing should be taken with caution against tiring the children.

Frequently, as a reward for good work, the class should be invited to choose the next song or exercise. The selections should be noted by the teacher, for they will indicate lines along which to make further experiments.

## 15. CONDUCTING AND TRAINING OF CHILDREN'S CHOIRS

At the outset it must be taken for granted that the trainer has a certain technical knowledge (*a*) of the possibilities and limitations of children's voices, (*b*) of the art of conducting, and (*c*) of the principles of artistic interpretation. Coupled with these there should be a sympathetic understanding of and power to manage children, a personality which will appeal to them, and a sense of humour.

At each practice a few minutes should be given to exercises. The resourcefulness of the conductor can make these the most stimulating part of the rehearsal. Simplicity and variety should mark them, and most important of all, the vitalising factor, rhythm. Breath control, tone, and attack are all improved by them. The remainder of the time will be spent in learning unison and part-songs of every conceivable type. Whether taught by ear or from copies, words, rhythm and tune should be learnt as quickly as possible. The style of the song and its interpretation should then be discussed with the choir. This kindles interest and artistic feeling, brings out individual ideas and develops a feeling of unity and responsibility. Apart from the general principles of massed singing (such as clean attack and good phrasing) the charm of a children's choir lies in its spontaneity, its natural stressing of words, and its evident delight in and understanding of the song itself (see also Part III, 17, "Conducting and Training of Adult Choirs", in which some suggestions apply equally to Junior Choirs).

Where a selection of singers is necessary, to ensure a keen beginning, the entrance test could take the form of a competition, varying in difficulty according to the age and capacity of the children. The test might be drawn from work done in the weekly singing class, e.g. (*a*) long sounds with changing vowels, (*b*) scale passages of some kind, (*c*) one verse of a well-known song—for enunciation. In the case of children new to the school a verse of something as simple as *God save the King* is quite a good test. Details of the test should be announced beforehand, and at the audition a few words of criticism should be given after each performance. This creates at once a standard in the child's mind. In selecting voices, good pitch, clearness and roundness are better than powerful tone. The children who are not quite good enough to be given a place can be put on a reserve list and encouraged to try next time. By this means there is always a waiting list of expectant candidates which can be drawn upon, and work in the weekly singing classes will be keener.

The foregoing principles apply to choirs of boys, or girls, or both, in every type of school, and of every age. In some districts the trainer will encounter problems of tone quality and dialect accents. These can usually be modified by a process of vowel and consonant practice. The varying ages of children in the choir of a small school constitutes a far greater problem. As it is not always possible to use songs suitable for all, it is better to choose for the older ones. Small children rise to an occasion, and experience proves that little ones would rather be thought "grown-up" than older ones "childish". It is well to encourage a sense of leadership among the seniors, and of importance among the juniors.

The stimulus of concert-giving and Festival work is good in moderation (and if the right spirit is shown), but the steady team work of a school choir is valuable from every point of view.

## 16. CONDUCTING AND TRAINING OF CHILDREN'S ORCHESTRAS

Usually the teacher in charge of the school music is expected to conduct the school orchestra. The main requisites in the conductor are enthusiasm and willingness to learn his job by doing it. Experience will teach him much, and if he is not above consulting orchestral players, in time he can get enough working knowledge to carry him over most of his elementary difficulties. Attention to the following details will help him to get a satisfactory grip of the work:

(1) Practice periods should be regular. One to one-and-a-half hours each is usually long enough.

(2) In arranging the performers, it is inadvisable to have all the better players on the 1st violin side, and the weaker ones on the 2nd violin side. They should be mixed, and a complete change over is desirable occasionally. Confidence is necessary at first, so blunders should not be too much noticed. Timid players will be helped by being placed next to those of more experience.

(3) In tuning their instruments, beginners can be

helped by more expert players. Aimless scraping should be checked, and the tuning process should be completed quickly. The sound A (new Philharmonic pitch) given from a pianoforte will provide the pitch.

(4) The players must understand clearly the movements used for beating time, which should be according to the orthodox system. Plenty of drill in *attack* should be given, until all can start confidently with the beat. The first beat given should be the first beat of the score, with an ample preliminary movement of the stick leading up to it. Players who have had some bars' rest should be given warning of re-entry several beats beforehand. A sudden signal is useless. Release of tone must be unanimous; practice should be given on long notes, using a "flick off" of the stick as the terminating signal. The restart after a pause needs the same care.

(5) In ensemble performance, the players must be encouraged to use eyes and ears: they must play with the beat and listen to the effect. Following late on the beat is a common fault. A unison passage can be used for practice.

(6) Playing out of tune is often due to lack of concentrated listening. Individual attention is necessary in dealing with this fault. For beginners some teachers use a fretted finger-board, others a more temporary expedient in the shape of gummed paper. When such methods are employed, the mechanical aid should be discarded as soon as possible and the players be encouraged to rely on memory of finger position checked by ear. The great advantage of frets is that they allow beginners to play simple orchestral arrangements very early in their training, and this is an added interest.

(7) A dead level tone should be avoided. There should be a wide difference between *piano* and *forte* and

gradations should be nicely gauged. Monotonous tone is often caused by playing music which is too difficult: attention is then wholly absorbed by the notes. An expressive beat will promote expressive playing; the left hand of the conductor should be used to indicate variations. The meaning of the gestures must be clearly explained to the players.

(8) Attention to orchestral balance is an important part of the conductor's task. He must assess clearly, and explain to the players, the function of each part: and he must listen keenly throughout.

(9) Before attempting a new piece of music the pupils should first listen to a good gramophone record of it, played by a complete and competent orchestra. In this way both the pupils and their conductor will obtain a valuable lesson on the interpretation of the piece, and also on details of pace, tone colour, phrasing and expression. After this the children's orchestra should play the whole piece through at approximately the right speed in order to get a general practical impression of it. Attention should then be given to securing correct notes, the instrumentalists being encouraged to play out (at a slightly slower pace if necessary). The parts should be taken separately, with special observation of position, fingering, and bowing, and the players be urged to practise in their own time. Next, the ensemble should be considered, and precision in attack and release emphasised. Last should come attention to expression and general polish. Each practice should include sight playing of pieces well within the capacity of the performers; the pieces must be played through without stopping, and the players must strive to be together at each bar. Boldness must be encouraged: timidity is fatal.

(10) String technique is a matter for the expert

teacher. Non-playing conductors should consult an expert on matters of fingering, position, and bowing, and have the parts marked. They should know a good posture from a bad, and learn to realise technicalities of tone production. Uniform bowing should be demanded. Technical points are a matter for illustration, however, and the best player should be called upon to demonstrate. Passages which are too hard for the weaker players should be simplified. This is better than having some players idle. The conductor's musicianship should be shown here.

(11) A small school orchestra will be greatly helped by having a pianist to give rhythmic and harmonic support. The best plan is to have two competent players, playing together from a carefully edited four-hand arrangement. The conductor must insist on unobtrusive playing. The function of the pianoforte is not to lead; nor should it reproduce the passage work of the strings. It should be used, just as the harpsichord was used in the days of Bach and Handel, to strengthen the bass (a children's orchestra will probably have few violoncellos and no double basses), to give general harmonic support and to impart vigour and confidence to the rhythmic attack.

The conductor will require considerable knowledge of music in order to prepare a suitable pianoforte part; if he has not had an adequate theoretical training himself he will do well to ask the help of some more experienced musician.

(12) School orchestras are not often able to secure capable players of wind instruments. The deficiency may be supplied in various ways. Sustained melodies may sometimes be written out for solo stringed instruments; quick and lively passages, and energetic passages for trumpets and other brass instruments, are

often better given to the pianoforte. Sometimes a harmonium or American organ will be helpful; but its deficient power of attack makes it often a hindrance rather than a help. There are other instruments such as the concertina, and even the humble tin or wooden whistle, often played by children, which can be used in a small orchestra. The concertina, if confined to the playing of melodies, will make a fair substitute for the oboe, and the flute parts may be supplied to some extent by the whistle.

## 17. CONDUCTING AND TRAINING OF ADULT CHOIRS

A conductor needs to be a sound musician, who has studied voice-training, can sing passages to his choirs in the way he wishes to have them sung, and can illustrate different kinds of tone production. He should be regular and punctual at rehearsal, business-like, and above all, inspiring. He should invariably map out beforehand all that he wishes to get through at any one rehearsal. He should of course be able to hear all the parts of any work practised, and should listen particularly to the inner and lower parts. At rehearsal (and especially at a final rehearsal) he should occasionally leave his desk, and listen at a distance to the general effect, paying particular attention to balance and clarity of words. The conductor's desk is often the worst position in a large hall for estimating the balance of various sections of the choir, of choir and orchestra, and of soloists and orchestra.

Both conductor and chorus should realise the value (both to themselves and to the audience) of singing the English language finely in public. Good declamation means not only the clear enunciation of vowels and consonants; it implies the power to discriminate the differing vocal *force* necessary to sing effectively, say, five crotchets in a row, where some syllables or words need accentuation, while others should be more in the background (less accented). In other words, *all* members of a well-trained chorus should sing their parts as a good soloist sings his or her part. Quick declamation ("patter") should be practised: it makes for mobile tongues and lips.

The conductor should test all applicants for admission to the chorus in sight-reading and sense of pitch. It may not be possible to insist on a really high standard of sight-reading, but this should be kept constantly before the chorus as an ideal; the singers should be encouraged to practise reading and the exact hitting of intervals at home. Ascending major intervals, which are easily sung out of tune, should especially be practised. Bad readers cause much waste of time at rehearsal and are always inclined to *drag* the music.

The conductor should make sure that each applicant has the requisite and *even* compass for his or her part. A tenor part should not be sung by a forced-up baritone. Mezzo-sopranos require careful and individual consideration; some will be better amongst the sopranos, if there is any sign that the upper notes will gain strength by practice, while others, who cannot stand the strain of continuous high passages, must be placed with the contraltos.

Each section, as well as the chorus as a whole, must be trained to make a short or long *crescendo* and a *diminuendo*, which is far harder, together; this is largely a matter of correct breathing. Since faulty breathing also produces flat singing, especially at the ends of the longer phrases, the conductor should give the chorus instruction in correct breathing. *Tremolo*, which is also due to bad breathing, must be carefully avoided; one tremulous voice can ruin the effect of a whole chorus.

Variety of tone will be needed for different contexts. In polyphonic music, each set of voices should mark and illustrate the declamation and phrasing that belongs to its own part; this may necessitate a *crescendo*, with a rising phrase, and a *diminuendo* with a falling phrase at different times in the different parts. A chorus must beware, too, of being cramped by bar-lines: a sense of free rhythm is essential. This treatment applies to music of all periods, though, of course, it is particularly necessary for the effective singing of music of the sixteenth and early seventeenth centuries.

All chorus-singers should learn to listen to parts other than their own: then they will realise that they are all parts of a whole, and should be now prominent, now in the background. They should learn their music by heart as much as possible: only thus will they be able to notice every lead of the conductor, and respond at once. This is essential at the beginnings and ends of phrases, and at all changes of time. Any raggedness or inequality will be most apparent in octave (so-called "unison") singing, which many chorus-singers regard as their easiest task.

In choosing works for performance (large or small choral works, with or without orchestra; or unaccompanied works, motets, madrigals, or part-songs), the conductor should see that the words are good poetry, and have been set by composers of repute: and as a final test, he should see that the composer has fully grasped the meaning and the declamation of the words. Amateur choirs should give occasional public performances either at a concert or in a competition festival: thus they can gain confidence and experience, and learn through criticism or by comparison with others how to sing better.

Choral Societies may, on occasion, turn their attention to opera, especially if a proper stage performance be feasible. Performances of popular and well-known comic operas are to be deprecated; it is much better to attack some work that is now unknown to the general public, so that the interpretation of the work can be fresh and new, instead of a slavish imitation of something which has become stereotyped. Research into seventeenth and eighteenth century operas and masques will be repaid. For example, any of the following are well worth study and performance: Purcell, *Dido and Aeneas*, *King Arthur*, and *The Fairy Queen*; Handel, *Semele*. Handel's dramatic oratorios, e.g. *Samson* and *Theodora*, are very suitable for stage production in a dignified form.

## 18. CONDUCTING AND TRAINING OF ADULT ORCHESTRAS

We discuss in Part IV, 4 and 5, "Organisation of Adult Choirs and Orchestras", some of the points which have to be considered when the foundations of an orchestra are being laid. Once this preliminary work has been done, the conductor has to consider carefully the lines of development and here we give hints that may be found useful at this stage.

In the early stages it is wise to choose music for those players whose competence is rather below the average of the whole orchestra, but once the orchestra is formed and working, harm can be done by keeping music too easy. Capacity must be kept on the stretch for part at any rate of each rehearsal.

The ideal conductor is the man or woman who can

play and discuss the technical problems of every instrument in the orchestra. This is manifestly impossible in the case of amateurs. Where, for instance, the conductor is a pianist or wind player unacquainted with string technique, it would be wise to get the leader to help to mark the bowing and fingering of the orchestral parts. The feeling of good bow discipline must be instilled early into the orchestra. Players who have sufficient rehearsals should be able to reach the point where everybody's bow touches the string at the same point at the same moment, and where bows move up and down absolutely together. The same principles apply to fingering, for this affects the choice of string for a particular note, which in its turn affects the tone. Balance between sections of the orchestra, and within the different sections, is important. Top-heaviness caused by a large number of violin players and only a few 'cellos and basses or (what is very common) weakness in the viola section, is not compensated by faulty balance in the other direction, in another part of the orchestra.

The players should be as much on the alert as the conductor to see that the part that carries the tune is prominent, and that no undue weight is given to any particular note in a chord.

In the wind section the same principles apply and it should be seen that the players breathe at the same moment whenever their parts are moving together. Another special point in this section is intonation: the quality of the instruments may not be very good and many of the notes may be out of tune. Faulty intonation can be corrected by embouchure, with patient attention by the player to every note that he plays. The art of listening to one's own performance is not easy to learn, but is of vital importance.

Balance between the various sections—wind and strings and percussion—is still more the affair of the conductor. An important principle here is transparency of tone: it is a useful rule to tell players that if they cannot hear the instrument that is playing the tune, they themselves must be playing too loudly. Listening to the tune is a rule which can never be too often emphasised in different ways by the conductor. The conductor must also watch rhythm, for from this comes the vitality without which no performance has any artistic value.

## 19. TRAINING OF CONDUCTORS

Remarkable results have been achieved in the last few years with classes for the training of conductors. One need not be a highly equipped musician to be able to impress on others the importance of making their own music, and to train successfully a village choral society or an amateur orchestra. The ideal demanded of the student who leaves Kneller Hall to become a military bandmaster—that he should be able to teach every instrument in his band—need not be aimed at. Judges who have paid repeated visits to annual musical events, such as musical competition festivals, have been astonished at the improvement in the standard of performance after the introduction of a conference or course for conductors. The conferences are most satisfactory when held at the beginning of the season (usually the early autumn) for a period of a half day, or more, with intervals for meals and informal conversation. The conference can usefully be followed by a course of about six meetings of an hour and a half or two hours each, taken by a professional conductor. The course should be organised by the committee of the local musical festival (Part IV, 6), some voluntary association interested in music (Part IV, 7), or the Local Education Authority. The subjects which should be discussed in a course for the training of conductors may be classified as follows:

(1) *Technique in the actual movements of conducting, with practice (if possible) for each member of the class.*

This should include a discussion of the merits and demerits of using the stick or open hand; the actual movements to be used in conducting various beats of the bar; the methods of showing expression, such as *staccato* and *legato*; the proper preparation of each beat, the easy swing of the hand and the avoidance of jerky movement except where needed for special efforts; starts and finishes, when it is particularly valuable for the class to form itself into an informal choir and for each member to conduct a few bars, or a few chordal pauses.

(2) *Hints on the study of the music before the first rehearsal.*

Here the importance should be stressed of studying the music as a whole first and of only beginning detailed study when the character of the complete work has been grasped. The relative importance and weight of the climaxes should be noted, and any point of difficulty in the use of the stick should be thought out before the rehearsal.

(3) *Suggestions for the management of rehearsals, and the preparation and approach to the performance by the conductor.*

Hints should be given on the plan of rehearsal, which might begin with a few breathing exercises, to open throats and stretch lungs before the new work is approached. Then should come the hardest task of the evening, the study of new work. The sopranos and altos may start the rehearsal alone and the tenors and basses stay alone at the end. To stimulate attendance, rehearsals should finish with the enjoyment of music already learned and known. At the end of each rehearsal the work done should be noted and members reminded of this at the beginning of the next, in order that they may be induced to attend regularly, and may realise that they have missed valuable work if they miss a rehearsal. Conductors should think out beforehand a scheme of work for the whole season, and have a detailed plan for each rehearsal (see Part II, 5, (2)).

(4) *Advice on the elements of voice-production and of instrumental technique* (see Part III, 2, 3 and 15–18).

(5) *Practical hints on the management of village and other concerts*, with special emphasis on the advisability of the conductor's delegating to others much of the business arrangement. Under this heading will come also such topics as the choice and length of programme; the interval; seating of the choir and orchestra; and propaganda.

# PART IV

## OTHER ASPECTS OF MUSIC

So far, the Report has dealt with the more direct ministrations of teacher to taught. There are other less direct influences, which, though not matters of actual teaching, have great effect upon the musical outlook of the people. Their effect is so definitely educational, that our task would be incomplete if we did not discuss the more important of them.

## 1. MUSIC AND THE CORPORATE LIFE OF THE SCHOOL

A short paragraph dealing with the corporate musical activity of schools of such varying types and opportunities as Junior and Preparatory Schools, Senior Classes and Modern Schools, Secondary Schools, and Public Schools cannot attempt more than an outline of possibilities.

It is happily becoming each year more evident that the care of those in charge of school music is being lavished as generously on the mass as on the individual, with the conviction that it is not less important to train future concert-goers to listen intelligently than to produce individual executants. Mass-singing, and class-singing (with its tributary activities of sight-reading and ear-training) are features that are naturally common to all types of schools, and periods devoted to these subjects offer the widest recreational value. From mass-singing even the most unmusical person is usually found to derive some enjoyment, and whether it be hymns and psalms for a school service, songs for a school concert, or a hurriedly improvised sing-song of an informal nature, here is a type of corporate activity which needs no special justification. The range of artistic appeal is manifestly wide, extending from the well-known instances of performances by the whole school of the *Messiah* and the *B minor Mass*, to the lusty-throated camp-fire. While the Public Schools (and some of the Preparatory Schools), with their chapels and organs, appear more fortunately equipped than others for their daily service, yet Junior, Modern, and Secondary Schools make special features of their morning assemblies for prayers in which, often, the music is provided by their own bands. In these schools (especially Junior Schools and Senior Classes) particularly careful preparation is made for the services for special occasions such as Empire Day, Armistice Day, and Church Festivals.

A vigorous musical life is undoubtedly an important factor in improving the tone of a school.

Although it affects only a small proportion of each school, the weekly orchestral practice cannot be overlooked as a corporate factor, since the orchestra plays such an important part in school concerts, informal sing-songs, prize days, "Open Days" and all other occasions for special celebration.

There is a pianoforte and gramophone in most schools (a player-piano and the wireless in some), and chiefly through them classes of varying sizes learn the art of listening, and sometimes the whole school has similar opportunities when assembled for mass-singing.

The beginning of each school day, with its assembly, gives a frequent opportunity for the expressive use of music. Hymn and Psalm and English lyric with fine settings sung by the whole school can give an inspiring beginning to the day's work, all the more effective if there is a school orchestra to accompany. There is much to be said to devoting the morning assembly on one or two days a week to music.

These are the broad features common to the corporate musical life of the majority of schools; a description of some of their individual variations will conclude this outline.

Peculiar to Junior Schools and Senior Classes (and some Modern and Secondary Schools) is the musical accompaniment for the march into the morning assembly for prayers, and the entry to and from the school buildings. The music is supplied by the pianoforte, the gramophone, or the violin class. Analogies are to be found in the O.T.C., Scout, and Girl Guide organisations where a sense of unity and discipline is helped by these means.

The "Open Days" of all types of schools, and "Music Clubs" of the Secondary Schools call for special mention. In the former, parents and friends see the school at work in all its activities, and music claims a big share in the proceedings. The "Music Clubs" that meet fortnightly or monthly cater for those specially interested in music by arranging lectures, debates, recitals, and concerts by selected forms in the school. In Preparatory Schools, the musical play is a popular item, and visits by professional soloists are fairly frequent.

In the Public Schools, the favourable range of age ($13\frac{1}{2}$ to $18\frac{1}{2}$), the resident music staffs, and a usually healthy concert fund make possible a great variety of local activities and concerts of high standard by professionals. With its organ, a trained four-part choir of the best singers in the school, and a large active unison element, the Public School chapel has unique advantages for corporate services.

The chapel choir is the nucleus of the school Choral Society. Instrumental and choral competitions between Houses are peculiar to Public and other schools which are run on the House system. Preparations for these competitions are largely helped by musical amateurs on the teaching staff. The results accruing from intensive preparation, the team spirit, and a friendly rivalry which pervades the whole school, are far-reaching in their effects.


## 2. CONCERTS FOR CHILDREN

Central concerts for children are now recognised as one of the most fruitful ways of broadening musical education. Their principal aims are to foster a love of the best music by giving children well-performed works of the great composers; to encourage in children the desire to make music themselves; and to build up a tradition in music.

Two series of concerts are available; those held in school hours; and those held at other times. For the first series attendance is compulsory for chosen children; admission must be free by the ruling of the education authority; and since these concerts come under the supervision of the Board of Education the audience must be previously prepared and to some extent must review the concert afterwards. For the second series attendance is voluntary, admission is by a moderate charge, and previous preparation is optional. Apart from these differences, the two series of concerts are similar. Both depend for their audience, the first series entirely, and the second very largely, upon the co-operation of the teaching staff. There is room for both series, and that held in school-time should aim at encouraging children to go to concerts out of school-time, during school-life, and in after-days. The two series are not competitive, but complementary.

The following points stand out amongst general experience:

(1) *Type of Concert.* An orchestral or choral programme, with some vocal or instrumental solos, appears to be the most useful type for the large-scale children's concerts. Chamber music, because of its intimate character, is more suitable for smaller audiences in the schools, where several senior groups can combine in one school hall. This may be a counsel of perfection: limitations of finance will sometimes make it necessary to include concerts by two or three soloists in the large-scale scheme. Similarly the expense of an orchestra and the shortness of the concerts make it desirable to use the players all the time, and not allow them to sit idle while a soloist performs.

(2) *Length of Concert and of Items.* A children's concert should rarely exceed one hour in length, and no item should take longer than seven to ten minutes. It has been observed repeatedly that *active* attention on the part of most of the audience ceases after about five minutes.

(3) *Musical Material.* Only the best music, within the capacity of the children, should be presented. The performance should reach the highest artistic standard. In choosing items it is well to remember that inexperienced listeners are most often attracted by strong rhythm, good melodic outline, and "programme" music. Nevertheless the practice of fixing a programme to music not so designed by the composer is to be deprecated. The device of attaching words to themes in classical music has serious disadvantages in the hands of the unskilled, and should be used with extreme caution.

The choice of suitable music is easier if the age and musical experience of the audience is homogeneous.

(4) *Choral Items by Audience.* As a relief from continual listening, the audience itself may take part sometimes, by humming or clapping themes, or by standing and singing.

(5) *Preparation for Concert.* Programmes should be circulated to schools in advance to allow preparation, which should be correlated as far as possible with the existing music scheme; *indeed the ideal concert programme should form the crowning point of a period of ordinary school music work.*

(6) *Introductory Talks.* At the concert, brief talks should precede the items, and the talks, as a whole, should occupy considerably less time than the music. Where the school preparation has been thorough, the remarks can be directed solely towards creating a suitable atmosphere. Indeed, little more than this can be done with advantage in any circumstances, if the talks are to be kept reasonably short. The success of the concert depends largely upon the skill of the speaker, who should be carefully chosen for the task.

## 3. OTHER MUSICAL INFLUENCES ON THE CHILD OUT OF SCHOOL

### (a) The Home

The conditions of home life vary so much in different families that it is impossible to make detailed suggestions of any value. Much depends on the parents' interest in music, as well as upon their financial resources. We cannot expect to find in every home that ideal family in which every member is a true lover of music, and the practice of ensemble music, vocal and instrumental, a matter of course. The days are perhaps gone when children were expected to perform for the entertainment of their parents, often for parents who did not even pay them the common courtesy of listening to the performance in silence. The very early years are as important for music as for other subjects. The best nursery rhymes and folk-songs, sung to children frequently from the first and learnt by them as early as can be, will lay a lasting foundation of sound taste.

Probably the commonest feature of musical life in the homes of to-day is the presence of the gramophone or wireless set. The benefits of these appliances need not be discussed. But they have their dangers as well. The mechanical reproduction of music is so easy that many people are tempted to regard these instruments merely as toys. Music—of some kind or other—can be turned on for any length of time. The dangers of making it available for everybody at all times are very real. If music is heard under the wrong conditions, it becomes merely an irritant to the nerves which may do us mental and nervous harm without any benefit or pleasure. Mechanised music should be turned on only when people are willing to listen to it in silence or when it serves some definite subsidiary purpose; the moment attention begins to wane and the music to lose its interest, it should be cut off, so that the ear and nerves may have rest.

Parents, whether musical or not, often find their musical children a nuisance. They should bear with them patiently. Music is for some children a refuge from the unpleasant realities of life, a secret world into which they can retire for that sense of privacy which all children imperatively require. Musical children can often enjoy music, if they are free of disciplinary constraint, for much longer periods than adult musicians can, though it may take the form of "strumming" and produce a plentiful supply of wrong notes. In some cases a passion for music may lead to self-absorption of a dangerous type; the remedy for this is not to forbid music, but to encourage the making of music in partnership with others, even if partnership can go no further than the pianoforte duet.

Apparently little is done in most families to encourage the child to read about music. Yet it should be obvious that the sooner this habit can be developed, so that it will be as natural for the youngster to read about music as about sport, or books, or other hobbies, the better for his musical development. Happily there is a steady increase of musical literature suitable for young readers —short and attractively compiled biographies, histories, etc. (see Appendix E, 11 (a)); there is also a musical journal for the young called *The Music Student* (see Appendix F). Even adult musical journals are not beyond young readers. The correspondence of a journal like *The Musical Times* reveals that students in the early 'teens find its articles within their comprehension.

### (b) PLACES OF WORSHIP

The singing of English in places of worship should, clearly, be of the best, both from the literary and the musical point of view. The Authorised Version of the Bible and the style of the Prayer Book are without parallel in English literature. It should be remembered that the Authorised Version was a new and inspiring thing to the sixteenth and early seventeenth century composers, and that the Prayer Book, and its version of the Psalms, was equally new and inspiring to the Restoration composers. Therefore the words of the hymns and the tunes to which they are sung should emulate these masterpieces.

Hymn tunes and chants, because they are bound to

be repeated over and over again, should be diatonic, dignified, rhythmical, and of reasonable compass in all parts (soprano, alto, tenor, and bass)—especially in the treble part for children. There should be no dragging, no *rallentandos* at the end of verses, nor pauses (except momentarily, for breath). Children and young people are generally alert and active; they do not want to drag their music, if left alone. Further, they will like the finest and best, if only they are allowed to know it. Organs or pianofortes (not harmoniums) should be used to accompany the choir and congregation. Village orchestras are often available now, and should play at service time, especially for the hymns (see Appendix B).

### (c) PLACES OF ENTERTAINMENT

The chief agencies which provide musical entertainment to-day are the band or orchestra in the public park, the theatre, restaurant, and picture palace; the street organ; and the cinema organ.

The band in the public park and the street organ play chiefly light, attractive music, the tunes of the moment—those that mother hums, that father whistles, that sister or brother sings or plays. They make an instant and easy appeal, they tickle the ear and haunt the memory. They do not require any concentrated attention. Since they lend colour to life, they are valuable; but their influence is social rather than musical.

The proportion of children who attend theatres or restaurants is very small, but the influence of music in the picture palace must be enormous. The numbers of children who go are formidable, while the quality of the music and of the environment in the public cinema is improving rapidly. Over thirty million people attend the cinema every week in the British Isles. In London alone more than half a million children of school age go to the "movies" at least once a week. The cumulative effect of the music they hear cannot be over-estimated. Music is an essential part of the film show. It underlines the scenes and creates the emotional atmosphere, even if it does not have the undivided attention of the patrons of the cinema. Second-rate halls with bad music are quickly disappearing, and even small towns now have "palaces" where the best films are projected and the music is cleverly arranged. It is now the rule for films to have their own pot-pourris of synchronised music. The whole range of music has been surveyed with a view to choosing what will make the most rapid and telling appeal to the average audience.* Thus, most children hear, in the cinema, better chosen and better performed music than anywhere else, except perhaps in school.

As the "sound" film improves in quality, it should give the world of musical education a most potent factor in training in intelligent listening. At present only a very few children can hear first-hand performances; but sound films should offer even more opportunities than does wireless for hearing master-pieces worthily performed. In the performance of opera, and many other types of work, the visual interest has an advantage over the wireless. When orchestral pieces are being played, the sound film can explain the instrumentation and show "close-ups" of sections of the orchestra as they enter. National music can be made by native artists in native dress.

At present the hearing of much cinema music cloys

---

* The criticism from the musical point of view, that the music is mutilated, can be over-stressed. What *is* important is the social effect of the music. This is too large a subject to go into here, but it is a matter with which musicians might well concern themselves.

the musical palate because of the high proportion of emotional and strongly coloured music. This makes the task of arranging children's concerts very difficult; children will not appreciate inferior performances of chamber music, for instance, when they have the attractive alternative at the cinema. While we do not suggest that the lead of the cinema should be followed in school and concert hall, it is possible to learn from it the need for wise selection and vivid performance.

### (d) MUSIC AND SOCIAL CONDUCT

Music is produced to-day with great ease and frequency in places of entertainment; gramophone and portable wireless set are ubiquitous and assault the ear in the most inappropriate places, on hillside and river. Child and adult alike are continuously battered by music on all sides. Music may be abused in many ways by over-zealous, selfish and thoughtless people. To the Greeks, music meant *good form* in all things; it meant *fitness* and gave a training in right conduct. The Greek idea might receive a modern interpretation.

We have suggested elsewhere that the music repertory set before children should be varied enough to suit all tastes. Now we add that the consideration shown to those who join with us in the practice of music must be extended to those who differ from us about the manner and occasion of their enjoyment of music. Music should contribute to the life of the community an attitude of social harmony and tolerance; if we do not recognise that there are times when music is out of place we fail in one of the virtues that music is supposed to foster. Lovers of music should be most careful not to cause annoyance to others; they may always hope that those who lack fervour will one day see the light, but the change will not come through the antagonising effect of over-enthusiasm. The same problem is met in a different form when the music class interferes with other lessons.

Teachers have, in fact, the new responsibility of setting a standard in the discriminating and considerate use of music in the home and in public, and by-laws are needed against the worst abuses.

## 4. ORGANISATION OF ADULT CHOIRS

In starting adult choirs it is commonly found both in towns and villages that the quickest approach is through the song club—sing-songs, community singing, gatherings at which everybody is encouraged to sing, not with the idea of learning something, but just for enjoyment. At first the songs must be chosen from well-known favourites: many of the singers will not take part when it is something they do not know, and as the first aim is to get them to enjoy singing together, it is important that they should have every inducement to sing. Singing on these lines can soon become a popular weekly event.

Once this is accomplished, a move may be made towards turning the sing-song into a choir or choral society. The church and chapel choirs may sometimes form the nucleus of a choral society (see Part IV, 7). Voice-training, reading, part-singing, and all that enters into good choral work can gradually become a part of the singing. At first, however, all teaching should arise from and be focused upon the particular song that is being sung; the actual exercise given should come from the song itself and not be merely an exercise. In this way the singers will begin to perceive how an exercise helps towards the result at which they are aiming and will be the more ready to undergo formal training.

Once the choir has been formed, there is the question of keeping the interest of its members. Useful agents in this are: tactful enthusiasm on the part of the conductor; watching for and training suitable members of the choir to take the place of the conductor in an emergency; keeping the sing-song as a permanent class side by side with the choir, for, having first offered a jumping-off place, it will be valuable as a recruiting ground.

Some of what has been said here may appear to contradict the precepts for more advanced training; but we must not forget that our concern is with *beginnings*, with the *arousing of interest*, and that serious work must nearly always have more informal beginnings.

## 5. ORGANISATION OF ADULT ORCHESTRAS

It has sometimes been argued that members of adult amateur orchestras would be better employed singing in a chorus, where their instrument is ready made, and probably of good quality, whilst orchestral instruments cost money and are often of poor quality. There is no answer to this beyond the fact that a certain type of mind gets more pleasure in playing an orchestral instrument than in singing in a choral society. Wind players especially have an independent part to keep up and their interest and musicianship are therefore stimulated to a far greater degree.

The organisation of orchestras naturally involves a greater financial strain than that of a choral society, and constructive help can perhaps best be given by quoting the experience of an orchestra associated for many years with the old Great Eastern Railway at Liverpool Street Station.

The orchestra was founded by a public-spirited director, Colonel William Johnson Galloway, and financed by him. It was over a hundred strong; most of the instruments, and the library, were the property of the orchestra. The system pursued was as follows. The members assembled at 5.15, or as near after as they could get away from work, and worked for about an hour and a quarter in various small rooms in the Bishopsgate Institute. They were grouped as follows: violins and violas with a violin professor, violoncellos with a violoncello professor, double basses with a double bass professor, and wood-wind and brass with an experienced military bandmaster. At the end of this period after a short interval they came together in the large hall of the Institute and rehearsed with their conductor for an hour and a half. The efficiency reached by this orchestra, owing to the special training given in the earlier part of the evening, was quite remarkable; they could rehearse and prepare, during the winter season, as many as six separate programmes and perform them with great efficiency and spirit. The technical level achieved can be shown by the fact that, at a time when it was found necessary to reduce railway staffs, the orchestra lost about twenty members, and all but two were able to earn a living by playing their instruments and became professional musicians.

It is obviously impossible for ordinary amateur orchestras to achieve such a standard, but it may be possible to adopt part of this procedure according to local conditions. Where, for instance, funds are not forthcoming for purchase of libraries, the Carnegie Loan Library has a useful collection of orchestral and choral material for hire at nominal rates (see Appendix H 3).

Conductors should look carefully into the possibility of using the services of players from any military band that may be within reach. The decision of the Army Council, made public in January, 1929, has made it possible for military bands to provide invaluable help to local orchestras at the low pitch which is now in general use for concerts in this country.

The question of the completeness of his orchestra is one of considerable difficulty to a conductor. It is not easy to find a pianist who will be able to play from a full score the parts of any instruments that are missing at rehearsal or performance. It is better to choose works for a smaller and not larger orchestra than is available. If, for instance, the orchestra is complete in wood-wind, but only has reduced brass, it is far better to play works by Mozart or Haydn, or the early works of Beethoven, and to give, say, the trombone player an extra bassoon or even a violoncello part and tell him to double with that instrument. In the same way, where a complete body of strings is available with only one or two wind instruments, it is far more satisfactory to use music written for strings and let any wind players use extra string parts.

## 6. MUSICAL FESTIVALS AND COMPETITIONS

The Musical Competition Festival is about fifty years old. The first meeting took place at Stratford (London) in 1882, followed by Kendal in 1885. The movement has developed with surprising rapidity; it is now one of the most vital forms of musical activity in the country and is doing a great work in improving performance and public taste. No other events outside school life bring so many people into practical contact with good music.

Quick development is a sign of vigorous life, but it has its dangers. It is not surprising that the festival movement has grown in some respects too rapidly for its organisation, and that there remain some departments whose educational value can be materially increased. In particular, in most festivals sight-singing classes are not popular and need more encouragement. Wherever the importance of the subject has been brought home to competitors, and the classes are well organised, the sight-reading has been extremely interesting and profitable. It is, we think, a mistake to make sight-singing a compulsory part of a contest until the subject has been popularised, and even then it should be only in certain special classes, such as those entered by schools where the subject is well taught and the standard good. Much harm to the cause of sight-singing has been done by the choice of too difficult tests, and (where the subject is new or the standard low) by the holding of competitions in public. Choirs naturally object to breaking down and being made to look foolish before a crowd. At festivals where the subject is not yet well established, we feel it is therefore advisable to hold the competitions in an anteroom, and to choose tests so simple that the risk of absolute failure is very small. Much might be done for the future of this subject by encouraging classes for solo sight-singing, especially among children. The tests should be quite short, and available in both notations. Small parties, such as trios and quartets, should also be encouraged to enter for sight-singing. In large choirs sight-singing is apt to be an unsatisfactory test, because there will probably be "passengers". Encouragement should be given to choirs to enter their singers in small sections.

There is not as a rule much ground for complaint on the score of the quality of the music selected. We feel, however, that it is not always discreetly chosen. Often the music is too difficult, or too severe, or unsuitable in other ways. At present, choirs (especially those in small centres) are often so much occupied in learning the notes that little attention can be paid to the basic principles of choralism, and still less to interpretation. Improved sight-singing would, of course, help here. There appears to be a tendency to show more zeal than discretion in the choice of old madrigals. Madrigal singing demands a special technique, which cannot be looked for in newly-formed choirs of poor material from small centres. Moreover, at festivals where Elizabethan madrigals have bulked largely in the syllabus over a number of years, smaller choirs tend to withdraw from the competition. It is desirable that choirs of all kinds should sing this fine old music, but they should be brought to the necessary stage of technique and taste gradually by means of attractive part songs that are well within their powers. The tests should also be of a type likely to make a ready appeal to them and to their friends, since much of the material used for competitive purposes forms the basis of the local choral society concert.

Turning to the choice of music for school choirs, we think that sufficient attention is not always paid to the consideration of vocal compass and ease of melodic line; tunes are frequently too chromatic and angular. Nor are the limitations of the average school pianist as an accompanist always remembered.

There is room for improvement, too, in the standard of music chosen for male-voice choirs  Too often committees are content to perpetuate a bad old type of male voice chorus of the descriptive, "point-to-point" character. There is now an abundance of male-voice music of excellent quality. In many places in which male-voice choirs are small, with a deficiency of singers able to take the top line, either as altos or first tenors, there is a need for music written for three voices (tenor, baritone, bass), in which the tenor part is kept as a rule within comfortable limits. There is not much music in existence for this combination, but no doubt it would be forthcoming if there were a demand for it.

Of late years a type of festival has developed (especially in the south of England) in which the competitive element is kept more or less in the background, and the activities of all are concentrated on the combined performance of a big work. Combined performances of smaller works are also a feature of some festivals. We feel that from an educational point of view this is a very important move. There are, of course, difficulties. The cost of a full-sized choral work is considerably more than that of two or three part-songs, and so choirs may find a financial difficulty. It is objected also that whereas a choir is able to sing at its local concert the short part-songs prepared for a festival, it is seldom able to give by itself a performance of a large choral work. Against these objections may be set certain great advantages. There is the stimulating experience of joining with other choirs in a massed performance of a fine piece of music. The choir that works through a season at the choruses of a big work has obtained an insight into the music that can be got in no other way. It is no small achievement that hundreds of singers in a district should thus annually become familiar with a masterpiece, which they might otherwise never even hear. Again, this type of festival develops the spirit of comradeship, and therefore does important service on the social side, whereas the purely competitive event contributes less in this way, and may even be anti-social to some extent through local rivalries.

The preliminary mass-rehearsal and the competitions form valuable preparations for the main event, the combined public performance which gives the festival its final justification: thus can a festival best serve and inspire its district.

The value of instruction classes for conductors cannot be over-estimated. Hints on their organisation and line of study will be found in Part III, 19, and Part IV, 7.

It is found that the degree of public support given to Competition Festivals varies very much. In some places it is considerable; in others, there is a regular annual loss. In the long run the best type of financial support is that which comes, not from a few wealthy donors, but mainly from the general public, through membership subscriptions and attendance at the festival. To encourage this the evening sessions, when the largest proportion of people are able to attend, should be made as attractive as possible. The ideal plan is to have one large work, and some of the smaller works set for the competitions, sung by the massed choirs, and a few solos by well-known professionals. In festivals which are purely competitive, the evening programmes might well consist of the *finals* of solo classes (the preliminary sessions having been held during the day), the pick of choral contests, a few well-varied instrumental classes, and an item or two from the best of the prize winners on some previous day of the festival, or even from some previous festival. The ideal should be a judicious combination of concert and competition. Any solo class in which the competitors exceed, say, half a dozen is apt to be an infliction rather than an attraction to all save the friends or teachers of the competitors. Sufficient time, too, should always be allowed for detailed criticism by the adjudicators. When adjudications are audible, simply expressed, frank but friendly, not without humour but entirely without sarcasm, and, above all, constructive, the general public will listen with enjoyment. Moreover, the educational value of a festival lies very largely in the adjudication from the platform; it teaches the general public as well as the competitors.

Sessions are made more interesting if the words of all concerted vocal music are printed in the programme.

Financial stability might be more often achieved than at present if committees would develop the plan of enrolling members of the festival, issuing, in return for subscriptions, a season ticket to cover the whole festival or tickets for separate sessions at reduced rates.

The festival movement possesses abundance of enthusiasm and great potentialities. With greater discretion, practical musical knowledge, psychological insight—a point that affects both audience and competitors—and business-like organisation we see no limit to what the festivals can do in improving the musical taste of a large section of the population, besides developing the social side of life.

## 7. THE FOSTERING OF MUSICAL EDUCATION BY LOCAL ORGANISATIONS

*As illustrated by the Cambridgeshire Council of Musical Education*

We give in Appendix H some particulars of established organisations such as the British Music Society, whose aim is to help music on a national scale. We feel, however, that there is also a need for local organisations which will undertake intensive work, using the county or the city as their unit. The Cambridgeshire Council of Musical Education, from whose initiative this Report springs, is one such organisation, and a description of its aims and activities may prove suggestive to other areas in which a similar body could be formed. Indeed, the Executive Committee of the local Musical Festival, or the Music Committee of the Rural Community Council, already forms in most places a body which could, and sometimes does, undertake work of this kind, although a reorganisation of its constitution would often be advisable. In order to enlist the fullest support, the Cambridgeshire Council's constitution embraces as many interests as possible. The membership is as follows: The Faculty of Music of Cambridge University, 5; Teachers' organisations, 9; the Local Education Authorities, 4; one representative each from the Federation of Women's Institutes, the British Legion, the Rural Community Council, the Federations of Boys' and Girls' Clubs, the University Musical Society and the Musical Club, the Young Men's Christian Association, the Workers' Educational Association, the Organists' Association; and six co-opted members.

The aims of the Council are:

(*a*)  To draw up recommendations for the Education Authorities concerning the place which music should occupy in schools; to prepare model syllabuses as a guide for those engaged in teaching music; to establish courses in music for teachers.

(*b*)  To hold a Festival of Music for Cambridgeshire.

(*c*)  To assist in the formation of choral and orchestral societies and in the provision of conductors, music, instruments, and soloists; to provide training courses for conductors.

(*d*)  To introduce, especially in the rural areas, concert tours and illustrated lectures.

(*e*)  To establish a free lending library of music.

(*f*)  To co-ordinate (through the Rural Community Council) the dates of musical events in the county.

The Council has three Committees: an Advisory Committee consisting of eight members who are expert musicians, to whom in the first place all technical matters of music are referred; a Festival Committee—an executive committee responsible for the organisation of the Festival of Music; and a Village Concerts and Choral Societies Committee, which arranges concerts in the villages, assists choral and orchestral societies in the rural area, and organises central classes for training amateur conductors.

We have not the space to describe how all these aims are carried out, but will confine ourselves, for the sake of an example, to the formation of village choral and orchestral societies, which has been a fruitful field of the Council's work. So often the material for a society is there, though it may not have occurred to anyone on the spot to exploit the possibilities. The Council arranges a concert (preferably including some community singing) in the village. A short talk on choral singing is given in the interval, and it is suggested that the church and chapel choirs should join to form the nucleus of a choral society. As often as not the society is in being before the hall empties that evening. The next step (and here is shown the council's policy of making the work as educational as possible) is to apply for the meetings of the society to be recognised under the County Education Authority's regulations for adult evening classes; the name of a suitable conductor is submitted to the Authority at the same time. In nearly every case the society realises the great advantages, both in the type of training and in finance, to be gained by meeting regularly as a County Evening Class. If they wish to have special rehearsals of some light opera, for instance, they have to meet outside the recognised class hours, and make their own financial arrangements with the conductor for extra periods. The syllabuses of the evening classes which have to be approved by the Local Education Authority cover valuable ground; and as the practical work in the classes consists largely of preparing the works for the Cambridgeshire Musical Festival, it will be seen that the music chosen radically affects the evening classes throughout the county. The continuance of the village societies must necessarily depend upon the keenness of members, but the fact that the County Authority with its paid conductor is behind them is a big factor in securing permanence.

Other agencies exist which are not dissimilar, notably the Worcestershire and the East Anglian Associations of Musical Societies; and some Rural Community Councils, particularly that in Kent, are actively engaged in encouraging music. The Cambridgeshire scheme differs chiefly in the width of its range and in its special concern for education.

## 8. CIRCULATING LIBRARIES OF MUSIC
## AND BOOKS ON MUSIC

The value of a music lending library to the teacher and student hardly needs emphasis, and there is no doubt that the music sections of our libraries contribute very materially to the diffusion of musical knowledge.

There are over two hundred collections in public libraries in this country, ranging from four thousand items to large collections of one hundred thousand, and with the county library systems at work in most counties, it should be possible for the teacher and amateur in isolated areas to have access to music collections of some sort. Those fortunate music lovers who are within easy reach of the Camm Library and Music Room at Bournemouth, and the Henry Watson collection at Manchester, the latter consisting of over 140,000 items, are in a distinctly enviable position. The Mitchell Libraries of Glasgow have a collection of 20,000 volumes and a special reading room for the use of music students.

The public libraries are now alive to the need for extensive music collections, and generally the ground is well covered. In addition there are many private libraries giving special facilities, notably the Carnegie Orchestral Loan Library (see Appendix H, 3).

One or two education authorities have established small collections of music, books on music appreciation, and gramophone records for the particular use of teachers in their schools. Other education authorities might well form small and specialised music libraries similar to these.

The Liverpool Branch of the Music Teachers' Association has organised a lending library which includes over 1500 items of sheet music (in the main, modern educational publications) and 200 books on music. The library is helpful to teachers, as there is a special librarian whose duty is to bring the newest publications to the notice of members, having regard to their particular needs. Members are allowed to have six pieces of music and one book for a period of ten days, after which they may either renew or exchange. A pianoforte is available, giving teachers an opportunity of trying over the music before deciding upon particular pieces.

In these days when mechanically reproduced music has brought frequent performances of important orchestral works, the music sections of libraries will need considerable development—particularly in the provision of full scores (see Part V, 41).

## 9. EXAMINATIONS, EXTERNAL AND INTERNAL, AND INSPECTIONS

External examinations and inspections can be of the highest value in setting a standard based upon a larger experience than anyone in the school itself possesses, and can serve to stimulate and encourage: those are their fundamental justifications.

Since many good musicians with little or no previous experience of class teaching have lately taken school positions, there is much need of a careful application of sound class method, and here, especially, INSPECTIONS can be most helpful. But inspections can only be fully serviceable if inspectors will get down to bedrock. The whole scheme of work of the school should be considered, in relation to its comprehensiveness, correlation, and grading, and it is well to study it first as a paper scheme, before testing its application throughout the school. There are many schools whose music teacher could not, without a good deal of thought, put upon paper at all definitely what he or she expects to do during a given term (or even during the next lesson). In such schools it will be found that, though some sort of plan is in the principal's possession, it has no graded continuity. An inspection that fails to reveal vital defects like these is useless, yet such inspections have been known to take place.

In inspecting a class the inspector needs to be keenly on his guard against the misleading effects of natural musical ability in two or three pupils. Again and again teachers will be found who have never recognised why a whole class may sing correctly and unanimously, yet occasionally make some extraordinary blunder with equal unanimity. The fact that in singing a whole class can demonstrate together has led many teachers into the mistake of assuming that such an activity as "Class Singing" is possible, which can, so far as sight-reading is concerned, only exist in somewhat the same sense as "Class Arithmetic" or "Class Geography". Learning to sing at sight has to be done by every individual for himself, and so in inspection the individual must be tested or at all events cross-sections be taken through the class in various directions so as to eliminate "leaders".

In view of the changed character of music syllabuses, teaching can no longer be judged merely by ear tests and sight-singing exercises, and by a song or two. Teachers are now expected to foster a love of good music, and should not be constrained to think it necessary to waste time in keeping a few simple songs in a polished condition, ready for an unannounced inspection.

It is common experience that when children are taken to concerts of masterpieces and lectures specially arranged by outside people, a week or so later little of what they have retained is "examinable". If it is agreed that concerts and lectures afford a valuable musical training, we feel that inspectors should remember that the same kind of training given in school cannot be tested in the ordinary way.

We suggest that when visiting the newly formed Modern schools, inspectors should approach their task with an open mind. The music syllabus, more than any other, perhaps, will be experimental for some years to come.

The value of OUTSIDE EXAMINATIONS in subjects of individual teaching depends entirely upon their wise use. They must not be so frequent and so seriously considered that they obsess pupil and teacher. However often, and however minutely, musical activity may be examined it should still remain an art and an enjoyment. Instrumental examinations tend to become ends instead of means. Further they often restrict the pupil's repertory, and because of the unwise drafting of syllabuses, involve far too great an expenditure of time and effort upon such things as scales and arpeggios. Moreover they do not offer nearly sufficient reward for skill in sight-reading which, after all, is almost as important to the musician as reading in a language is to the student of that language.

Outside examinations, then, should be used *thoughtfully*. They may not suit every pupil at every age. They may offer an admirable stimulus to certain pupils (perhaps to all able pupils at some stage or other in their careers) but they should be recognised as tonics requiring proper safeguards in administration.

The choice of music as a subject in UNIVERSITY ENTRANCE EXAMINATIONS needs to be carefully considered. Examiners have found that large numbers are entered who are in no way prepared, and it may be that the mere fact of their taking pianoforte or violin lessons has been supposed to qualify them to "have a shot"! Very thorough preparation is necessary in these examinations, and before it is begun teacher and principal should consider the syllabus carefully in relation to the needs of each individual pupil. The examination should sum up and carry somewhat further the normal musical work of the pupil's school life: it may then be called a musical "School Leaving Examination", and be suitable for every pupil with ability. But sometimes it will be found to be rather a musical "University Entrance Examination", a beginning of a more serious course of music study and practically useless to any pupil who is not going to proceed either to a music degree or to an arts degree with music as one of its subjects. An examination that looks back into the school is, then, the right sort of examination for every musical-minded pupil, whilst one that looks forward into the university is wrong for every pupil except the one who is going to take music there.

The Panel of Investigators appointed by the Secondary Schools Examinations Council, in their Report upon the School Certificate Examination issued in October 1932, comment critically upon syllabuses and many types of question set in the Music papers. They point out that the Music examination does not commend itself to schools, and that teachers regard the examination as being beyond the abilities of the average pupil of sixteen. The Panel concludes: "There is no reason why this examination should not be an inspiration and a stimulus to the musical education of the country. If this result is to be secured, the examining bodies, and the examiners, must be in closer touch with the conditions of school work all over the country. With radical modifications the examination would become generally popular, and attract a large number of candidates. It is at present in no respect comparable with the examinations in other subjects ".

Finally a few words may be added upon internal examinations. They should not be allowed to become occasions of dread, but they *can* be made occasions of stimulus to effort. Probably they are in general a neglected means of showing the teacher where he is failing, and it is in the teacher's own interest to remedy the neglect. A good deal more might be done to examine step-by-step progress, in a quick ten-minutes' informal test of all the individuals of the class, on the principle that it is always better to pay current cash than to allow debt to accumulate. Sight-singing is based on ear-training, and that, like the study of mathematics, can only be carried out by minute steps. The pupil who misses one step is probably left behind for ever after. A monthly test of the class can be made, with one minute for each pupil, in such a way that all are mentally active throughout the tests and the examination constitutes a valuable class lesson. A record can be made by one of the pupils, at the teacher's dictation, as the tests proceed, and at the end attention should be called more to the marking of the individual in relation to his previous markings than in relation to that of other individuals. It is said that Heaven rejoices more over the repentance of a sinner than over the righteousness of a just man that needs no repentance; in the music class there are usually gifted individuals whose high marks are less creditable than some little gain of skill in those of more normal musical ability.

## 10. COMMUNITY SINGING

The recent revival of community singing calls for
notice in a survey of musical education. The united
singing of a crowd has a power out of all proportion to
the sum of the efforts of the individuals who constitute
the crowd. The ideal in community singing is attained
occasionally in religious services when all present have
been prepared by a common emotion such as is stirred
by a seasonal observance, a national event, or an im-
pressive sermon. An inspired conductor can develop
a similar enthusiasm in other gatherings. Community
singing is of two main kinds: (1) the deliberate kind,
when folk assemble for the purpose, and (2) the incidental kind, when they are convened primarily for
other objects. From a musician's point of view it is
desirable that in both cases the singing should be
musical and orderly. It is not necessary that all voices
should be trained and refined, but there must be a
certain unanimity of attack and agreement of harmony.
Attack is the responsibility of the conductor: let him
fill his office with efficiency and dignity and avoid
temptations to cheap humour. Some say community
singing should be in unison, but this restricts the singing
to the short compass which is common to all voices;
if possible, therefore, community singing ought to include some singing in harmony. Unanimity of harmony requires previous rehearsal or the provision of
books. Some enthusiasts recommend folk-song as the
natural expression of a people's feeling in music; but
can it be seriously maintained that the folk-song of the
English peasant of an earlier century is the natural
vehicle of expression of the town dweller of to-day?
The advocates of an exclusive use of folk-songs and
national songs ignore the fact that many of these seem

supremely dull to the modern man. The advocates of
nothing but unison singing also ignore the advances in
musical education during the last generation. In fact,
the problem of the choice of music has yet to be fully
solved. A field for community singing, at present but
little explored, exists amongst the passengers on ocean-
going vessels. The provision of suitable song books is
an inexpensive way of adding to the amenities of a sea
voyage. (For suitable song collections, see Appendix A.)

# PART V

## RETROSPECT AND CONCLUSIONS

We devote the first part of this final section of the Report to a short survey of recent progress in musical education and end it with a summary of our main conclusions. "The period usually assigned to the revival of music in England dates from almost exactly 50 years ago. It dawned at a very dark hour. In the third quarter of the nineteenth century the state of our music was deplorable."* This state of affairs is not surprising; music was neglected or ignored alike by the Education Department, the Universities and the Public Schools. The excuse given for the lack of encouragement of singing was that "at present the Privy Council did not find their inspectors were able to give that thorough examination which they ought to give, for the musical education of the upper and middle classes had been neglected, and it was difficult to find gentlemen competent to examine in the notation of music".†

The change has been remarkable, and there have been three main lines of advance. First came the improvement in sight-singing with the introduction of the Tonic Sol-fa Notation and, later, of proper ear-training; next improved methods of voice-training abolished that bane of all musically minded people,

* Sir Henry Hadow on "Fifty Years of Music", in *The Times* of March 16th, 1932.

† From a speech in the House of Commons (1871) by Mr Forster, Vice-President of the Board of Education, in reply to the criticism that music was omitted in the 1871 Code.

the "Board School voice"; and thirdly, we have seen the growth of intelligent listening to music, which has derived so much help from the advent of mechanical reproduction.

The introduction of the fixed *doh* by Hullah hindered the early progress of *sight-singing*, for the failure of the method much increased the difficulties of the pioneers of Tonic Sol-fa, led by John Curwen. Attempts to teach sight-singing from Staff Notation, though persistent, produced little result, because of the difficulties which the notation seems to have presented to the child mind. Real headway was not made until the Tonic Sol-fa Notation came into general use, and revolutionised sight-singing in the schools. The tide was turning most rapidly just over 40 years ago; between 1884 and 1892 the number of children learning songs by rote only (without the help of either notation) fell from 1,997,572* to 965,196 (in 18,593 and 10,623 schools respectively). The number who learnt from notation rose in that period from 1,282,586 to 2,920,749 (in 9169 and 18,834 schools respectively). The number of schools in which the Tonic Sol-fa Notation was taught rose from 6773 to 16,368 in those eight years.

More recently serious attention has been paid to ear-training, and sound aural foundation, in place of the old basis of "theory", has broadened musical understanding. The power to read easily from Staff Notation is more intelligently acquired, and progress from modulator work to graded sight-reading studies and actual music more quickly made.

In ear-training itself the tendency has been to sing phrases in place of single notes; and to extemporise answers vocally instead of writing them.

Although there has been on the whole this marked

* From Board of Education Statistics.

change for the better, a distinct loss of ground has been noticeable in quite recent years in what may be called the technique of class-work—sight-singing, ear-training and even voice-production. It has come about mainly through the musical appreciation movement. While this movement has had enormously beneficial results, it has deflected the minds of teachers from the objective facts of music. It has deprived the young, to an alarming extent, of consistent study in the elements of notation. The set-back may be due in part to the fact that for a teacher who has not made a special study of the work, it is more difficult to interest children and to keep good discipline in sight-singing than in appreciation. Notation is a comparatively simple matter *if well taught*, but the present lack of clear guidance has resulted in a superficial reading of the signs with no real controlling knowledge in the background. There is no fundamental antagonism between the two aspects of music teaching: they can be fused into one on the lines of the scheme given in Part II for Modern Schools (Part II, 2, (i)).

A contributory factor in this set-back is the anxiety that children should master the Staff Notation before they leave school.* But those who belittle the value of Tonic Sol-fa in relation to Staff Notation defeat their own ends. Children reach the Staff Notation most quickly and safely by way of Sol-fa.

Improved *voice-production*, the second main line of advance, has had many enthusiastic supporters. Those who have only heard school children singing at Festivals since the war, will not know to what harshness the voice can degenerate with neglect or wrong

* We heartily agree with the statement in the Board of Education's *Report on the Primary School* (1931), p. 187, that the earlier the Staff Notation is taught the better.

methods of voice-production. The sweetness and simplicity of the singing in many if not most Primary Schools to-day is natural in the best sense; but it only remains natural owing to the very careful steps which teachers take to guard against forced and breathy tone, and to preserve flexible and forward production. Good voice-production in singing has far-reaching effects on speech, and pure speech helps to lower class barriers; and it must not be forgotten that in the song sweetly sung, children come nearer to perfection than in anything else.

We have already referred to the need for a more careful balance between practical technique and *musical appreciation*, the third main branch in which great progress has been made. Enthusiasm for the new movement brought the inevitable crop of excesses, and stories were woven even into music that had no sort of "programme". The *Report on the Primary School* says with studied moderation: "The subject of Musical Appreciation has lately occupied the attention of teachers, perhaps to the detriment of other branches of musical training. At first undue emphasis was laid upon the importance of programme music, or music that painted a picture. Other and more important aspects were overlooked. The best results have been obtained where younger children have accompanied the music with movement. In this way the essential mood of a piece of music may be grasped, the interplay of themes noticed, and the general form of the piece understood".

The influence of the movement has been wholly good in all other directions. It is in line with the general broadening of education. It is important because leisure is increasing, and it teaches a good use of leisure. Music, in fact, chiefly through the gramophone and the wireless, is becoming one of the main counter-attractions to the less admirable forms of amusement. Probably its influence in this respect is now nearly as great as that of books. The development of broadcasting, especially, puts fresh responsibility on teachers, for the advance in musical standards which it has already brought can be hastened' with help from the schools.

Besides the three main movements which we have just reviewed, many other factors have contributed to the country's progress in musical education. We refer briefly to some of these. First, the uphill fight to get pianofortes into schools: few schools to-day are without at least one. Gramophones are now frequently found in the larger schools, although they are seldom provided by the Local Education Authority; and the numbers of player-pianos and wireless sets are steadily growing.

One of the greatest improvements has been an increased discrimination in the choice of songs to be sung in schools.

Choirs, violin-classes, and, less rapidly, school orchestras, have grown in number in recent years. In Manchester interesting developments have been the joint School Children's Orchestra and the Elementary Schools' Choir, founded in 1923 and 1925 respectively. In 1929 the choir performed with the Hallé Orchestra at one of the Hallé concerts. In a report on Music in Manchester Schools (see Appendix E, 1), special mention is made of the growth in the sense of citizenship amongst members of the two organisations.

Secondary Schools have shared in the general advance, but girls' schools to a far greater degree than boys'. Indeed, in the whole range of the state system, music has had its least recognition in boys' Secondary

Schools. In adult education a greatly increased membership of choral and orchestral classes has been the most striking evidence of growth (for example, Part IV, 7).

In England, the Board of Education and many Local Education Authorities have done much, after a period of hesitation at first, to encourage music in education. For example, the Education Authorities of London, Manchester, Sheffield, Bradford, Newcastle-upon-Tyne and Plymouth have appointed directors of music. Scottish schools, speaking generally, are more generously provided with music specialists than the English. Aberdeen, Dumbarton, Edinburgh, Clackmannan and Fife appoint directors of music, who are in charge of their respective areas and have under them a number of supervisors. Each supervisor is responsible for a group of primary schools, helping the music teachers in those schools, and he generally teaches all the music in the central secondary school of his district. Thirty-three authorities appoint specialist teachers in music. Glasgow has no director of music, but a number of supervisors.

Northern Ireland made a good start with its new educational system by appointing a director of music, and in Wales the work of the Welsh National Council of Music is well known.

Our survey so far has viewed the changes in the State Schools. The progress in Public Schools and Universities has been no less marked, if different in nature. In Preparatory Schools, on the other hand, no comparable advance can be recorded. It is the common experience of Public School music masters that in nine cases out of ten boys come to them with no true musical foundation, and that sight-reading especially has been neglected. At the Public Schools themselves class music is not yet the order of the day: but choral and school singing, and the numbers of private pupils and of school orchestras have grown exceedingly. The position of music at the Universities, too, has improved greatly since the turn of the century and more recently has been further strengthened by the inclusion of music as a subject for an Arts degree at more than one University.

The rise of Competition Festivals dates back just 50 years; in 1882 the Stratford and East London Festival was founded, and in 1885 Miss Mary Wakefield founded the Kendal Festival. The numbers of Festivals increased so greatly that in 1921 the Federation of Musical Competition Festivals was incorporated. To-day there is hardly a single village that is not within reach of a Festival. There are now 216 Festivals which are members of the Federation in the United Kingdom, twenty-five in other parts of the Empire, and a few which are not affiliated. Considerable numbers of musicians devote a large proportion of their time to judging at the Festivals. In considering whether England is a musical nation, the question is not whether its people are moved by music. Of that there is no doubt. What we must consider is whether the people exercise their capabilities in the best way. The Festivals are indigenous. The fact that they go from strength to strength, whilst Grand Opera cannot produce a worthy season even with a heavy subsidy, suggests that the English people may be the wisest judges of the direction in which their musical energies are best spent. If public money is to be used to encourage music, the Festivals are as worthy an object of help as any, and the conclusions given below emphasise this point. Many performances of big choral works by massed village choirs are of the highest artistic excellence—

equal and often superior to what is heard in some large choral concerts in London.

Despite these advances music still gets grudging treatment in many schools, with curtailed time and "tired" periods in the time-table. The music class is sometimes used as a dumping ground for children with insufficient intellect to learn more reputable subjects. "Any fool can do music" is the slogan in some staff-rooms. Where this attitude exists, discipline in the music classes is difficult to keep, and if the music course is not taken seriously the intellectual stimulus will be weak. In some schools where there is a bad tradition, the music teachers can correct it by increasing their own efficiency. If the music schemes in these schools are made more educational and systematic, Heads will be impressed. They will realise that a well-conducted music course has a striking influence on the spirit of the school; that music, although not a "relief" subject in the old sense, exercises mind and body differently from other subjects and in such a way as to act as a leaven for the rest of the time-table; that music has its value as an examination subject for the Higher and School Certificates and for other public examinations; that it enhances, through school singing, the choir and the orchestra, the value of many school functions, whilst there is no better way to foster the team spirit than by these activities and through inter-House music competitions; that music has, in fact, its practical uses as a school subject even if they doubt its greater significance. That the Consultative Committee on the Primary School had no doubts is shown by the following quotation: "Bodily poise and balance, a habit of natural and expressive emotion, are not merely physical accomplishments which add grace to life, but are intimately connected with intelligence and character. Such forms of excellence have sometimes in the past been regarded as among the ornaments of existence with which the schools attended by the majority of the population were not directly concerned. If, however, they are to become, as they might and should, a national possession, the outward sign of a common culture and civilisation, it is precisely in the primary schools that they should be cultivated. Dancing, singing, music, and the drama are the means of cultivating them".

This retrospect began with a quotation from Sir Henry Hadow's article from *The Times*, and ends with another which discusses the most recent way in which music has come to affect the life of the community: "We are much indebted to the British Broadcasting Corporation for bringing the best music to our homes, and for bringing it in such abundance and variety; it will be a national loss if we allow ourselves to be satisfied with listening and let our practice fall into desuetude. This... affects the whole future of the art in England, for England has grown to be a musical nation not only by hearing but by actively producing the music which it hears. We cannot yet appreciate the extent or reality of the danger; we can only suggest that it needs vigilance and some measure of common action".

Whatever the present difficulties, and even though some recommendations which follow seem now to be counsels of perfection, we believe the most faint-hearted will take hope from the remarkable progress of the last fifty years: and that all concerned with musical education will be encouraged to attempt yet greater things.

## CONCLUSIONS

### Part I

1.  The full enjoyment and understanding of music can only be experienced from active participation, and the value of music as a subject in school depends mainly upon the physical, intellectual, and social stimulus of singing, rhythmic exercises, sight-reading, ear-training, and work in choir and orchestra. The practical work should be related whenever possible to music of acknowledged worth. We consider that this more concrete personal practice has still too small a share in musical education, and that on the whole the balance needs redressing on the side of practical work against the less constructive art of listening.

2.  All children should take music as a normal class subject, and every school should devote a minimum of two half-hour periods a week to class singing, ear-training, and sight-reading.

3.  All teachers of school and college music should have had training in group teaching and should have knowledge of the future musical needs of those they teach. This is particularly important in the case of lecturers in Training Colleges and University training departments where the effects of wrong training are so far reaching.

It cannot be too strongly emphasised that, valuable as the Tonic Sol-fa method may be, it offers no short cut to the teacher of class singing. The method must be thoroughly grasped by the teacher before it is used in school.

4.  No school should be without at least one pianoforte in good condition and tune. Where there are several pianofortes in a school, one should be a good instrument for concerts, and for the use of more advanced pupils.

5. There is room for a representative National Council of Musical Education* to publish reports of experiments in schools, graded lists of music, lists of gramophone records and player-piano rolls, and other information not otherwise available; to give advice to teachers, administrators, librarians and others when asked; to raise money for musical education and to help local councils of musical education, rural music schools and other bodies formed to foster musical education; to encourage organisations concerned with music, such as the Committees of Musical Festivals, to undertake educational work; to co-ordinate external examinations in music, music libraries and other activities in which central consultation would be useful.

## PART II

6. Careful grading of music schemes within schools and between one type of school and another is vital. Local Education Authorities should be as exacting in this respect with music as with any other subject. Not infrequently schools start new entrants from the beginning without taking account of any previous teaching in music. On the other hand, schools for older children have, sometimes, to take the most elementary work because earlier studies in music have been neglected.

7. The repertory of songs sung in school, which should be large, should be the possession of the child rather than of the class or teacher. Each child should compile a music notebook and add to it throughout school life. Periodically classes should sing through the songs learnt in the previous years.

8. There is a shortage of music teachers (especially men teachers) in Primary Schools, Senior Classes and

* A scheme for the formation of such a Council is in course of preparation by the Committee.

Modern Schools, and the distribution of those who can teach music is uneven. In particular the talents of many musical young teachers are not used through their being appointed to schools which already have enough teachers of music. Improvement could be effected if musical teachers who at present do not teach music would agree to be moved to schools which are musically under-staffed; and if young teachers with qualifications in music were always given their first appointments in schools in which they could teach this subject. Local Education Authorities could also help to improve the position by issuing a monthly bulletin to schools which had a musical, but not musically qualified, teacher and wished to work a standard scheme of work. The bulletins would be based on the standard scheme, and would give notes of lessons, with non-copyright musical illustrations.

9. All *Preparatory Schools* should have class music (including ear-training, sight-singing, and voice-production) throughout the school as part of the normal curriculum and not as an "extra". Public Schools will continue to be severely handicapped in giving a reasonable musical education until Preparatory School music *generally* is comparable in standard with that in the State Schools. The greatest stumbling block is the deplorable condition of sight-reading, which should have been well mastered by the age of fourteen in the Preparatory School.

10. The special difficulties of the *smaller State Schools* in rural areas add to the need for careful planning of the music in them. Schemes can be made progressive on the lines suggested in Part II, 3.

11. In *Secondary Schools* the music has reached a much more creditable stage on the whole amongst girls than amongst boys. Boys' schools should not underrate the

value of music, nor should they allow music to stop when the pressure of examinations begins to be felt or because of the change of voice. Whereas most Secondary Schools start music with a great advantage over the Public Schools, they will usually be found to have lost their pride of place if comparisons are made amongst the seniors of the two types of school.

12. In *Public Schools* boys who have private lessons should be allotted two school periods a week; the timetable should include two periods of class music a week, at any rate in the middle and lower school. Boys of exceptional talent should be encouraged to proceed to a musical degree at the Universities with a view to making music their life's work. Music masters should be paid an inclusive salary, and music, whether learnt individually or in class, should not be charged as an "extra".

13. The Authorities should encourage students to take music in the *Training Colleges* when possible as an advanced course. Music is increasing its scope in schools, and, as we mention in conclusion 8, there is a dearth of qualified teachers. The belief that a College course is not needed if one already has some facility in music is wholly wrong. A student with a knowledge of music has more time to study teaching methods and for this reason is the most suited for a course in music. So important, in fact, is this preliminary knowledge, and so rarely is it found, that prospective students, who intend to teach music, should make special preparation during the year before entry.

Training in teaching methods is particularly necessary for the effective teaching of little children.

14. When allocating students to the respective *Training College* courses in preparation for the teaching of Infants, Juniors, or Seniors, it is well to bear in mind

that there is particular scope for able students with advanced musical knowledge in the new Modern Schools. There is a danger of leading too great a proportion of musical students to prepare for work in Infants' or Junior Schools, because of the recognised need for music in those schools.

15. More accommodation is needed for practising the pianoforte in many *Training Colleges*. Special grants from the Board of Education towards the cost of such accommodation would, it seems, be money well invested. Eventually some degree of pianoforte playing should be compulsory for all taking music as a subject.

16. In view of the amount of music which is illegally copied in schools, it is important that students should be instructed at the *Training College* in the applications of the Copyright Act to music, and words set to music.

17. In beginners' classes in *Adult Education,* when members have had little previous musical training, the first approaches should be informal and social, rather than strictly instructional in nature.

18. We recommend that expenditure on the classes mentioned in the foregoing conclusion should be recognised by the Board of Education under the Regulations for Further Education. The work is an essential preliminary step to classes which Local Education Authorities already provide. As a condition of grant a limit could be fixed to the number of meetings after which the group would have to start more formal study, and the grant could be varied according to the proportion who continued the work.

19. The most satisfactory basis for the meetings of Choral and Orchestral Societies, except the very largest, and for other *Adult Education* groups, is that of organised courses under the Regulations of the Board of Education.

20. Local Education Authorities should have a list of people in their areas capable of taking adult choral and orchestral classes or of giving lectures on music to adults.

21. At *Universities* we consider that the ideal arrangement would be to have a special building, with a concert hall, library, lecture, practice and club rooms, in which all the music, official and unofficial, of the University can have its focus.

22. It should be possible to take music as one of the subjects in an Arts degree at all British *Universities*. Practical work should be included in the course.

23. It is desirable that *Universities* should provide, in addition to the indispensable course in theoretical studies, some instruction in the art of teaching music. This is particularly important during the fourth year Training Department course for intending teachers. At present music is very seriously neglected in many University Training Departments. Another subsidiary course which is highly desirable is one in liturgical music for those intending to take holy orders or to become church musicians.

## PART III

24. Singing need not be discontinued during adolescence, but care is needed in the use of the voice for both sexes during the period of change.

25. There is still a general need for better reading of music at sight. Difficulty with sight-reading is the greatest single factor in retarding the progress of music and in discouraging individuals from continuing their music after leaving school. Sight-reading exercises should be very carefully graded, because learning to read depends upon moving by easy stages and overcoming one new difficulty at a time. Schools and

libraries should have sets of music specially chosen by experts for sight-reading purposes—for singing, pianoforte, strings, and other instruments.

26. The curriculum in special schools or classes for backward children should include a far greater number of singing lessons than is now usual. Ten formal singing lessons a week, besides odd moments between other lessons, has not been found an excessive allowance. Singing taught in the right way will bring a more intelligent response from mentally defective children than any subject, except perhaps handwork. Teachers who specialise in schools of this kind should *always* be trained to teach singing.

27. The stimulating effect of music on the intelligence and health of backward children is far from being fully understood, and a careful investigation into the matter should give valuable results.

28. A gramophone has become an essential part of the musical equipment of every school. We desire, however, to warn schools against a lazy or excessive use of the gramophone: when used as an easy means of amusing a class it is merely harmful.

The extra outlay for a player-piano in place of a pianoforte would be justified at any rate in the larger schools.

29. There is a shortage of good amateur conductors: the growth of local choirs and orchestras, which are the bulwarks of music in this country, depends upon a proper supply. No organisation which has it in its power to hold courses for conductors can be too zealous in carrying out this duty.

## PART IV

30. There is need for more *concerts for children*. Music Schools, Training Colleges, Choral Societies,

and Orchestras could help by inviting local children to rehearsals or by repeating performances of suitable programmes.

31. The growth of *mechanically reproduced music* has introduced the need for an addition to our code of manners; we have to recognise musical litter as a nuisance, and the time has come when the public needs the protection of by-laws against the indiscriminate use of the new resources.

32. Many of the *competitive musical festivals* have grown too rapidly for their organisation, and should do their utmost to improve standards rather than to expand further. Consolidation is often more needed than expansion.

33. Sight-singing needs much more encouragement at *festivals* than it has had so far. The ideal is to make it compulsory in all classes, but great care should be taken not to make the competition unpopular at first by too difficult tests in public.

34. Discrimination is needed in choosing festival test pieces, especially, at present, for schools and male voice choirs.

35. A most praiseworthy tendency amongst certain types of festival is to reduce the time spent on the competitions, and to make the combined performance of a big work the main object of the festivals. Money prizes have, fortunately, disappeared almost entirely.

36. Festivals should try to obtain the greater part of their income from the general public, through membership subscriptions and attendance at the festival. The evening session, when most people can attend, should therefore be made as attractive as possible.

37. The Board of Education should consider recognising for grant, contributions made by Local Education Authorities in aid of festivals which have

educational value. The more valuable a festival is from the musical point of view, the more difficult it usually is to finance.

38. Schools should be encouraged by the authorities to prepare the festival music in school hours, and attendance at the festivals should count as attendance at school for the purposes of the Board of Education's regulations. Entrance fees which would thus be illegal in the case of state schools could be included in the contribution made by the Local Education Authority (see previous conclusion).

39. Tickets sold at festivals and at concerts given by local choral and orchestral societies should be exempt from entertainments tax.

40. Every county and large town should have its own organisation, on the lines of the Cambridgeshire Council, to undertake intensive pioneer work in musical education: the Rural Community Council or the Committee of the local Musical Festival could often do the work, thereby avoiding an extra organisation, but in both these cases there should be a special Committee to deal exclusively with musical education in the area (see conclusion 5).

41. *Public libraries* should be encouraged to extend their music sections, in music, full scores, books on music and gramophone records.

42. In the Matriculation, School Certificate, and other *external examinations* considerable changes are needed in existing syllabuses and types of question if music is to compare in popularity with other examination subjects, especially in the direction of making the tests more practical. More uniform standards would be assured in these different examinations if closer co-ordination could be effected (see conclusion 5).

# APPENDICES

The lists of music and books in Appendices A to E are intended to help teachers when choosing music. They are suggestive, not exhaustive. In some cases the works have been classified and graded. In others, an alphabetical arrangement has been found the most convenient. In all cases the names of the publishers are given; a list of publishers, which shows the abbreviations used in the appendices, appears below.

It should be remembered that prices are subject to fluctuation.

## LIST OF PUBLISHERS WITH ABBREVIATIONS

| | | | |
|---|---|---|---|
| A.B. | Associated Board | Col. | Columbia Graphophone Co. |
| A.U. | Allen & Unwin | | |
| An. | Anglo-French | Cr. | Cramer |
| Ap. | Appleton | Cra. | Cranz |
| Ar. | Arnold | Cu. | Curwen |
| As. | Ashdown | De. | Dent |
| Asc. | Ascherberg | Du. | Durand |
| Au. | Augener | Duc. | Duckworth |
| B.H. | Breitkopf & Härtel | Ed. | Édition l'Oiseau Lyre |
| Ba. | Bayley & Ferguson | El. | Elkin |
| Be. | Benjamin | En. | Enoch |
| Ben. | Benn | Ev. | Evans Bros. |
| Bi. | Silas Birch | Fo. | Forsyth |
| Bl. | Black | Fou. | Foulis |
| Bo. | Boosey & Hawkes | Gi. | Gibson |
| Bos. | Bosworth | Gin. | Ginn |
| Bot. | Bote & Bock | Gr. | Gramophone (Publications) Ltd. |
| C.U.P. | Cambridge University Press | | |
| | | Gra. | Gramophone Co. (H.M.V.) |
| Ca. | Cassell | | |
| Ch. | Chester | Graf. | Grafton |
| Cha. | Chatto & Windus | H.M.S. | His Majesty's Stationery Office |
| Cl. | Clowes | | |
| Cla. | Clarendon Press | Ha. | Hawkes (now Boosey & Hawkes) |
| Co. | Constable | | |

| | | | |
|---|---|---|---|
| Hai. | Hainauer | Nov. | Novello |
| Ham. | Hamelle | O.U.P. | Oxford University Press |
| Hamm. | Hammond | P.P. | Paterson's Publications |
| Har. | Harrap | Pa. | Paxton |
| He. | Heugel | Pal. | Palmer |
| Hey. | Heywood | Par. | Parsons |
| Ho. | Hope's Educational Co. | Parlo. | Parlophone |
| Hu. | Hug | Pe. | Peters |
| I.P. | Independent Press, Ltd. | Pi. | Pitman |
| J. | Jenkins | Pu. | Putnam's Sons |
| Ke. | Keith Prowse | Re. | Reeves |
| Keg. | Kegan Paul | Rei. | Reinecke |
| Ker. | Kerr | Ri. | Ricordi |
| Ki. | Kistner | Ric. | Grant Richards |
| King | King | Ro. | Rogers |
| L.G.B. | Leonard, Gould & Bolttler | Rou. | Routledge |
| | | S.J. | Sidgwick & Jackson |
| L.S.D.E. | London School of Dalcroze Eurhythmics | S.P.C.K. | Society for Promoting Christian Knowledge |
| La. | Larway | S.S. | Schofield & Sims |
| Lan. | Lane | Sa. | Saville |
| Le. | Lengnick | Sam. | Sampson Low, Marston |
| Led. | Leduc | Sc. | Schott |
| Ler. | Lerolle | Se. | Seuart |
| Li. | Litolff | See. | Seeley |
| Lo. | Longmans Green | Si. | Simrock |
| M.E.C. | Manchester Education Committee | St. | Stainer & Bell |
| | | Sw. | Swan |
| Mac. | Macmillan | U. | Universal |
| Mc. | McDougall's | W.G. | Wells Gardner, Darton |
| Me. | Methuen | W.N. | Williams & Norgate |
| Mo. | Mowbray | W.P. | Warren Phillips |
| Mu. | Murdoch | We. | Weekes |
| N.C. | News-Chronicle Pub. Depart. | Wer. | Werner Laurie |
| | | Wi. | Williams |
| N.W. | Ivor Nicholson & Watson | Y.B.P. | Year Book Press |
| Ne. | Nelson | Z. | Zimmermann |

## APPENDIX A

# LIST OF SONG BOOKS

## 1. FOR INFANTS' AND JUNIOR SCHOOLS

Arranged in broad order of difficulty, the easiest first.

(a) *Traditional:*

1. *English Nursery Rhymes,* selected and edited by L. Edna Walter. 7s. 6d. Bl.
2.\* *Songtime,* by Percy Dearmer and Martin Shaw. 4s. 6d. net. Cu.
3. *Children's Singing Games,* edited by Alice B. Gomme and Cecil J. Sharp. In five sets. 1s. each. Nov.
4. *British Nursery Rhymes,* edited by Frank Kidson, accompaniments by Alfred Moffat. 4s. Au.
5. *The Standard Book of Traditional Songs and Tunes for Little Folk,* edited by Mrs Murray MacBain. 3s. 6d. net. Ev.
6. *Thirty-five Nursery Rhymes,* collected and arranged by Arthur Somervell. 2s. net. Bo.
7. *The Songs of the Children,* edited by Lilian E. Bucke. Set I, 3s. 6d. net. Wi.
8. *Nursery Rhyme Quadrilles,* arranged by Louise Edwards-Carter. 1s. Nov.
9.\* *The Orchard Rhymes,* by Ethel Boyce and Dora Bright. 2s. Nov.
10. *Nursery Songs from the Appalachian Mountains,* arranged by C. J. Sharp. In two series. 6s. each. Nov.
11. *Seventeen Nursery Songs from the Appalachian Mountains,* arranged by C. J. Sharp, selected from the two series. 1s. Nov.
12. *Brahms' Children's Songs.* 2s. 6d. net. Cu.
13. *Children's Songs,* arranged by Johannes Brahms. 8d. Nov.

\* These books contain also some original compositions.

14. *The Wonderful Inn*, by May Sarson, a play in one scene built round *Brahms' Children's Songs* (the music is included). 1s. 6d. Nov.

15. *French Nursery Rhymes*, selected and arranged by A. Thirion. In two series. 1s. net each. Wi.

16. *French Nursery Songs*, with accompaniments by Percy F. Fletcher. 4s. net. Cu.

17. *Polichinelle, old Nursery Songs of France*, by J. R. Monsell. 7s. 6d. net. O.U.P.

18. *A Song-Garden for Children*, adapted from the French and German by Harry Graham and Rosa Newmarch, music edited by Norman O'Neill. 3s. net. Ar.

19.* *Little Dutchy, Nursery Songs from Holland*, by Alex de Jong. 7s. 6d. net. Har.

20. *The Laureate Song Book*, Part I, adapted and composed by Thomas F. Dunhill. 2s. Melody only, 9d. Ar.

21. *English Folk-Songs for Schools*, collected and arranged by S. Baring Gould and Cecil J. Sharp. 6s. Cu.

(*b*) *More recent compositions:*

22. *Nursery Rhyme Pieces*, by Ernest Read. 2s. 6d. net. Wi.

23. *Chiddlewinks, Thirteen Songs for Children*, by Alec Rowley. 2s. 6d. net. Cu.

24. *Old Rhymes with New Tunes*, by Richard Runciman Terry. 3s. 6d. net. Lo.

25. *More Old Rhymes with New Tunes*, by Richard Runciman Terry. 3s. 6d. net. Lo.

26. *Still More Old Rhymes with New Tunes*, by Richard Runciman Terry. 3s. 6d. net. Lo.

27. *The Elephant and his Friends in the Ark*, by Louie E. de Rusette. 2s. net. Pi.

28. *Before Bedtime: Ten Singing Games*, by Geoffrey Shaw. 2s. 6d. net. Cu.

29. *Six Fairy Story Game-Songs*, by Ida M. Cartledge. 1s. Nov.

* These books contain also original compositions.

30. *Fairy Story Game-Songs.* Set II, by Cecil Sharman. 1*s*. Nov.

31. *Autumn Days, a Song-Cycle for Young Children*, by Cecil Sharman. 6*d*. Nov.

32. *Animal Songs*, by Louie E. de Rusette. 2*s*. 6*d*. net. Cu.

33. *Twelve Kindergarten Game Songs*, by George Rathbone and Percy E. Fletcher. 1*s*. Nov.

34. *Little Dog Dinkie, and other Song-Stories*, by Ruby E. Copland. 2*s*. 6*d*. net. Cu.

35. *The For Children by Children Song Book*, collected and arranged by J. Michael Diack. 2*s*. and 4*d*. P.P.

36. *Wumblements*, by Alec Rowley. 2*s*. 6*d*. net. Cu.

37. *Children's Sing-Song from Sweden*, by Alice Tegner. Book I, 2*s*. 6*d*. net. Book II, 2*s*. net. Au.

38. *Six Playroom Songs*, by Herbert Frank Nicholls. 2*s*. 6*d*. net. Cu.

39. *Five Kiddies' Songs*, by Gladys G. Murray. 2*s*. net. Wi.

40. *For My Grandchildren: Ten Simple Songs for Children, Traditional and other Rhymes*, by T. Maskell Hardy. 2*s*. 6*d*. net. Cu.

41. *Eight Children's Songs*, by Rossetter G. Cole. 1*s*. 6*d*. Nov.

42. *Twelve Songs for the Very Young*, by Paul Edmonds. 2*s*. Cr.

43. *Riddle Songs*, by H. A. Chambers. In two sets. 8*d*. each. Nov.

44. *Six Rhythmic Singing Games*, arranged by May Sarson. 1*s*. Nov.

45. *A Treasury of Twenty Songs for Little Singers*, by Bruce Gibbon. 3*s*. 6*d*. Har.

46. *Higgledy Piggledy: Twelve Songs for Small Children*, by Arthur Somervell. 1*s*. 6*d*. net. Bo.

47. *The Bells of London: A Collection of Nursery Rhymes and a Carol*, by Paul Edmonds. 2*s*. 6*d*. net. Cu.

48. *Higgledy Piggledy: Thirteen Songs for Children*, by Paul Edmonds. 2*s*. 6*d*. net. Cu.

49. *Nursery Rhymes: a Set of Seventeen Songs*, by Joseph Fredericks. 2*s*. Wi.

50. *Little People's Song Book* (*Chansons Enfantines*), English and French words, by Gabriel Grovlez. 3s. 6d. net. Au.

51. *Dickory's House, and Five other Songs for Singing and Action*, by Anne Harding Thompson. 1s. Nov.

52. *Nursery Rhymes of London Town*, by Eleanor Farjeon. In four books. 2s. net each. An.

53. *Nature Song*, by Martin Shaw. In two books. 4s. each. Cr.

54. *Songs of Elfin Town*, by E. Dorothea Barcroft. 2s. net. Bo.

55. *Traditional Songs*, by Frank H. Lockyer. 3s. 6d. net. Sa.

56. *Six Unison Songs*, words by William Blake, music by Rutland Boughton. 8d. Nov.

57. *New Tunes to New Rhymes*, by Doris and Alec Rowley. 2s. net. L.G.B.

58. *Songs of the Little Brown House*, by Kenneth A. Wright. 3s. 6d. net. Sa.

59. *Rhymes and Rhythms*, by Edgar Moy. 10d. net. St.

60. *Little Bo-Peep and Six other Rhymes*, by Mabel Browning Fairlie. 1s. 6d. net. We.

61. *Six Songs for Children*, by Ethel Boyce. 2s. net. Wi.

62. *Rhythmic Pictures*, with song and action, by Nessie Elder and Robert McLeod. In two books, 2s. 6d. each. Bo.

63. *A Garland*, a collection of songs, collected or composed by Ursula Greville: old songs arranged by Maurice Jacobson. 3s. 6d. net. Cu.

64. *Aunt Mary: Six Songs for Children*, by Noel Johnson. 2s. net. Wi.

65. *Songs from "Punch"*, by Eleanor Farjeon. 3s. 6d. net. Sa.

66. *Aunt Lucy: Six Songs for Children*, by Noel Johnson. 2s. net. Wi.

67. *Fairy Pipes: Songs for Children*, by D. H. Wassell. 3s. net. Sa.

68. *Mermaid Songs*, by D. H. Wassell. 3s. 6d. net. Sa.

69. *Playbox, Ten little Songs of Childhood,* by Gerrard Williams. 3*s.* 6*d.* O.U.P.

70. *The King's Breakfast,* words by A. A. Milne, music by H. Fraser-Simson. 3*s.* 6*d.* net. Me.

71. *Three Songs for Children,* by Granville Bantock. 1*s.* 6*d.* net. Wi.

72. *Birthdays,* by Doris and Alec Rowley. 10*d.* net. St.

73. *Robert Louis Stevenson's Songs for Children,* by Edith Swepstone. In two books. 2*s.* 6*d.* net each. Cu.

74. *Pillicock Hill,* by Alec Rowley. 3*s.* 6*d.* O.U.P.

75. *Round the Year Songs,* words by Enid Blyton, music by Alec Rowley. 1*s.* 6*d.* Nov.

76. *The Months,* words by Doris Rowley, music by Alec Rowley. In two books. 10*d.* net each. St.

77. *The Roundabout Song Book,* Part I for Juniors. 2*s.* 6*d.* and 1*s.* Ne.

78. *Kookoorookoo and other Songs,* words by Christina Rossetti, music by various composers. 2*s.* 6*d.* Y.B.P.

79. *Kikirikee,* sequel to *Kookoorookoo.* 3*s.* Y.B.P.

80. *Nonsense Songs,* by Stanley Marchant. 4*s.* Nov.

81. *A Chap-Book of Rounds,* by Eleanor Farjeon. In two parts. 6*d.* each. O.U.P.

82. *Songs for My Little Ones from "Punch",* by Sir Frederic H. Cowen. 6*s.* net. Sa.

83. *Pet Marjorie's Rhymes,* by Robert McLeod. 3*s.* 6*d.* net. P.P.

84. *Fourteen Songs from "When We Were Very Young",* words by A. A. Milne, music by H. Fraser-Simson. 7*s.* 6*d.* net. Me.

85. *Teddy Bear and other Songs from "When We Were Very Young",* words by A. A. Milne, music by H. Fraser-Simson. 7*s.* 6*d.* net. Me.

86. *More "Very Young" Songs,* words by A. A. Milne, music by H. Fraser-Simson. 7*s.* 6*d.* net. Me.

87. *The Hums of Pooh,* words by A. A. Milne, music by H. Fraser-Simson. 7*s.* 6*d.* net. Me.

88. *Songs from "Now We are Six",* words by A. A. Milne, music by H. Fraser-Simson. 7*s.* 6*d.* net. Me.

89. *Four Junior School Songs with some optional two-part*, by Jaques-Dalcroze. 6*d*. Nov.
90. *The Clarendon Song Books*, edited by W. G. Whittaker, Herbert Wiseman, and J. Wishart: including Nursery Rhymes, Folk, Classical, and Modern Songs. I, I a, II, and II a. 2*s*. 6*d*. each. Melody edition, 6*d*. net each. O.U.P.
91. *Thirty Unison Songs for Junior Classes*, by modern composers. 2*s*. Voice part only, 8*d*. Nov.

## 2. FOR SCHOOLS, COLLEGES, AND GENERAL USE

92. Bach, *Bach School Song Book*, edited by J. Michael Diack. In two vols. 2*s*. each. P.P.
93. Beethoven, *Beethoven's Songs*, English version by the Rev. Dr Troutbeck. In three vols. 2*s*. 6*d*. each. Nov.
94. Boys, For, *Heritage of Song, A*, edited and arranged by Robert McLeod. A song book for adolescent boys. 5*s*. Melody edition, 1*s*. Cu.
95. —— *School Song Book for Boys*. 2*s*. 6*d*. net. Bo.
96. —— *The Boys' Book of Songs*, Nos. I and II (Clarendon Song Book Series), edited by W. G. Whittaker, Herbert Wiseman, and J. Wishart. Including Folk, Classical, and Modern Songs and Rounds and Canons. 2*s*. 6*d*. O.U.P.
97. —— *Youth's Own Song Book*, a collection of well-known airs arranged in simple four-part harmony, including National Songs and Airs, Rounds and Catches, Sailors' Songs and Chanteys, Traditional Songs, Hymns, Carols, and Spirituals. 6*d*. net. Pa.
98. Brahms, *Brahms' Songs, Twenty-two*. 2*s*. 6*d*. Nov.
99. —— *Johannes Brahms*, selected songs, edited and arranged for school use by James Easson. 3*s*. Melody and words, 9*d*. Le.

100. Canons: *Eight Two-part Canons*, by various composers. 1s. Nov.

101. —— *Twelve Vocal Canons for Female or Boys' Voices*, by Charles Wood. 3s. net. Y.B.P.

102. Chanteys: *A Book of Shanties*, by C. Fox Smith. Music with explanatory notes. 6s. net. Me.

103. —— *Capstan Chanteys*, collected and arranged by Cecil J. Sharp. 1s. Nov.

104. —— *Pulling Chanteys*, collected and arranged by Cecil J. Sharp. 1s. Nov.

105. —— *The Shanty Books*, collected by R. R. Terry. In two vols. 6s. net each. Cu.

106. *Characteristic Songs and Dances of all Nations*, with historical notes and a bibliography, edited by Alfred Moffat. 5s. Ba.

107. Christmas Carols: *Christmas Carols*, edited by L. Edna Walter, harmonised by Lucy E. Broadwood, illustrated by J. H. Hartley. 3s. 6d. net. Bl.

108. —— *Christmas Carols*, Vol. II, Part II of *The Motherland Song Book*, selected by Geoffrey Shaw. 1s. net. St.

109. —— *Christmas Carols New and Old*, edited by Sir John Stainer. 5s. Nov.

110. —— *Christmas Songs and Carols*, by various composers. In nine sets. 8d. each. Nov.

111. —— *Cowley Carol Book*, edited by the Rev. G. R. Woodward, Parts I and II. 2s. each. Mo.

112. —— *English Carol Book*, edited by Martin Shaw and Percy Dearmer. In two series. 2s. 6d. each. Words 3d. Mo.

113. —— *Folk-Song Carols*, arranged by Cecil J. Sharp. 1s. Nov.

114. —— *Oxford Book of Carols, The*, edited by R. Vaughan Williams, Martin Shaw and Percy Dearmer. 6s. net. Complete words edition, 4s. Words only without music or notes, 1s. 6d. O.U.P.

115. —— *Six Christmas Songs*, Op. 8, by Peter Cornelius. 8d. Nov.

116. Christmas Carols: *Twelve Carols for Children*, by F. Pascal. 1*s*. net. Wi.
117. —— *Twelve Christmas Carols*, by F. Pascal. 1*s*. net. Wi.
118. *Clarendon Song Books*, edited by W. G. Whittaker, Herbert Wiseman and J. Wishart, a graded series of books containing Nursery Rhymes, Folk, Classical and Modern Songs. Books I, I a, II, II a, III to VI. Music, 2*s*. 6*d*. each. Melody edition, 6*d*. net each. O.U.P.
119. *Classical Song Books*, in five vols. 2*s*. 6*d*. each. Nov.
120. *Classical Songs, Fourteen Two-part*. 2*s*. Nov.
121. *Classical Songs, Thirteen Two-part*. 2*s*. Nov.
122. *Classical Songs, Twenty-five*, selected. 2*s*. Melody edition 8*d*. Nov.
123. *Classical Songs, Twenty-six*, selected. 2*s*. Melody edition, 8*d*. Nov.
124. *Community Song Book*, edited by Gibson Young. 4*s*. 6*d*. Melody edition, 9*d*. Cu.
125. *Concinamus*, arranged by E. T. Sweeting. Folk and National Songs. 3*s*. net. St.
126. Descants: *Cambridgeshire Song Book*, National Airs with Descants, arranged by Alan Gray. 1*s*. net. Voice part only, 8*d*. net. St.
127. —— *Christmas Carols with Descants*. 8*d*. Nov.
128. —— *National Airs with Descants*, arranged by Nicholas Gatty and Alan Gray, in two books. 1*s*. 3*d*. net each. St.
129. —— *National Songs with Descants*, selected and arranged by Geoffrey Shaw and H. A. Chambers, in seven sets. 8*d*. each. Nov.
130. —— *Ten Descants to National Songs*, by Arthur Somervell. 1*s*. net. Bo.
131. —— *Twelve British Songs*, arranged with Descants by Eric H. Thiman. 1*s*. 3*d*. net. Au.
132. *Echoing Green, The*, and other songs (two- and three-part) for female or boys' voices, by Victor Hely Hutchinson, words by Blake. 1*s*. 6*d*. El.

133. *Eight Nursery Rhymes for Children's (unison) or Ladies'
(three-part) voices*, by H. Walford Davies. 1s. 6d.
Bo.

134. *English Posy, An*, selected or composed by Ursula
Greville, old songs arranged by Maurice
Jacobson. 3s. 6d. Melody edition, 6d. Cu.

135. *English Songs of the Georgian Period*, edited by Alfred
Moffat, notes by Frank Kidson. Companion
volume to 165. 5s. net. Ba.

136. Folk Songs: *Beautiful Folk Songs of France, The* (French
words), arranged by Austin de Croze. Book I, 2s.
Book II, illustrated, 4s. Nov.

137. —— *Bohemia, Folk Songs from*, edited by J. Michael
Diack. 2s. P.P.

138. —— *Collected Folk-Songs*, by Cecil J. Sharp and
R. Vaughan Williams. 3s. Nov.

139. —— *English Country-side Songs*, edited by Alfred
Moffat. 3s. net. Ba.

140. —— *English Folk-Songs for Schools*, arranged by
S. Baring Gould and Cecil J. Sharp. 6s. Melody
edition, 2s. Cu.

141. —— *Flemish Folk Songs*, music by Jan Broeckx,
English words by Adrian Ross. 3s. Bo.

142. —— *Folk-Songs*, collected and arranged by Cecil
Sharp and R. Vaughan Williams. In nine sets.
1s. each. Nov.

143. —— *French Folk Songs, Six*, arranged by Heller
Nicholls. 4d. Y.B.P.

144. —— *Little Song Book of the Nations, A*. 1s. 6d.
O.U.P.

145. —— *North Countrie Ballads, Songs and Pipe Tunes*, edited
by W. G. Whittaker. Two parts, 6s. each; words
and melodies (both books in one), 2s. 6d.
Cu.

146. —— *Old Welsh Folk-Songs*, edited by W. S. Gwynn
Williams. 5s. net. Melody edition, 9d. Cu.

147. —— *Russian Songs, One Hundred*, edited by Rimsky-
Korsakov. B.H.

148. Folk Songs: *Songs of the West: Folk Songs of Devon and Cornwall*, collected from the mouths of the people, by S. Baring Gould, H. Fleetwood Sheppard, and F. W. Russell. Musical editor, Cecil J. Sharp. 12s. 6d. net. Me.

149. —— *Songs of Eastern Europe*, edited by J. A. Kappey, English words only by Clara Kappey. 5s. Bo.

150. —— *Songs of France*, French and English words, the latter by Maria X. Hayes. 5s. Bo.

151. —— *Songs of Germany*, German and English words, the latter by Maria X. Hayes, edited by J. A. Kappey. 5s. Bo.

152. —— *Songs of Italy*, Italian and English words, the latter by Maria X. Hayes. 5s. Bo.

153. —— *Songs of Scandinavia*, edited by J. A. Kappey, English words only by Clara Kappey. 6s. Bo.

154. *Follow my Leader*, by Harold Mason. 1s. 9d. Ne.

155. *Garland of Songs, A*, Classical and National Songs, arranged for consecutive singing by W. G. McNaught. In three sets. 8d. each. Nov.

156. *Golden Treasury of Song, A*, Vol. I, edited by Norman O'Neill. Vol. II, Vol. III, Part songs for female voices. 4s. net each. Melody edition, 1s. 6d. net. Bo.

157. *Golden Treasury of Song for Children*, Classical Songs. 4s. net. Words and melody, 1s. Bo.

158. Handel: *Eighteen Songs by Handel*. 2s. Nov.

159. —— *Handel School Song Book*, edited by J. Michael Diack. In three vols. 2s. each. P.P.

160. *Historic British Songs* (sixteenth, seventeenth and eighteenth-century sources), arranged by R. Dunstan and C. E. Bygott. 1s. 3d. S.S.

161. *Hundred Best Short Songs, The*, selected by Elena Gerhardt, Sir George Henschel, and J. Francis Harford. In four vols. 3s. each. P.P.

162. *Kingsway Songs, The First Book of*. 2s. 6d. net. Ev.

163. *Laureate Song Book, The*, Part II, adapted and fitted with new settings by Thomas F. Dunhill. National Songs. 2s. Ar.

164. Mendelssohn: *Mendelssohn's Two-part Songs*. 1s. Nov.

165. *Minstrelsy of England, The*, edited by Alfred Moffat, notes by Frank Kidson, including some popular songs from sixteenth century to middle of eighteenth century. 5s. net. Ba.

166. *Motherland Song Book*—Official Publication of the League of the Arts for National and Civic Ceremony. For unison and mixed voices. Vol. I, for Peace and General Celebrations. Vol. II, Part I, Sea Songs, arranged by Martin and Geoffrey Shaw. Vols. III and IV, Sea Songs, arranged by R. Vaughan Williams: Vol. V, Hymns, edited by Percy Dearmer (words) and Martin Shaw (music). 1s. each except Vol. V, which is 1s. 6d. St.

167. *Music for the Home*, edited by Sir Landon Ronald, including Classical Songs, Arias from Grand Opera, Selections from famous pianoforte compositions, Cryes of London, and Marches. 3s. 6d. N.C.

168. *Musical Appreciation through Song*, by R. Dunstan and C. E. Bygott. Teachers' book 12s. 6d., pupils' book 2s. 9d. S.S.

169. *National Song Book*, Vol. I, edited by C. V. Stanford. 6s. Bo.

170. *National Song Book*, Vol. II, edited by Harold Boulton and Arthur Somervell. 3s. Bo.

171. *News-Chronicle Song Book*, edited by T. P. Ratcliff, including Community Songs, Plantation Songs, Sea Shanties, Negro Spirituals, Children's Songs, Hymns, and Carols. 2s. 6d. net. N.C.

172. *New Fellowship Songbook*, arranged by H. Walford Davies, Hundred Songs for indoor or open-air singing as solos or in chorus, with or without accompaniment. 1s. 9d. net to 4s. 6d. net. Nov.

173.  *Old English Songs,* in three sets. 8*d.* and 1*s.* each. Nov.
174.  *Oxford Album of Standard Songs,* edited by Steuart Wilson. 2*s.* 6*d.* O.U.P.
175.  *Oxford Song Book,* Vol. I, collected and arranged by Percy C. Buck. 7*s.* 6*d.* net. Melody edition, 1*s.* O.U.P.
176.  *Oxford Song Book,* Vol. II, collected and arranged by Thomas Wood. 7*s.* 6*d.* net. O.U.P.
177.  *Pictures in Song,* edited by Robert McLeod, in four vols. 2*s.* 6*d.* net each. Ba.
178.  *Pocket Sing-Song Book,* including Folk and National Songs, Rounds, Hymns and Carols. 1*s.* 6*d.* Words only, 4*d.* Nov.
179.  Purcell: *Fifteen Songs by Purcell,* edited by Arthur Somervell. 4*s.* Nov.
180.  —— *Moon, The,* unison and two-part Songs by Purcell, arranged by W. G. Whittaker. 1*s.* 6*d.* net. O.U.P.
181.  —— *Seventeen Songs by Purcell,* edited by Arthur Somervell. 4*s.* Nov.
182.  —— *Twenty Favourite Songs.* 4*s.* net. Au.
183.  —— *Twelve Songs by Purcell,* edited by William Cummings. 4*s.* Nov.
184.  Rounds: *Graduated Rounds* (93), by various composers. 1*s.* Nov.
185.  —— *Rounds and Canons,* by Beethoven, edited by W. G. Whittaker. 1*s.* O.U.P.
186.  —— *Rounds and Canons,* by Haydn, edited by W. G. Whittaker. 2*s.* 6*d.* O.U.P.
187.  —— *Rounds and Canons,* by Schubert. Three parts, each 3*d.* O.U.P.
188.  —— *Rounds and Canons,* by Mozart, edited by W. G. Whittaker. 1*s.* 6*d.* O.U.P.
189.  *S.A.B. Book, The,* by Cyril Winn, arranged for three-part singing with melody in bass clef. 1*s.* net. Bo.
190.  Schubert: *Thirty Songs by Schubert.* 2*s.* Nov.
191.  —— *Twelve Favourite Songs,* edited by A. H. Fox-Strangways and Steuart Wilson. 3*s.* O.U.P.

192. *Scottish Students' Song Book.* 5s. net. Words only, 2s.
     Ba.
193. Shakespeare: *Songs from Shakespeare* (earliest known
     settings), edited by J. Frederick Bridge. 3s. Nov.
194. —— *Songs from Shakespeare, with Dances,* compiled by
     Mrs G. T. Kimmins. 2s. 6d. Nov.
195. —— *Songs from Shakespeare's Plays,* edited by T. Maskell
     Hardy. Parts I and II, 3s. 6d. each. Melody
     edition, 9d. each. Cu.
196. *Songs from the Poets* (unison and two-part), by Alec
     Rowley. 3s. 6d. net. Sa.
197. *Songs of the British Islands,* edited by W. H. Hadow,
     including One Hundred National Melodies.
     6s. Melody edition, 1s. 6d. Cu.
198. *Songs of Four Nations,* arranged by Arthur Somervell.
     £1. 1s. Cr.
199. *Songs for the Young,* Set I, Classical. 2s. 6d. Au.
200. *Twice Fifty-five Community Songs, More than,* arranged
     for singing in parts or unison, including Patriotic
     and Folk Songs, Traditional Airs, Hymns,
     Rounds and Canons. 6d. Bo.
201. *Twice Forty-four Sociable Songs,* collected and arranged
     by Geoffrey Shaw, for unison and part singing.
     6d. Bo.

### CANTATAS, ORATORIOS AND OPERAS

Vocal scores are published by Augener, Boosey, Breitkopf
and Härtel, Chappell, Chester, Curwen, Novello, Oxford
University Press, Peters, Pitman, Ricordi, Schott, Universal and others.

## APPENDIX B

## LIST OF HYMN BOOKS

### 1. FOR YOUNG CHILDREN

*Hosanna* (illustrated), edited by T. Grigg-Smith, Charles Wood, and Hubert Middleton. 4*s.* net. S.P.C.K.

*Song Time* (Section N comprises hymns), by Percy Dearmer and Martin Shaw. 4*s.* 6*d.* net. Cu.

### 2. FOR SCHOOLS AND COLLEGES

*Songs of Praise*, musical editors, Martin Shaw and R. Vaughan Williams. Enlarged edition (1931). 6*s.* net. Words only, 1*s.* 9*d.* net. O.U.P.

*Songs of Praise for Day Schools.* 1*s.* 3*d.* net. O.U.P.

*Songs of Praise for Boys and Girls.* 3*s.* 6*d.* net. Words only, 1*s.* net. O.U.P.

*Hymns for Use in Schools.* 1*s.* 3*d.* net. O.U.P.

*Public School Hymn Book*, edited by Committee of the Headmasters' Conference. 5*s.* Words only, 2*s.* 6*d.* and 1*s.* 3*d.* Nov.

*School Worship*, musical editor, G. Thalben-Ball; includes Orders of Worship and Prayers, and indexes for Junior, Intermediate and Senior Departments. 5*s.* net. Words only, 10*d.* and 1*s.* I.P.

*A Book of Worship for Youth*, being Parts 2 and 3 of *School Worship*. 4*s.* 6*d.* net. Words only, 9*d.* and 11*d.* I.P.

*A Students' Hymnal (Emynau'r Myfyrwyr)*, including *Hymns of the Kingdom* and 123 Welsh Hymns, musical editor, Sir Walford Davies. Harmonised edition, 6*s.* 6*d.* Melody edition, 1*s.* 6*d.* O.U.P.

*Hymns of the Kingdom*, being the English section of *A Students' Hymnal*, musical editor, Sir Walford Davies. Harmonised edition, 4*s.* 6*d.* net. Melody edition, 8*d.* net. O.U.P.

### 3. FOR CHURCHES

*Songs of Praise,* see B, 2 above.

*English Hymnal,* musical editor, R. Vaughan Williams.
6s. net. Melody edition, 2s. 6d. net. Words only, 1s. 9d.
net. O.U.P.

*Hymns Ancient and Modern,* new edition (1924), musical editor,
Sydney H. Nicholson. 3s. 6d. Words only, 1s. 9d. Cl.

*Hymns Ancient and Modern,* Plain-song edition, musical editor,
Sydney H. Nicholson. 6s. net. Melody edition, 2s. 6d.
net. Words only, 1s. net. Cl.

*The Oxford Hymn Book,* musical editor, Basil Harwood.
5s. 6d. net. O.U.P.

*Songs of Syon,* musical editor, Rev. G. R. Woodward. 10s. Sc.


### APPENDIX C

# LIST OF ORCHESTRAL AND CHAMBER MUSIC

## 1. ORCHESTRAL MUSIC (SCHOOL ORCHESTRAS)

Miniature full scores of many orchestral works and
chamber music, from 1s. upwards, are available from most
publishers and dealers.

### (a) *Strings and Pianoforte*

*Easy:*

Carse, A. *Festival March.* Au.
—— *Minuet.* Au.
—— *Norwegian Dances.* Au.
—— *English Dance Tunes.* Au.
—— *Gavotte and Musette* (Lulli). Au.
Dyson, G. *In Pixie-land.* Wi.

Fletcher, P. E. *Graceful Measures*. Cu.
*Junior Orchestral Series* (ed. E. Read). Wi.
"*Maidstone*" *Violin Music*. Mu.
Mozart. *Bell Gavotte* and *Priests' March*. Cu.
*Polychordia Library* (Primary and Lower Grades). St.
*School Band Music*. No.
Woodhouse, C. *Minuet and Waltz*. Ha.
—— *Carmen March*. Ha.
—— *Processional March*. Ha.
—— *Rustic Dance*. Ha.

*More Advanced:*

Carse, A. *The Amateur Orchestra*. Wi.
Fletcher, P. E. *Folk-tune and Fiddle Dance*. Cu.
Gluck. *Ballet Music* (from *Orpheus*), two books. O.U.P.
Handel. *Il Ballo* (from *Alcina*). O.U.P.
—— *Minuet* (from *Berenice*). O.U.P.
—— *Pieces from* "*Water Music*". Nov.
—— *Two Bourrées from* "*Water Music*". Nov.
Haydn. *Serenade from Quartet*. Ha.
Macfarren. *Bourrée in C*. Nov.
"*Maidstone*" *Orchestral Library*. Mu.
Mendelssohn. *Cornelius March*. Nov.
—— *War March of the Priests*. Nov.
Mozart. *Dance Suite*. O.U.P.
—— *Minuet and Trio*. O.U.P.
*Polychordia Library* (Middle Grade). St.
Rameau. *Rigaudon de Dardanus*. Nov.
Schmidt (ed.). *The String Orchestra* (several books). B.H.
Tours. *March in G*. Nov.
Young, W. See (*m*), (*n*) and (*o*), below.

*Advanced:*

Bach. *Concerto in G minor*. O.U.P.
Cimarosa. *Overture to* "*Il matrimonio segreto*". Cu.
Coleridge-Taylor. *Four Characteristic Waltzes*. Nov.
Cowen. *Four English Dances*. Nov.
Davies, H. Walford. *Solemn Melody*. Nov.

Elgar. *Serenade (Wand of Youth)*. Nov.
German. *Henry VIII Dances*. Nov.
—— *Nell Gwynne Dances*. Nov.
Mackenzie. *Benedictus*. Nov.
Mozart. *Suite ("Idomeneo")*. Cu.
*Polychordia Library* (Higher Grade). St.
Schmidt (ed.). *The String Orchestra* (the more difficult numbers). B.H.
Schubert. *Minuet and Trio* (Octette). Nov.
Vaughan Williams. *Charterhouse Suite*. St.

## (b) *String Orchestra*

*Easy to Moderate:*
Bach—Dunhill. *The Anna Magdalena Suite*. O.U.P.
Blagrove. *Class Music for Strings*. Wi.
Byrde—Jackson. *Thou come kiss me now*. O.U.P.
Elgar. *Elegy*. Nov.
Elvey. *Gavotte a la mode ancienne* (Pianoforte ad lib.). Nov.
Gurlitt. *Overture "Marionettes"*. Au.
—— *Overture "Comedietta"*. Au.
Handel—Dunhill. *Five short Pieces*. O.U.P.
Henselt. *Ave Maria*. B.H.
Mozart. *Seven Minuets with Trio* (three parts). B.H.
—— *Six Country Dances* (three parts). B.H.
—— see (a), above.
Purcell. *"The Old Bachelor" Suite*. O.U.P.
Robjohns (ed.). *The Chamber Orchestra*. Wi.
Saint-George. *1re Petite Suite*. Au.
Scharwenka, Op. 71. *For the Young*. B.H.
Schubert. *Minuet in D major*. B.H.
Tschaikowsky. *Douce Rêverie et Petite Valse*. Ha.
Warlock, P. (ed.). *Six English Tunes*. O.U.P.
—— *Six Italian Dances*. O.U.P.

*More Advanced:*
Bach. *Aria in E major*. B.H.
Boccherini. *Minuet*. Au.

Boyce. *Suite*. Wi.
Foster. *Folk-Song Suite*. Nov.
Gluck. *Musette from "Armida"*. Au.
Handel. *Scherzo from Concerto in G minor*. Au.
—— *Larghetto from Concerto in B minor*. O.U.P.
Haydn. *Nachtwächter Minuet*. Au.
Jacob. *Denbigh Suite*. O.U.P.
Kreug. *Norwegian Suite*. Nov.
McEwen. *Suite of National Dances*. Wi.
Purcell—Coates. *Suite*. Nov.
Purcell—Holst. *The Gordian Knot untied* (wind *ad lib.*). Nov.
Rameau. *Chaconne and Musette*. Au.
Rowley. *Christmas Suite*. Nov.

*Advanced:*

Bach. *The "Giant" Fugue*. O.U.P.
—— *Prelude and Fugue in G minor* (arr.). Nov.
—— *Suites* 1–6 (arr.). O.U.P.
Carse. *Arrangements of Symphonies*. Au.
—— *Variations on "Barbara Allen"*. Nov.
Corelli. *Concerto Grosso in C minor*. O.U.P.
Dunhill. *Chiddingfold Suite*. Nov.
—— *Dance Suite*. Cu.
Elgar, Op. 20. *Serenade*. B.H.
Fletcher, P. E. *Two Bagatelles*. Nov.
Geminiani. *Concerto Grosso in C minor*. O.U.P.
Gluck. *Overture to "Orpheus"*. O.U.P.
Holst. *"St Paul's" Suite*. Cu.
McEwen. *The Jocund Dance*. O.U.P.
Mozart. *Eine kleine Nachtmusik*. B.H.

*Advanced:*

Stuteley, G. *Salt o' the Sea*. O.U.P.
Vivaldi. *Concerto in E minor*. O.U.P.
Wall. *Pastorale and Bourrée*. O.U.P.

## (c)  Strings and Wind

*Easy:*

Hunt (arr.). *Various Pieces* (with Flute, Clarinet and Cornet). Bo.
"*Maidstone*" *Violin Library* (with Clarinet and Cornet). Mu.

*More Advanced:*

Blow—Harrison. *Venus and Adonis* (Flute, Oboe, Clarinet, Bassoon *ad lib.*). Wi.
Carse. *The Amateur Orchestra* (Flute, Oboe, Clarinet, Bassoon *ad lib.*). Wi.
—— (ed.). *Two Series* (Flute, Oboe, Clarinet, Bassoon *ad lib.*). Au.
—— *Variations on* "*Barbara Allen*". Nov.
Gluck. *Ballet Music from* "*Orpheus*" (Flute *ad lib.*). O.U.P.
Handel. *Il Ballo* ("*Alcina*") (Oboe, Flute, Bassoon *ad lib.*). O.U.P.
—— *Minuet* ("*Berenice*") (Flute, Oboe, Clarinet, Bassoon *ad lib.*). O.U.P.
Hausmusik (Pianoforte, Strings and any Wind Instrument). *Standard Symphonies and Overtures, etc.* B.H.
Hunt. *Arrangements.* Bo.
"*Maidstone*" *Orchestral Library* (Clarinet and Cornet). Mu.
Mozart—Rootham. *Six Dances* (Flute, Oboe, Horns and Bassoon *ad lib.*). O.U.P.
—— *Gavotte* ("*Idomeneo*") (Flute or Oboe, Horns, Bassoon *ad lib.*). O.U.P.
Rootham. *St John's Suite* (Strings, Clarinet, Hautboy or English Horn, French Horn or Trumpet, Trombone and Percussion; or, alternatively, Strings and Pianoforte throughout). O.U.P.
Scarlatti, A. *Toccata, Aria, Minuetto and Giga* (Flute, Bassoon and Tympani *ad lib.*). O.U.P.
Thomas, A. *Gavotte from* "*Mignon*" (Flute, Clarinet, Cornet). Cu.
Tschaikowsky. *Chant sans paroles* (Flute, Clarinet, Cornet). Cu.

*Advanced:*

Bach. *Choral Prelude "Wachet auf"* (Flute, Oboe, Clarinet, Trumpet or Horn). O.U.P.
—— *Sinfonia to Church Cantata* 75 (Trumpet and *ad lib.* Flute, Oboe, Violin). O.U.P.
—— *Sonatina from Church Cantata* 106 (two flutes). O.U.P.
Milford, R. *Suite for Oboe and Strings.* O.U.P.
Scarlatti, D. *Four Dances* (Flute, Bassoon and Tympani *ad lib.*). O.U.P.
Williams, Gerrard. *Four Traditional Tunes.* O.U.P.
—— *Three Scottish Tunes* (Flute, Clarinet, Cornet and Tympani *ad lib.*). O.U.P.
*Standard Symphonies and Overtures in "Hausmusik" series.* B.H.
*Various Symphonies,* arr. Strings and Flute. Au.

### (d)  Toy Symphonies

Carse. *Childhood's Happy Days.* Au.
Conradi. *Christmas Overture.* Au.
Gurlitt. *Toy Symphony.* Au.
Haydn. *Toy Symphony.* Au.
Romberg. *Toy Symphony.* Au.

## 2.  CHAMBER MUSIC

### (a)  Duets for Two Violins alone

Carse. *Three easy duets.* Au.
Dancla. Op. 23, *Three easy duets* (first position). Au.
—— Op. 24, *Three easy duets.* Au.
—— Op. 25, *Three Duos concertants.* Au.
Pleyel, Op. 8. *Six Duos.* Pe.
—— Op. 44, *Three Duos.* Pe.
Ries, H. *Progressive Duos,* nine books. Au.

### (b)  Duets for Violin and Cello

Pleyel, Op. 30. *Duets.* Pe.
Stutschewsky. *Modern and Classical Pieces,* four books. Sc.

(c)  *Duets for Violin and Viola*

Haydn, Op. 93. *Three Sonatas.* Au.
Kalliwoda, Op. 208. *Duets.* Pe.

(d)  *Trios for Two Violins and Pianoforte*

Carse. *Three Waltzes.* Au.
Corelli. *Six Sonatas.* Au.
Dancla. *Six Little Pieces,* two books. Sc.
Handel. *Three Sonatas.* Pe.
Hermann (ed.). *Ensemble Music.* Au.
Humperdinck. *Abendsegen.* Sc.
Moffat. *The First Position.* Si.
—— *Suite in the Olden Style.* Si.
—— *Sixteen Classical Transcriptions.* Sc.
—— (ed.). Locatelli, *Sonata in G.* More difficult. Si.
—— Rameau, *Two Minuets.* Sc.
Saint-George. *L'Ancien Regime* (two Suites). Au.
See also (m), below.

(e)  *Three and Four Violins and Pianoforte*

See (n) and (o), below.

(f)  *Trios for Strings alone*

Dalmaine. *Six Trios,* three violins. Fo.
Dancla. *Six Easy Trios,* three violins. Sc.
Schroder. *Trios* (first position), three violins. Ki.
—— *Trios* (higher positions), three violins. Ki.

(g)  *Trios for Two Violins and Cello*

Boccherini. *Trios for two Violins and Cello.* Li.
Corelli. *Six Sonatas.* Si.
Handel. *Fifteen Sonatas.* Sc.
Mozart. *Twelve German Dances.* Sc.
—— *Twelve Minuets.* Sc.
Pleyel. *Three Trios concertants.* Sc.
Wood-Warlock. *Trio.* Au.

(h) *Trios for Two Violins and Viola*
Haydn. *Divertimento in C* (No. 3). B.H.

(i) *Trios for Violin, Viola, and Cello*
Haydn. *Three Trios.* Li.
—— *Two Divertimenti.* U.
Schubert. *Trio in B♭.* Li.

(j) *Trios for Pianoforte, Violin, and Cello*
*Albums for Trio* (Progressive Books I–IV). U.
*Albums for Trio,* Books I–VI (Carse). Au.
Bridge, F. *Miniatures* (three books). Au.
Carse. *Five Easy Trios.* Au.
Gibbs, Armstrong. *Country Magic.* Cu.
Gurlitt, Op. 129. *Easy Trio in G.* Au.
Kupfer. *Two Easy Trios.* Si.
Rowley, A. *The Puppet Show.* O.U.P.
—— *Four Contrasts.* O.U.P.
—— *A Short Suite.* O.U.P.
Sitt. *Two Easy Trios.* Pe.
Trew, A. *Triolets* (easy). O.U.P.

(k) *String Quartets (two Violins, Viola, and Cello)*
Carse. *Three Dances.* Au.
Dancla. *Three Easy Quartets,* Op. 208. Sc.
Hermann. *Easy Quartet Movements.* Sc.
Howell, D. *Dance* (from *Christmas Eve*). O.U.P.
Köhler. *Easy Quartet* (first position). Sc.
Kupfer. *Four Pieces* (three Violins and Cello). Si.
Rowley, A. *Phyllis and Corydon.* O.U.P.

(l) *Pianoforte Quartets (Pianoforte, Violin, Viola, and Cello)*
Pleyel, Op. 48. *Six Sonatinas.* Au.
—— Op. 44. *Three Quartets.* Au.
Reinecke. *Quartet in easy style.* Rei.

### (m) Quartets for Pianoforte, Two Violins, and Cello
#### (Sometimes optional)

Arne. *Sonata in E minor.* Nov.
Blow. *Two Sonatas.* Ed.
Boccherini. *Sonata in C minor.* Si.
Boyce. *Sonata in A.* Sc.
—— *Sonata in E minor.* Nov.
Corelli, Op. 4. *Six Sonatas.* Au.
Handel. *Six Trio Sonatas.* Au.
—— *Nine Trio Sonatas.* Sc.
—— *Largo alla Siciliana.* Au.
Lulli. *Gavotte and Minuet.* Au.
Purcell. *Four Sonatas.* Au.
—— *Golden Sonata.* Au.
—— *Twenty-two Sonatas.* Ed. (In preparation.)
Saint-George. *L'Ancien Regime.* (Two suites.) Au.
Young, W. *Three Sonatas and Four Suites.* (Contrabass optional.) O.U.P.

### (n) Quintets for Pianoforte, Three Violins, and Cello
#### (Sometimes optional)

Young, W. *Seven Sonatas.* (Contrabass optional.) O.U.P.

### (o) Sextet for Pianoforte, Four Violins, and Cello

Young, W. *Sonata XI.* (Contrabass optional.) O.U.P.

### (p) Chamber Music with Wind Instruments

Beethoven. *Serenade* (Flute, Violin, Viola) (difficult). Li.
Mozart. *Two easy Divertimenti* (Pianoforte, Oboe, and Bassoon). B.H.
Popp, Op. 505. *Jugend Trios* (Flute, Violin, Pianoforte, Cello *ad lib.*). Li.
—— Op. 522. *Six easy solo Quartets* (Pianoforte, Flute, Violin, Cello).
—— Op. 521. *Six easy Trios* (Flute, Violin, Pianoforte). (Steingräber edn.) Bos.

Schumann. *Märchenbilder* (Pianoforte, Clarinet, Viola). Bos.

Vivaldi. *Pastorale* (Flute or Oboe, Cello, Organ or Pianoforte). Nagel, Hanover.

(*q*) *Easy Solos for Wind Instruments and Pianoforte*

(i) *Flute and Pianoforte:*

Alwyn. *Three Easy Pieces.* Wi.
Carse. *Pipe Tune.* Au.
—— *Romance.* Au.

(ii) *Clarinet and Pianoforte:*

Carse. *Happy Tune.* Au.
—— *Reverie.* Au.
Donnington. *Two Pieces.* Wi.
Read, E. *Song without words.* Wi.

(iii) *Oboe and Pianoforte:*

Caine, E. *Andante.* Wi.
Carse. *A Dance Measure.* Au.
—— *Regreto.* Au.

(iv) *Bassoon and Pianoforte:*

Foster, Ivor R. *Serenade.* Wi.
—— *Rondo.* Wi.


# APPENDIX D

# LIST OF PIANOFORTE MUSIC

The lists are divided into seven grades; the standard of each grade approximates to: I, the 5 finger group; II, *The Merry Peasant* (Schumann); III, Clementi, *Sonatina No. 1*; IV, Beethoven's *Minuet in G*; V, A Chopin Mazurka; VI, Mendelssohn's *Spring Song*; VII, A Beethoven Sonata.

## SECTION (i): FINGER EXERCISES—SCALES AND ARPEGGIOS

Beringer. *Daily Technical Studies* (with Scales and Arpeggios). Bos.

Cortot. *Principes Rationnels de la Technique Pianistique.* Se.

Czerny, Op. 337. *Forty Daily Studies.* Au. & Nov.

Fowles. *Studies in Part Playing.* Au.

Hanon. *Pianist Virtuoso*—60 Exercises (with Scales and Arpeggios). Sc.

Kleinmichel. *Twelve Special Studies for Finger Strength.* Be.

Krug. *Exercises for the Independence of the Fingers.* Nov.

Leschetizky. *His Method* (Prentner). Cu.

O'Neill. *Exercises for the Weaker Fingers.* Nov.

Pischna. *Technical Studies.* Pe.

Safonoff. *New Formula for Teacher and Student.* Ch.

Schmitt. *Finger Exercises.* Au. & Nov.

Scott. *Modern Finger Exercises.* El.

Somervell. *Ten Minutes Technique.* Cu.

## SECTION (ii): GRADED STUDIES

### GRADE I

Rowley. *Twelve Little Fantasy Studies for the First Year.* Ha.

—— *Poetical Studies,* Book 1. As.

*The New Czerny,* Book 1. Ke.

### GRADE II

Rowley. *Fantasy Studies for the Second Year,* Book 1. Ha.

—— *Poetical Studies,* Book 2. As.

*The New Czerny,* Book 2. Ke.

Thümer. *New School of Studies,* Book 1. Au.

### GRADE III

Bertini, Op. 100. *Twenty-five Studies* (small hands). Au.

Burgmüller, Op. 100. *Twenty-five Studies.* Au. & Nov.

*The New Czerny,* Book 3. Ke.

Rowley. *Fantasy Studies for the Second Year*, Books 2 and 3. Ha.
—— *Poetical Studies*. As.
Stamaty, Op. 37. *Studies* (2 books). Au.
Thümer. *New School of Studies*, Book 2. Au.

## GRADE IV

Burgmüller. *Eighteen Characteristic Studies*. Au. & Nov.
Le Couppey, Op. 20. *Agility*. Au.
*The New Czerny*, Book 4. Ke.
Stamaty, Op. 38. *Etudes*. Au.
Toch, Op. 59. *Ten Etudes* (Modern). Sc.

## GRADE V

*The New Czerny*, Book 5. Ke.
Godard, Op. 149. *Etudes Melodiques*, Books 1 and 2. Le.
Heller, Op. 47. *Studies*. Au. and Nov.
Moszkowski, Op. 91. *Dexterity and Style* (2 books). Au.
Toch, Op. 57. *Ten Middle Grade Etudes* (Modern). Sc.

## GRADE VI

*The New Czerny*, Book 6. Ke.
Godard, Op. 149. *Six Etudes Rythmiques*. Le.
Haberbier. *Poetical Studies* (3 books). Pe.
Heller, Op. 45–46. *Etudes* (2 books). Au. & Nov.
Jensen, Op. 32. *Twenty-five Etudes* (3 books). Pe.
MacDowell, Op. 39. *Twelve Studies*. El.
Moszkowski. *Esquisses Techniques* (2 books). Au.
Swinstead. *Six Studies* (Modern). O.U.P.
Toch, Op. 56. *Ten Recital Studies* (Modern). Sc.

## GRADE VII

Chopin. *Etudes*. Au. & Nov.
Clementi. *Gradus* (Tausig). Pe.
Cramer. *Etudes* (Bülow). Pe.
Czerny, Op. 740. *Art of Finger-practice*. Au. & Nov.

*The New Czerny*, Book 7. Ke.
Godard, Op. 149. *Six Etudes de Concert.* Le.
Henselt, Op. 5. *Twelve Etudes de Salon.* Au.
—— Op. 2. *Twelve Grand Characteristic Studies.* Au.
MacDowell. *Twelve Virtuoso Studies.* El.
Moscheles, Op. 70. *Twenty-four Studies.* Au.
Toch, Op. 55. *Ten Concert Studies* (Modern). Sc.
York Bowen, Op. 46. *Twelve Studies* (Modern). Asc.


## SECTION (iii): THE EARLY CLASSICS
### Grades II–III

*At the Court of Queen Anne* (20 Easy Pieces). Ch.
*Bach and the Old Masters* (Bien). We.
*Bach for Beginners* (Books 1 and 2). Ha.
*Beringer's School of Easy Classics* (twelve vols.). Au.
*Mozart and the Old Masters* (Bien). We.
*Old English Worthies.* Ha.
*Simple English Classics* (Glyn) (100 tunes of the sixteenth to
    seventeenth centuries). Le.


### Grades IV–V

Bach. *Two-Part Inventions and Short Preludes and Fugues.* Wi.
*Eighteenth Century Music* (The Four Bach Sons). Sc.
*Old English and French Masters* (arr. Beringer). Au.
*Old English Roundelays and Dances* (two books). Le.
Scarlatti (arr. Beringer). *School of Early Classics.* Au.


### Grades VI–VII

Bach. *Three-Part Inventions.* Au. & No.
—— *Forty-eight Preludes and Fugues:*
       (*a*) Associated Board (Samuel and Tovey). A.S.
       (*b*) Novello (Brooke). Nov.
       (*c*) Peters. Pe.
       (*d*) Ashdown. As.

Bull (arr. Bantock). *Selected Pieces*. Nov.
Byrd (arr. Bantock). *Selected Pieces*. Nov.
Couperin. Two books. Pa.
*Craxton-Moffat Series* (separate numbers). Cr.
*Early English Harpsichord Music* (separate numbers). Ha.
*Giles Farnaby* (arr. Bantock). Nov.
*In the days of Frederick the Great* (two books). Le.
*Masters of the Rococo Period* (two books). Le.
*Old English Suite* (Bantock). Nov.
Purcell. *Suites*. Au. & Nov.
—— *Ten Pianoforte Pieces*. Nov.
*Some Old World Classics* (V. Warner). Bos.

## TRANSCRIPTIONS
Godowski. *Renaissance* (three books). Sc.
MacDowell. *From the Eighteenth Century* (two books). El.

# SECTION (iv): SONATINAS AND SONATAS (THE CLASSICS)

## GRADE I
*Early English Sonatinas*. Vol. I. Ha.

## GRADE II
Beethoven. *Sonatina in F*, Op. 49, No. 2. Au. & Nov.
Clementi. *Six Sonatinas*. Au. & Nov.
Dussek. *Six Sonatinas*. Au. & Nov.
*Early English Sonatinas*. Vols. II and III. Ha.
Mozart. *Six Sonatinas*. Sc.

## GRADES III–IV
Beethoven. Nos. 19 in G minor and 25 in G. Au. & Nov.
Clementi. *Sonata*, No. 5 in D. Au.
Haydn. Nos. 2, 4, 9, 11, 17. Au.
Mozart. Nos. 5, 16, 19. Pe.
Schumann. *Sonatinas*. Au. & Nov.

## GRADES V–VI–VII

Beethoven. *Sonatas* (selected). Au. & Nov.
Clementi. No. 2 in G. Au.
Dussek. *Sonatas*. Cra.
Haydn. Nos. 5, 6, 7, 10, 12, 13, 14, 15, 16, 18, 22. Au.
Mozart. *Sonatas*. Pe.
Schubert. *Sonatas*. Pe.
Weber. *Sonatas*. Cra.

## VERY DIFFICULT

Beethoven. *Later Sonatas*. Au. & Nov.
Brahms. *Three Sonatas*. Au. & Nov.
Chopin. *Sonatas*. Au. & Nov.
Liszt. *Sonata in B minor*. Au. & Nov.
Schumann. *Three Sonatas*. Au. & Nov.

## SECTION (v): PIECES AND ALBUMS

### GRADE I (Tutors and 5 finger group)

Bavin. *Piano Class Method*. Ha.
*Mrs Curwen's Pianoforte Method*. Cu.
Donald Gray. *The Musical Gateway* (Tutor). Bo.
Matthay and Swinstead. *The Pianist's First Music Making*. An.
Moy. *Well Begun*.
Rowley. *The Easiest Way* (Tutor). En.
—— Op. 37. *Characters* (Thirteen Easiest Pieces). Pe.
Sekles. *Tune Building*. Sc.

### GRADE II

Baynon. *Up Hill Down Dale*. Nov.
Carroll. *Scenes at a Farm*. Fo.
—— *The Country Side*. Fo.
Carse. *Toyland Tunes* (two books). Au.
Diller and Quaile. *First and Second Solo Albums*. Ha.
Gretchaninov. *Piano Album* (1). Sc.

Kullak. *Kinderleben*. Nov.
Lee. *Ten Little Pieces* (compass of six notes). O.U.P.
Moy. *From the Beginning*. Ha.
Sarson. *Told with a Tune*. St.
Swinstead. *Recreations* (book 2). Ha.
—— *The Very First Album*. Cr.

### GRADE III

Austin. *Twelve Tunes for Young Musicians*. La.
—— *Playtime Pieces* (Book 1). La.
Bath. *Doll's House Suite*. Nov.
Carroll. *Forest Fantasies*. Fo.
—— *Sea Idylls*. Fo.
Diller and Quaile. *Third Solo Book*. Ha.
Dunhill. *Lyric Thoughts*. An.
Greenhill. *A Woodland Posy*. Nov.
Lee. *The Mermaid*. Cr.
Moy. *Seven Miniatures*. Ha.
Niemann. *The Cheery Music Master*. Pe.
Poldini, Op. 53. *Album for the Young* (two books). Le.
Rebikoff. *Silhouettes*. Le.
Rowley. *The Circus*. As.
—— *From a Toy Cupboard*. As.
Spurling. *Six Short Easy Pieces*. Nov.
Swinstead. *Recreations*, Book 2. Ha.

### GRADE IV

Austin. *Playtime Pieces* (Books 2 and 3). La.
Bridge. *Miniature Pastorals*. Ha.
Dunhill. *Eyes of Youth*. Le.
—— *A Garden of Melodies*. Le.
—— *Holiday Snaps*. Ar.
Farjeon. *Toys*. Ar.
Gade. *Christmas Pieces*. Au. & Nov.
Greenhill. *A Country Holiday*. Nov.
Gretchaninov. *Piano Album* (2). Sc.
Grieg, Op. 12. *Lyric Pieces*. Pe.

Grovlez. *A Child's Garden*. Ch.
Heller. *Album for the Young*. As.
Ireland. *A Child's Sketch Book*. Ha.
Jensen. *Songs and Dances*. As.
Mendelssohn. *Six Christmas Pieces*. Au. & Nov.
Moszkowski. *Dix Petites Morceaux*. Sc.
Moy. *Soldier Tunes*. Ha.
—— *Fanciful Sketches*. Ha.
—— *Sea Sketches*. Cr.
Niemann. *My Piano Book* (two vols.). Pe.
Rebikoff. *Mood Sketches*. Le.
Rowley. *Sailor Tunes*. Ha.
—— *Miniature Dance Suite*. Ha.
—— *From My Sketch Book*. Pe.
—— *The Changing Year*. As.
Schubert. *Scherzo in B Flat*. Au. & Nov.
Schumann. *Album for the Young*. Au. & Nov.
de Severac. *En Vacances* (two books). Ch.
Spurling. *Our Village in Summer*. Nov.
—— *Our Village in Winter*. Nov.
Swinstead. *Leisure Moments*. As.
—— *Six Little Pieces*. As.
—— *Five Idylls*. An.
Tschaikovsky. *Album for the Young*. Au. & Nov.
Williams. *On My Own*. O.U.P.

## Grade V

Austin. *Musical Verses*. La.
—— *Ditties and Dances* (Book 2). La.
Bridge. *Miniature Pastorals* (Second Set). Ha.
Chopin. *Mazurkas*. Au. & Nov.
Dunhill. *Times and Seasons*. As.
—— *Elfin Glade*. Cr.
—— *Puppet Dance*. Wi.
Greenhill. *Springtime in the Forest*. Nov.
Howells. *Sailor Dance*. Cr.
MacDowell. *Six Fancies*. El.
—— *Forgotten Fairy Tales*. El.

Moszkowski, Op. 77. *Dix Pieces Mignonnes* (two books). Sc.
Moy. *Three Impressions.* O.U.P.
—— *From a Country Garden.* Cr.
Niemann, Op. 59. *Masken* (two books). Pe.
Poldini. *Poupée Valsant.* Ri.
—— *Petites Poesies* (two books). Hai.
Rebikoff. *Album* (1). Sc.
Rowley. *Here we come a-piping.* Wi.
—— *Humoresque.* As.
Sarson. *Hey Diddle Diddle.* St.
Schutt. *Pour tou les Ages* (two books). Le.
Schytte. *Berceuse.* Wi.
Scott. *Album for Girls.* El.
—— *Album for Boys.* El.
Tschrepnine. *Dix Pieces Gaies.* Ch.

## GRADE VI

Albeniz. *Espana,* six pieces. Sc.
Austin. *Mist on the Hills.* La.
—— *Meadowland and Mountain.* El.
Berger. *Flower-Pieces.* Pa.
Carse. *Eccentric Dance.* Au.
—— *Three Miniatures.* Nov.
Chopin. *Valses.* Au. & Nov.
Dohnanyi. *March on a Ground Bass.* Le.
Dunhill. *Three Short Pieces.* Wi.
—— *From the Forest of Faerie.* Sw.
—— *Distant Angelus.* O.U.P.
Farjeon. *Pictures from Greece.* Au.
—— *Tone Pictures* (Book 3). Au.
Fletcher. *Reflections.* Nov.
Grovlez. *L'Almanach aux Images.* Au.
Heller. *Twenty-four Preludes.* Au.
—— Op. 99. *Fantasie-Stück.* Au.
Korngold. *Epilog.* Sc.
MacDowell. *Woodland Sketches.* El.
—— *Four Poems.* El.
—— *Six Poems after Heine.* Ha.

Moy. *Snapshots.* Ha.
Poulenc. *Novellette*, No. 1. Ch.
Rebikoff. *Album* (2). Sc.
Rowley. *Walking Tune.* Cr.
Schutt. *Etude Mignonne.* Le.
—— *Canzonetta.* Le.
Scott. *Verperale.* El.
Swinstead. *Pierette.* Wi.
—— *Humoresque.* Wi.
Tschaikovsky. *The Months.* Au. & Nov.

### GRADE VII

Albeniz. *Iberia* (four books). Ch.
Bax. *A Country Tune.* Mu.
—— *The Maiden with the Daffodil.* Wi.
—— *Apple-Blossom Time.* Au.
Bridge. *Dainty Rogue.* Au.
—— *Hearts Ease.* Au.
—— *A Fairy Tale* (Suite). Au.
—— *Three Sketches.* Ha.
—— *The Dew Fairy.* Au.
Debussy. *Children's Corner.* Du.
Delius. *Five Pieces.* U.
—— *Three Preludes.* An.
Dvořák. *Waltzes* (two books). Le.
—— Op. 8. *Silhouettes.* Le.
—— Op. 98. *Suite.* Le.
Fauré. *Huit Nocturnes* (complete). Ham.
—— *Six Barcarolles et Cinq Impromptus.* Ham.
Goossens. *Kaleidoscope.* Ch.
Grieg. *Lyric Pieces*, various. Pe.
Ibert. *A Giddy Girl.* Ler.
Ireland. *The Darkened Valley.* Au.
—— *Ragamuffin.* Au.
—— *The Island Spell.* Au.
—— *Four Preludes.* Ha.
—— *Rhapsody.* Ha.
—— *February's Child.* Sc.

Jensen. *Romantic Studies*. Pe.
—— *Erotikon*. Au.
—— *Album* (selection). Au.
Liadow. *Album* (selection). Ha.
MacDowell. *Sea Pieces*. El.
—— *New England Idylls*. El.
Moy. *Moonbeams*. Cu.
—— *Caprice*. Sc.
Niemann. *Porcelain*. Pe.
—— *Pickwick*. Si.
—— *Hamburg*. Pe.
Palmgren. *Night in May*. Au.
—— *Prelude-Nocturne*. Ch.
—— *Album*. Ch.
Quilter. *Four Country Pieces*. Ha.
Rowley. *The Sea*. As.
—— *Seven Preludes*. Au.
—— *The Aquarium*. Sc.
Schutte. *Carnival Mignon*. Le.
—— *Vignettes*. Le.
—— *Souvenirs de Jeunnesse* (two books). Le.
Scott. *Two Pierrot Pieces* (separate). Bo.
—— *Lotusland*. El.
—— *Water Wagtail*. El.
—— *Handelian Rhapsody*. El.
—— *Poems*. Sc.
—— *Suite*. Sc.
Scriabin. *Album* (selection). Ha.
Sjogren. *Erotikon*. Hai.
Stojowski. *Album* (selection). Sc.
—— *Romantic Pieces*. Pe.
—— *Chant d'Amour*. Pe.
Williams. *Pot-Pourri*. Nov.
Wright. *Fantasy Pictures from a Pantomime*. Ha.
York Bowen. *Three Suites*. An.
—— *Nocturne*. O.U.P.
—— *Caprice* (2). Ri.
—— *Mood Phases*. O.U.P.

## SECTION (vi): VARIATIONS (all grades)

Bach. *Goldberg Variations.* Pe.
Beethoven. *Several Sets.* B.H.; Pe.
Brahms. *Handel Variations.* Au. & Nov.
Farjeon. *Variations in A.* Au.
Grieg. *Ballad.* Pe.
Glazounov. *Variations in F sharp minor.* Ha.
Haydn. *Variations in F minor.* Au.
Liadov. *Variations on a Theme of Glinka.* Ha.
Medtner. *Second Improvisation.* Z.
Mendelssohn, Op. 54. *Variations Serieuses.* Au. & Nov.
Mozart. *Variations in A and F.* Au. & Nov.
Paderewski, Op. 11. *Theme and Variations.* As.
Reger, Op. 81. *Variations on a Theme of Bach.* Bot.
Schumann. *Etudes Symphoniques.* Au. & Nov.
Schutte. *Figurante de Petite Variations.* Le.

## SECTION (vii): MODERN SONATINAS
### (in order of difficulty)

Rowley. *Four Sonatinas.* Pe.
Farjeon. *Miniature Sonata.* Au.
Poldowski. *Sonatine.* Ch.
Koechlin. *Cinq Sonatinas* (separately). Ch.
Niemann. *Sonatina Giocosa.* Si.
York Bowen. *Short Sonata.* Sw.
Ravel. *Sonatine.* Du.

## SECTION (viii): SONATAS (before 1914)
### (in order of difficulty)

Grieg. *Sonata in E minor.* Pe.
MacDowell. *Four Sonatas.* El.
Scott. *Sonata.* El.
Glazounov. *First and Second Sonatas.* Ha.
McEwen. *Sonata in E minor.* Nov.
Dale. *Sonata in D minor.* Nov.

## SECTION (ix): SONATAS (modern—in order of modernity)

Palmgren. *Sonata.* Au.
York Bowen. *Sonata.* Sw.
Jongen. *Suite en forme de Sonate.* Ch.
Ireland. *Sonata.* Au.
Bridge. *Sonata.* Au.
Bax. *Two Sonatas.* Mu.
Tansman. *Sonate, No. 2.* Sc.
Kadosa. *Sonata, No. 2.* Sc.
Schulhoff. *Sonata, No. 2.* Ch.
Wiener. *Sonatas (3).* Sc.
Scriabine. *Sonatas (10).* Ch.
Sessions. *Sonata.* Sc.
Sorabji. *Two Sonatas.* Cu.

## SECTION (x): COLLECTIONS (various)

*Album Russe,* 2 vols. Le.
*Berner's Edition of Graded Pieces* (various, separately). Wi.
*Gradations* (E—ME—MD—D) (separately). Pe.
*Graded Classics,* six books (preparatory to Higher Intermediate). As.
*Graded Series* (VE—E—ME—MD). Sc.
*New Piano Book* (E—ME—MD), modern works, three books. Sc.
*Rediscovered Classics* (six books). Ha.
*Scandinavian Masters* (two books). Au.
*Twenty-Four Lyric Sketches* (Elementary—Junior—Intermediate). Ro.

## SECTION (xi): SIGHT READING

Borland. *Pianoforte Sight-Reading Practice* (three parts). Hamm.
Gray. *Come and Play.* Bo.
Greenfield. *Graded Sight Readers* (three vols.). Wi.

Lee. *Graded Sight Tests* (three books). Le.
Moy. *Sight Reading Pieces* (E—M—D) (three books). Cr.
Raymond. *Graded Sight Reader* (four vols.). We.
Rook. *Graded Sight Reader* (four vols.). As.
Scott. *Graded Sight Reader* (two vols.). We.
Somervell. *Sight Reading* (six books) (VE to D). Sw.
Wallace. *Graded Sight Reader* (three vols.). W.P.

## SECTION (xii): TIME EXERCISES

Whittaker. *Graded Time Exercises*, for pianoforte students, with French tune names. Cu.

## SECTION (xiii): LEFT-HAND WORKS
### (one hand only, in order of difficulty)

Driver. *Left-hand Pieces*. Bo.
Rowley. *Colla Sinistra*. Ha.
Swinstead. *Six Studies*. Ha.
Germer. *Twenty-five Studies*. Hu.
Bridge. *Improvisations*. Ha.

## SECTION (xiv): DUETS
### GRADE I

Carse. *A little Concert* (two books). Au.
—— *The Path of Progress* (Book 1). Le.

### GRADE II

Carse. *Progressive Duets* (Book 1). Au.
Diller and Quaile. *Green and Blue Duet Albums*. Ha.
—— —— *First and Second Duet Books*. Ha.

### GRADE III

Carse. *Progressive Duets* (Book 2). Au.
—— *Sight Reading Duets* (Books 1 and 2). Au.
Lee. *Alice in Wonderland*. O.U.P.

## GRADE IV

Campbell. *Hornpipe.* Pa.
Carse. *Progressive Duets* (Book 3). Au.
—— *Sight Reading Duets* (Book 3). Au.
Gretchaninov, Op. 99. *Im Grünen.* Sc.
Lee. *Diversions.* Le.
Moy. *Four Scenes.* O.U.P.
O'Neill. *All Fours.* O.U.P.
Rowley. *The Child Heart* (two books). As.
—— *Divergencies.* As.

## GRADE V

Brahms, Op. 39. *Waltzes.* Le.
Dunhill. *Pastime and Good Company* (two books). O.U.P.
Farjeon. *On the Water.* Pa.
Inghelbrecht. *La Nursery* (four books). Ch.
Moszkowski, Op. 96. *Master and Pupil.* En.
Schutt, Op. 54. *Waltz Märchen.* Le.
Shaw. *Six Sea Songs.* Nov.
Shaw (Geoffrey). *Six Traditional Melodies.* Nov.
Thompson. *Four Duets* (separate). O.U.P.
*Lyric Series Graded Duets* (separate) (E to MD). Ha.

## GRADES VI AND VII

Arensky. *Six Pièces Enfantines.* Au.
Dvořák. *Slavonic Dances.* Le.
—— *The Bohemian Forest.* Le.
Grieg, Op. 14. *Two Symphonic Pieces.* Pe.
—— Op. 37. *Valse Caprices.* Pe.
—— Op. 35. *Norwegian Dances.* Pe.
Hahn. *Berceuses.* He.
Jensen, Op. 46. *Welling Music.* Bos.
—— Op. 62. *Silhouetten.* Bos.
—— Op. 59. *Abendmusik.* Pe.
Koechlin. *Quatre Sonatines Françaises.* O.U.P.
Ladnurault. *Lullaby.* O.U.P.
Moszkowski. *Twelve Spanish Dances.* Pe.

Moszkowski, Op. 81. *Six Pièces.* Sc.
—— *Valses.* Au.
—— Op. 2. *Menuet.* Au.
—— *From Foreign Parts.* Au.
Raff. *Tarantella.* Au.
Schmitt. *Sept Pièces.* Le.
—— *Feuillets de Voyage.* Du.
—— *Huit Courtes Pièces.* He.
Schubert, Op. 51. *Trois Marches Militaires.* Nov.
York Bowen. *Two Suites.* St.

## SECTION (xv): WORKS FOR TWO PIANOFORTES

Original compositions for two pianofortes (four hands), all moderately difficult to difficult, have been written by the following composers:

A. Arensky, M. Asantschewsky, L. Aubert, J. S. Bach, A. Bax, P. Bazelaire, M. Bonis, J. Brahms, A. Bush, F. Busoni, F. Chopin, M. Clementi, A. Coedes-Mongin, F. Couperin, C. Cui, C. Debussy, N. Demuth, R. Gliere, H. Gnessin, B. Godard, T. Gouvy, P. A. Grainger, A. de Greef, A. Gretchaninow, E. Grieg, R. Hahn, T. Harsanyi, B. Haynes, E. B. Hill, H. Hodge, E. Horne, M. Infante, S. Jadassohn, T. Kirchner, Ch. Koechlin, Kronke, L. D. Mannes, G. Martucci, Melan-Gueroult, I. Moscheles, W. A. Mozart, L. Nicolaiew, S. Palmgren, E. Parlow, I. Philipp, Ed. Poldini, S. Rachmaninow, M. Reger, C. Reinecke, J. G. Ropartz, C. Saint-Saëns, F. C. Schmitt, R. Schumann, L. Schytte, A. Simon, C. Singing, A. Somervell, G. Taille-ferre, L. Vuillemin, B. Williams, and A. Winkler.

## APPENDIX E

# LIST OF BOOKS ON MUSIC

### Classified under the following headings

1. Teaching Methods.
2. Infants' and Junior Training.
3. Voice Training for Choirs.
4. Ear Training and Musical Appreciation.
5. Melody and Harmony.
6. Counterpoint.
7. Composition.
8. Musical Form and Analysis.
9. Rudiments.
10. Vocal Sight Reading.
11. History of Music and Musicians.
12. Dictionaries and Encyclopaedias.
13. Pianoforte.
14. Stringed Instruments.
15. Learning Instruments in Class.
16. Orchestra.
17. Conducting.
18. General.
19. Music through Movement.
20. Mechanically reproduced Music.

### 1. TEACHING METHODS

*Class Singing*, by W. G. Whittaker. 6s. O.U.P.

*Compleat Teacher, The*, by Arthur Somervell. In four books. Teachers' edition. 2s. 6d. net each. Bo.

*How to Teach Class Singing*, by Granville Humphreys. 3s. 6d. net. Re.

*First School Music Course for Secondary Schools*, by W. J. Gibbs. 6s. C.U.P.

*Music in Manchester Schools*, by Walter Carroll. 1s. M.E.C.

*Language of Music, The*, by E. Stanley Roper and J. Wickham Hurd. 5s. O.U.P.

*Making of Musicians, The*, by T. H. Yorke Trotter. 3s. 6d. net. J.

*Memorising Music*, by Gerald Cumberland. 6s. Ric.

*Music and Boyhood—Music in Public and other Schools*, by Thomas Wood. 3s. 6d. O.U.P.

*Music Class, The,* by Herbert Wiseman and J. Wishart.
2*s.* 6*d.* Ker.
*Music for All,* by Cyril Winn. 6*d.* Rou.
*Music for Children,* by Muriel Storr. 6*s.* S.J.
*Music for School and Home,* by J. T. Bavin. 2*s.* net. Bi.
*Music of Life,* by Charles T. Smith. For Senior Classes and
Modern Schools. 4*s.* King.
*Music Teacher's Part in a General Education Scheme, The,* by
Stewart Macpherson. 4*d.* net. Wi.
*Music throughout the Secondary School,* by Margaret Donington.
2*s.* 6*d.* O.U.P.
*Musical Education of the Child, The,* by Stewart Macpherson.
3*s.* 6*d.* Wi.
*Musical Foundations,* by John E. Borland. 3*s.* 6*d.* O.U.P.
*Psychology applied to Music Teaching,* by Mrs Spencer Curwen.
10*s.* 6*d.* Cu.
*Public Schools and their Music,* by A. H. Peppin. 5*s.* 6*d.* net.
O.U.P.
*Report on the Experimental Course in Music at the Mary Datchelor
School, Camberwell.* 4*d.* net. H.M.S.
*School Teacher's Music Guide, The,* by L. C. Venables. 6*s.* net.
Cu.
*Shorthand for Musical Dictation,* by Arthur Somervell. 6*d.*
Cu.
*Singing-Class Teacher, The,* by F. C. Field-Hyde. 5*s.* 6*d.* Wi.
*Standard Course, The,* by John Curwen. 7*s.* 6*d.* net. Cu.
*Successful Music Teacher, The,* by Herbert Antcliffe. 1*s.* 6*d.*
Au.
*Teacher's Manual, The,* by John Curwen. 15*s.* net. Cu.
*Teaching of Music, The,* by R. T. White. 4*s.* Co.

### Courses for Pupils

*Compleat Teacher, The,* by Arthur Somervell. Pupils' edition
(exercises only). 3*d.* each. Bo.
*Good Musician, The,* by James Easson, R. C. McCrone, and
Mabel Chamberlain. A pupil's course leading to Matriculation. Three books (others in course of preparation).
1*s.,* 1*s.,* 1*s.* 3*d.* Nov.

## 2. Infants' and Junior Training

*Action Songs and Singing Games*, by F. H. Bisset. 6d. P.P.

*Dulcimer Stories*, by Louie E. de Rusette. 2s. 6d. net. Cu.

*Ear Training*, see section under this heading for *Infants and Junior Children*.

*Making of Instruments: Creative Music*, by Satis N. Coleman. 17s. 6d. Pu.

> *Pipers' Guild Handbook, The*, by Margaret James. 2s. Cr.
>
> *Shepherds' Pipes and Tunes for them*, by E. M. G. Liddell. 3s. net. Y.B.P.

*Music in the Kindergarten and Lower Forms*, by Lilian E. Bucke. 5s. net. Wi.

*Music in the Nursery School*, by Lilian E. Bucke. 3s. 6d. net. Wi.

*Playways in Musical Training*, by Mrs Murray MacBain. 3s. 6d. Ev.

*Percussion Bands: Children's Band, The*, by Louie E. de Rusette. 2s. 6d. net. Cu.

> *Children's Percussion Bands*, by Louie E. de Rusette. 3s. 6d. net. Keg.
>
> *Music for Percussion Bands*, published by Curwen, Boosey and Hawkes, Novello, Joseph Williams.

*School Band-Book, The*, by Stephen S. Moore. 3s. 6d. Ne.

*Physical Exercises, Dances and Games in the Infant School*, by Margaret Hughes. 4s. 6d. Nov.

*Vocal Sight Reading*, see section under this heading for *Infants and Junior Children*.

*Voice Training*, see section under *Voice Training for Choirs*, (a) *For Children's Choirs*.

## 3. Voice Training for Choirs

(a) *For Children's Choirs*:

*Art of Training Choir Boys, The*, by G. C. Martin. 3s. Nov.

*Boys' Choirs*, by Sydney H. Nicholson. 6d. P.P.

*Choir-Boy in the Making, The*, by Charles H. Moody. 2s. 6d. O.U.P.

*How to train Children's Voices*, by T. Maskell Hardy. 2s. Cu.

*School Choir Training*, by Margaret Nicholls. 3s. Nov.

*School Choirs*, by Herbert Wiseman. 1*s*. P.P.

*Song Teaching*, by Lucy M. Welch. 6*s*. net. Cu.

*Training of Children's Voices, The*, by Walter Carroll. 2*s*. 6*d*. Fo.

*Voice Culture for Children*, by James Bates. Complete, 5*s*. 6*d*.
Nov.

*Voice Training for Choirs and Schools*, by C. B. Rootham.
4*s*. 6*d*. C.U.P.

*Voice Training for Schools*, by L. C. Venables. 2*s*. 6*d*. Cu.

*Young Singers*, by James Bates. 1*s*. St.

See also list under *General Teaching Methods*.

(*b*)  *For Adult Choirs:*

*Amateur Choir Trainer, The* (Church Choirs), by Henry
Coleman. 3*s*. 6*d*. net. O.U.P.

*Choirs—Mixed Voice, Female Voice and Male Voice*, by Hugh S.
Roberton. 6*d*. P.P.

*Choral Technique and Interpretation*, by Henry Coward. 7*s*. 6*d*.
Nov.

*Five minutes daily exercises in Vocal Technique*, by J. M. Diack.
1*s*. 6*d*. P.P.

*Hints on Choir Training for Conductors and Choralists*, by W. G.
McNaught. 3*d*. Nov.

*Vocal Exercises in Tone Placing and Enunciation*, by J. M. Diack.
3*s*. 6*d*. P.P.

*Voice, The*, by W. A. Aikin. 10*s*. 6*d*. net. Lo.

*Voice Placing and Training Exercises*, by George Dodds. 2*s*. 6*d*.
O.U.P.

*Voice Training*, by W. S. Drew. 3*s*. 6*d*. O.U.P.

(*c*)  *Interpretation:*

*Interpretation in Song*, by H. Plunket Greene. 7*s*. 6*d*. Mac.

*Madrigal Singing*, by Charles Kennedy Scott. 7*s*. 6*d*. O.U.P.

*Song-Interpretation*, by W. S. Drew. 3*s*. 6*d*. O.U.P.

4.  EAR TRAINING AND MUSICAL APPRECIATION

(*a*)  *Infants and Junior Children:*

*Aural Culture*, Book I, by Stewart Macpherson and Ernest
Read. 5*s*. Wi.

*Ear Training, including Musical Appreciation and Rhythmic Movements*, by Mabel Chamberlain. 6*s*. Nov.

(*b*) *General:*

*Appreciation Class, The,* by Stewart Macpherson and Ernest Read. 5*s*. Wi.

*Aural Culture,* by Stewart Macpherson and Ernest Read. In 3 parts. 5*s*. and 7*s*. Wi.

*Ear Training and Musical Dictation,* by E. Home. 2*s*. Keg.

*Foundations of Practical Ear Training,* by Annie Lawton. In 2 vols. 4*s*. 6*d*. net. and 2*s*. net. O.U.P.

*Improvising,* by E. Home. 2*s*. Keg.

*Listener's Guide to Music,* by Percy Scholes. 3*s*. 6*d*. O.U.P.

*Music and its Appreciation,* by Stewart Macpherson. 5*s*. Wi.

*Musical Appreciation,* by E. Home. 2*s*. Bo.

*Musical Appreciation, Elements of,* by W. G. Foxell. 3*s*. 6*d*. Nov.

*Musical Appreciation, First Lessons in,* by Thomas R. Mayne. 2*s*. 6*d*. De.

*Musical Appreciation in the Schools (Why and How?),* by Percy Scholes. 1*s*. 6*d*. O.U.P.

*Musical Dictation,* by Frederic Ritter. In 2 parts. 1*s*. 6*d*. and 3*s*. Nov.

*Musical Groundwork,* by F. H. Shera. 3*s*. 6*d*. net. O.U.P.

*Specimen Aural Tests,* by Janet Salsbury. 1*s*. 6*d*. net. We.

## 5. MELODY AND HARMONY

*Beginner's Guide to Harmony, The,* by Percy A. Scholes. 2*s*. 6*d*. net. O.U.P.

*Composition of Simple Melodies,* by Robert T. White. 2*s*. 6*d*. Nov.

*Ear, Eye and Hand in Harmony Study,* by Ernest Fowles. 5*s*. net. O.U.P.

*Elementary Harmony,* by C. H. Kitson. In 3 vols. 3*s*. 6*d*. net each. O.U.P.

*Evolution of Harmony,* by C. H. Kitson. 10*s*. 6*d*. O.U.P.

*First Steps in Harmonizing Melodies,* by Ethel Home. 2*s*. 6*d*. O.U.P.

*Five-part Harmony*, by F. E. Gladstone. 3*s.* Nov.

*Foundations of Practical Harmony and Counterpoint*, by R. O. Morris. 7*s.* 6*d.* Mac.

*Harmonising Melodies*, by Cuthbert Harris. In 3 books. 2*s.* 6*d.*, 2*s.* 6*d.* and 8*d.* Nov.

*Harmony for Beginners, Contrapuntal*, by C. H. Kitson. 3*s.* 6*d.* net. O.U.P.

*Harmony for Schools*, by F. E. Gladstone. 4*s.* Key 2*s.* 6*d.* Nov.

*Harmony Chart*, by Arthur Somervell. 1*s.* Cla.

*Harmony in Pianoforte Study*, by Ernest Fowles. In 2 vols. 4*s.* net and 10*s.* 6*d.* net. Cu.

*Melody and Harmony*, by Stewart Macpherson. 12*s.* 6*d.* Wi.

*Melody Making, First Steps in*, by Ernest Read. 1*s.* 6*d.* net. Wi.

*Method of Teaching Harmony, A*, by F. G. Shinn. In 2 parts. 6*s.* and 7*s.* 6*d.* Au.

*Modulation*, by James Higgs. 3*s.* Nov.

*Part-Writing for Beginners*, by J. W. Ivimey. 8*d.* Nov.

*Primer of Harmony*, by John B. McEwen. 2*s.* Ri.

*Student's Harmony, The*, by Orlando Mansfield. 6*s.* net. We.

*Unfigured Harmony*, by Percy Buck. 7*s.* 6*d.* net. O.U.P.

## 6. COUNTERPOINT

*Art of Counterpoint*, by C. H. Kitson. 7*s.* 6*d.* net. O.U.P.

*Contrapuntal Technique*, by R. O. Morris. 8*s.* 6*d.* O.U.P.

*Counterpoint*, by J. F. Bridge. 3*s.* Nov.

*Counterpoint*, by F. E. Gladstone. Part I, 3*s.*; Part II, 2*s.* 6*d.* Nov.

*Counterpoint Chart*, by Arthur Somervell. 1*s.* Cla.

*Counterpoint for Beginners*, by C. H. Kitson. 4*s.* 6*d.* net. O.U.P.

*Rules of Counterpoint*, by W. S. Rockstro. 3*s.* Au.

See also book by R. O. Morris under *Melody and Harmony*.

## 7. COMPOSITION

*Composition*, by J. Stainer. 3*s.* Nov.

*First Steps in Musical Composition*, by J. B. McEwen. 4*s.* Au.

*Modern Musical Composition*, by F. Corder. 10*s.* 6*d.* Cu.

*Musical Composition*, by C. V. Stanford. 6s. net. Mac.
*Orchestra, and how to write for it, The*, by F. Corder. 15s. Cu.

## 8. MUSICAL FORM AND ANALYSIS

*Analysis of Form*, by H. A. Harding. 4s. 6d. Nov.
*Applied Forms*, by Ebenezer Prout. 7s. 6d. Au.
Bach: *Forty-eight Preludes and Fugues*, by Frederick Iliffe.
    4s. 6d. Nov.
Beethoven: *Beethoven's Sonatas*, by H. A. Harding. 3s. Nov.
    *Beethoven's Sonatas*, by Stewart Macpherson. 1s. 6d.–3s. 6d.
    each. Wi.
    *Beethoven's Pianoforte Sonatas*, by C. Egerton Lowe. 4s. Nov.
    *Beethoven's Pianoforte Sonatas*, by A. Forbes Milne. 2 vols.
    1s. 6d. each. O.U.P.
    *Beethoven's Sonatas, Analysis of*, by Janet Salsbury. 1s. 6d.
    net. We.
    *Beethoven's Symphonies*, by George Grove. 9s. Nov.
*Form in Pianoforte Music*, by C. Egerton Lowe. 2s. 6d. net.
    Hamm.
Mozart: *Analysis of Mozart's Sonatas*, by Janet Salsbury.
    2s. We.
    *Mozart and the Sonata Form*, by J. Raymond Tobin. 5s. Re.
    *Mozart's Sonatas*, by Stewart Macpherson. 2s. each. Wi.
*Musical Form*, by Ebenezer Prout. 7s. 6d. Au.
*Musical Forms*, by E. Pauer. 3s. Nov.
*Sonata Form*, by W. H. Hadow. 4s. Nov.

## 9. RUDIMENTS

*Academus Rudiments Primer*, by R. Barrett-Watson, J. L.
    M'Kinlay, and R. H. Thomson. Text Book, 4s.;
    Questions Book, 4s. O.U.P.
*Elements of Music, The*, by John B. McEwen. 2s. Ri.
*Elements of Staff Notation, The*, by Paul Edmonds. 5s. net. Pi.
*Handbook of Music for use in Training Colleges and Senior Schools*,
    by Winifred E. Houghton. 2s. 6d. The Secretary,
    117a Fordwych Road, London, N.W. 2.
*Rudiments of Music*, by C. H. Kitson. 2s. 6d. net. O.U.P.

*Rudiments of Music*, by Stewart Macpherson. 2s. 6d. and
   1s. 6d. Wi.
*Studies in Musical Graces*, by Ernest Fowles. 6s. Ro.
*Theory of Music*, by J. A. O'Neill. 1s. 6d. Nov.

## 10. VOCAL SIGHT READING

*Infants and Junior Children:*

\*_Elementary Sight-Singing Course_, by George Lane. In two
   parts. 8d. each. Nov.
\*_Eye Training in Music_ (Teacher's Book), by Mabel Chamber-
   lain. 2s. 6d. Nov.
   \*_My Music Book_ (Pupil's Book), by Mabel Chamberlain.
   8d. Nov.
*Junior Staff Sight Reader, The*, by Cuthbert Forster. 3d. net. Ba.
*Large-Type Sight Reader for Beginners*, by Walter Everitt.
   5d. Bo.
\*_Mental Effect—a Basis for Singing at Sight from either Notation_,
   by T. Maskell Hardy. 2s. 6d. net. Cu.
*Primary Staff Reader, The*, by Hugh Hunter. 2d. net. Ba.
\*_Staff Notation Sight Singing for Beginners_, by R. Dunstan and
   C. E. Bygott. In two books. 5d. each. S.S.

*General:*     (a) *Including Teaching Method*

*Dual-Notation Course, The*, by L. C. Venables. In four parts.
   Teacher's edition 2s. 6d. each. Pupil's edition 3d. each.
   Cu.
*Fifty Steps in Sight Singing* (both Notations), by Arthur
   Somervell. 2s. 6d. Cu.
*Folk Song Sight Singing Series*, edited by Edgar Crowe, Annie
   Lawton and W. G. Whittaker. In twelve graded books.
   6d. cloth; 4d. paper. O.U.P.
*School Sight-Singing Reader*, by W. G. McNaught. Nov.
   *Staff Notation*: Graded Course, Books 137 and 138, each in
   two parts: 4d. each part.
   *Tonic Sol-fa Notation*: Graded Course, Books 154 and 155,
   each in two parts: 4d. each part.

       * These include Teaching Method.

*Sight Singing through Song* (Staff Notation), by R. Dunstan. Graded Course in seven books (including Junior Course). 6*d.* to 8*d.* each. Pianoforte edition 2*s.* 9*d.* each. S.S.

*Singing at Sight,* by G. E. Linfoot. Teacher's Book, complete. 7*s.* Ho.

### (*b*) *Exercises only*

*Classical Sight Readers, The* (Staff Notation), by James Easson, R. C. McCrone and D. C. Walker. In five books. 4½*d.* and 5*d.* each. Mc.

*Compleat Teacher, The,* by Arthur Somervell. Four books. Pupil's edition. 3*d.* each. Bo.

*Descant Staff Sight Reader, The,* by Cuthbert Forster. 4*d.* net. Ba.

*Fluent Reader, The* (Staff Notation), by Tom Adamson and Jas. P. Edmond. In four books. 4*d.* to 6*d.* Ba.

*Master Melodies for Schools,* by Herbert Wiseman and John Wishart. In two books. 4*d.* net each. Ker.

*Melodies and Tests for Sight-Singing and Musical Dictation,* by F. C. Field-Hyde. Book I, Tonic Sol-fa and Book II, Staff Notation. Complete 4*s.* Wi.

*Practice in Staff Notation—Exercises from The Elements of Staff Notation,* by Paul Edmonds. 1*s.* Pi.

*Progressive Sight Tests,* Staff Notation, Unison (Book 332); Two- and Three-part (Book 334); Tonic Sol-fa Notation, Unison (Book 333); Two- and Three-part (Book 335). 6*d.* each book. Nov.

*Progressive Staff Reader, The,* by Hugh Hunter and D. C. Walker. In four books. 3*d.* to 4*d.* net each. Ba.

*Rapid Sight Reader, The,* by Arthur Somervell. In three books. 3*d.* each. Bo.

*Singing at Sight,* by G. E. Linfoot. In six parts. 4½*d.* each. Ho.

*Studies in Sight-Singing for Elementary Pupils* (Staff Notation), by Ernest Read. 2*s.* net. Wi.

*Two Hundred Tunes for Sight Singing* (Staff Notation), by C. S. Lang. 2*s.* 6*d.* net. Y.B.P.

*Adults (Mixed Voices):*

*Handbook for Choralists,* by Harvey Grace, with studies by
Edward G. Bairstow, Harold E. Darke, T. F. Dunhill,
Julius Harrison, Geoffrey Shaw. 1s. 6d. Supplement
1s. Nov.

## 11. HISTORY OF MUSIC AND MUSICIANS

### (a) For Young People:

*Books of the Great Musicians,* by Percy Scholes. Vols. I, II and
III, 4s. 6d. net each. O.U.P.

*Book of the Great Music,* by James Easson. 2s. 6d. net. O.U.P.

*Good Adventure,* by Elfrida Vipont, stories based on musical
facts. 6s. Hey.

*Music and its Makers,* by Janet Weakley. 3s. 6d. Har.

*Music and its Story,* by Robert T. White. 7s. 6d. net. C.U.P.

*Music Stories for Girls and Boys,* by Donzella Cross. 3s. 6d. net.
Gin.

*Music through the Ages,* by Maud V. Stell. 3s. 6d. De.

*Story-Lives of Great Composers,* by E. M. G. Reed. 3s. 6d. Ev.

*Youth's Own Book of Great Composers: Bach, Beethoven, Chopin,
Handel, Haydn, Mendelssohn, Mozart, Purcell, Schubert,
Schumann,* by Thomas Tapper and Gertrude Azulay.
6d. each. Bo.

### (b) General:

*Art of Music,* by C. H. H. Parry. 7s. 6d. Keg.

*Bach,* by C. H. H. Parry. 9s. Pu.

*Bach, J. S.,* by Philipp Spitta, translated by Clara Bell and
J. A. Fuller Maitland. 3 vols. 26s. 6d. Nov.

*Bach, The Historical Approach,* by C. Sanford Terry. 7s. 6d.
O.U.P.

*Bach's "Brandenburg" Concertos,* by J. A. Fuller Maitland.
1s. 6d. O.U.P.

*Bach's Orchestra,* by C. Sanford Terry. 21s. O.U.P.

*Bach: The Cantatas and Oratorios, The Mass in B minor, The
Passions,* by C. Sanford Terry. 1s. 6d. each. O.U.P.

*Fugitive Notes upon Some Cantatas and the Motets of J. S.
Bach,* by W. G. Whittaker. 12s. 6d. O.U.P.

*Origin of the Family of Bach Musicians*, by C. Sanford Terry. 12s. 6d. net. O.U.P.

*Beethoven*, by Paul Bekker. 10s. 6d. De.

*Beethoven*, by Harvey Grace. 7s. 6d. net. Keg.

*Beethoven*, by Romain Rolland. 4s. 6d. Keg.

*Beethoven and his Forerunners*, by D. G. Mason. 10s. Mac.

*Unconscious Beethoven, The*, by Ernest Newman. 10s. 6d. Par.

*Brahms*, by E. Markham Lee. 2s. 6d. net. Sam.

*Brahms*, by J. A. Fuller Maitland. 10s. 6d. Me.

*Brahms's Orchestral Works*, by E. Markham Lee. 1s. 6d. net. O.U.P.

*Busoni, Ferruccio, a Biography*, by Edward J. Dent. 21s. O.U.P.

Chamber Music: *Cyclopedic Survey of Chamber Music*, by W. Willson Cobbett. In two vols. £5. 5s. net. O.U.P.

*Chamber Music*, by Thomas Dunhill. 12s. 6d. Mac.

*Chamber Music, The Development of*, by Richard Walthew. 1s. Bo.

*Chopin*, by J. C. Hadden. 4s. 6d. De.

*Handbook to Chopin's Works, A*, by G. C. Ashton Jonson. 8s. 6d. Re.

*Concert-goer's Library of Descriptive Notes, The*, by Rosa Newmarch. Four vols. 3s. 6d. net each. O.U.P.

*Contemporary British Composers*, by J. Holbrooke. 15s. Pal.

*Contemporary Music, A Survey of*, by Cecil Gray. 7s. 6d. O.U.P.

*Debussy and Ravel*, by F. H. Shera. 1s. 6d. O.U.P.

*Delius*, by Philip Heseltine. 6s. Lan.

*Elgar*, by John F. Porte. 7s. 6d. Keg.

*English Madrigal*, by E. H. Fellowes. 3s. 6d. net. O.U.P.

*English Music*, by W. H. Hadow. 3s. 6d. net. Lo.

*French Music of To-day*, by Jean Aubry. 4s. 6d. Keg.

*French Music, Introduction to*, by Jean Aubry. 2s. 6d. Ch.

*Grieg to Brahms, From*, by D. G. Mason. 10s. Mac.

*Growth of Music*, by H. C. Colles. Three vols. 3s. 6d. each. O.U.P.

*Handel,* by Romain Rolland. 4*s.* 6*d.* Keg.

*George Frederick Handel,* by Newman Flower. 21*s.* Ca.

*Handel's Oratorio "The Messiah",* by Edward Bairstow.
  1*s.* 6*d.* net. O.U.P.

*Haydn,* by Michael Brenet. 6*s.* O.U.P.

*Joseph Haydn,* by D. G. A. Fox. 1*s.* 6*d.* net. O.U.P.

History. *Columbia History of Music through Ear and Eye,
  The,* by Percy Scholes. In course of publication. 1*s.* 6*d.*
  each book. O.U.P. See also *Mechanically reproduced
  Music.*

  *Growth of Music,* see above.

  *History of Music,* by Percy Buck. 6*d.* Ben.

  *History of Music,* by F. L. Ritter. 8*s.* 6*d.* Re.

  *History of Music,* by W. S. Rockstro. 2*s.* Au.

  *History of Music,* by C. V. Stanford and C. Forsyth.
    10*s.* 6*d.* Mac.

  *History of Music, Short,* by E. Home. 5*s.* We.

  *History of Music in England,* by Ernest Walker. 10*s.* 6*d.*
    O.U.P.

  *Listeners' History of Music,* by Percy Scholes. Three vols.
    6*s.* net each. O.U.P.

  *Miniature History of Music, A,* by Percy Scholes. 1*s.* 6*d.* net.
    O.U.P.

  *Music,* by Ursula Creighton. 7*s.* 6*d.* net. Cha.

  *Oxford History of Music, The,* edited by W. H. Hadow.
    Various writers. Vols. I and II, "The Polyphonic
    Period"; Vol. III, "The Seventeenth Century";
    Vol. IV, "The Age of Bach and Handel"; Vol. V,
    "The Viennese Period"; Vol. VI, "The Romantic
    Period". 17*s.* 6*d.* each. O.U.P.

*Summary of Musical History,* by C. H. H. Parry. 4*s.* 6*d.* Nov.

*Master Musicians,* by J. C. Hadden. 5*s.* Fou.

*Masters of Music,* by Sydney Grew. 6*s.* Fou.

*Modern Music, The Problems of,* by Adolf Weissman. 6*s.* De.

*Modern Music, Its Aims and Tendencies,* by Rollo Myers.
  2*s.* 6*d.* Keg.

*Modern Musicians,* by J. C. Hadden. 5*s.* Fou.

*Music and its Creators,* by Neville D'Esterre. 6*s.* A.U.

*Musical Instruments and their Music, 1500–1750,* by Gerald R. Hayes. Vol. I, 4s. 6d., Vol. II, 10s. 6d. O.U.P.

*Musicians of Former Days, Some,* by Romain Rolland. 4s. 6d. Keg.

*Musicians of To-Day,* by Romain Rolland. 4s. 6d. Keg.

*Moussorgsky—The Russian Nationalist,* by M. Calvocoressi, translated by A. Eaglefield Hull. 4s. 6d. Keg.

Mozart. *Life of Mozart,* by Edward Holmes. 2s. De.

 *Mozart—The Story of his Life as Man and Artist,* by Victor Wilder, translated by Franz Liebich. 5s. Re.

 *Mozart's Operas,* by Edward J. Dent. 12s. 6d. Cha.

*New Music, The,* by George Dyson. 8s. 6d. O.U.P.

Opera. *A Miniature History of Opera,* by Percy Scholes. 1s. 6d. net. O.U.P.

 *Opera, The,* by R. A. Streatfeild. 8s. 6d. Keg.

 *Stories from the Operas and More Stories from the Operas,* by Gladys Davidson. 8s. 6d. net each. Wer.

 *Sullivan's Comic Opera,* by Thomas F. Dunhill. 10s. 6d. net. Ar.

 *Thousand and One Nights of Opera, A,* by Frederick H. Martens. 10s. 6d. Ap.

 *Wagner and the Reform of the Opera,* by Edward Dannreuther. 6s. Au.

*Plainsong,* by T. Helmore. 4s. 6d. Nov.

*Progress of Music, The,* by George Dyson. 5s. net. O.U.P.

Purcell. *Henry Purcell,* by Dennis Arundell. 3s. 6d. net. O.U.P.

 *Henry Purcell,* by W. Cummings. 2s. 6d. Sam.

*Ravel,* see Debussy and Ravel.

*Russian Music, History of,* by Montagu Nathan. 7s. 6d. Re.

*Scarlatti, Alessandro—His Life and Works,* by Edward J. Dent. 12s. 6d. Ar.

Schubert. *Schubert's Songs,* by Richard Capell. 15s. net. Ben.

 *The Symphonies,* by A. Brent-Smith. 1s. 6d. net. O.U.P.

Schumann. *Robert Schumann,* by Frederick Niecks. 10s. 6d. De.

 *Schumann,* by A. Patterson. 4s. 6d. De.

*Schönberg, Arnold*, by Egon Wellesz, translated by W. H. Kerridge. 6s. net. De.

*Scriabin, A Great Russian Tone Poet*, by A. Eaglefield Hull. 4s. 6d. Keg.

*Shakespearean Music in the Plays and Early Operas*, by J. F. Bridge. 10s. 6d. De.

*Short Lives of Musicians*, edited by H. J. Taylor. 4d. each. We.

*Story-Lives of Master Musicians*, by Harriette Brower. 7s. 6d. Har.

*Studies of Great Composers*, by C. H. H. Parry. 3s. 6d. Rou.

*Studies in Modern Music*, by W. H. Hadow. Two vols. 8s. 6d. each. See.

*Tchaikovsky*, by Edwin Evans. 4s. 6d. De.

*Tchaikovsky, Orchestral Works*, by Eric Blom. 1s. 6d. O.U.P.

*Twelve Good Musicians, from John Bull to Henry Purcell*, by F. Bridge. 5s. Keg.

*Vaughan-Williams, An Introduction to the Music of*, by A. E. F. Dickinson. 1s. 6d. O.U.P.

Wagner. *Wagner as Man and Artist*, by Ernest Newman. 12s. 6d. Lan.

*Wagner*, by Ernest Newman. 3s. 6d. Lan.

*The Musical Design of "The Ring"*, by A. E. F. Dickinson. 1s. 6d. O.U.P.

## 12. DICTIONARIES AND ENCYCLOPAEDIAS

*Cyclopaedic Dictionary of Music*, by Ralph Dunstan. 25s. Cu.

*Dictionary of Modern Music and Musicians*, edited by A. Eaglefield Hull. 35s. De.

*Dictionary of Musical Terms*, by Edmondstoune Duncan. 5s. Ro.

*Dictionary of Musical Terms*, by Arthur Greenish. 3s. 6d. Wi.

*Dictionary of Musical Terms*, by John Stainer and W. A. Barrett. 11s. 6d. and 2s. 6d. (abbreviated). Nov.

*Dictionary of Musicians*, edited by Edmondstoune Duncan. 3s. 6d. Re.

*Dictionary of Musicians*, by William Cummings. 3s. Nov.

*Dictionary of the Tonic Sol-fa System*, by W. R. Phillips. 2s. 6d. Nov.

*Grove's Dictionary of Music and Musicians,* edited by H. C. Colles. In 5 vols. 25*s*. each. Mac.

*New Encyclopedia of Music and Musicians, The,* edited by Waldo Selden Pratt. 12*s*. 6*d*. net. Mac.

## 13. PIANOFORTE

*Act of Touch in all its Diversity, The,* by Tobias Matthay. 10*s*. 6*d*. Lo.

Analysis of works by Bach, Beethoven, and Mozart, see *Musical Form and Analysis.*

*Art of Pianoforte Practising, The,* by C. Egerton Lowe. 2*s*. Nov.

*Centre Points in Pianoforte Study,* by Ernest Fowles. 4*s*. Cu.

*Dictionary of Pianists and Composers for the Pianoforte, A,* by E. Pauer. 3*s*. Nov.

*Hand Gymnastics,* by T. R. Prentice. 2*s*. 6*d*. Nov.

*Happy Pianist, The,* by Enid Grundy. 2*s*. 6*d*. net. O.U.P.

*History of the Pianoforte,* by A. J. Hipkins. 4*s*. Nov.

*History of Pianoforte Music, The,* by H. Westerby. 12*s*. 6*d*. Keg.

*Modern Pianoforte Technique,* by Sydney Vantyn. 2*s*. 6*d*. Keg.

*On Memorising,* by Tobias Matthay. 2*s*. net. O.U.P.

*Pianoforte, The,* by Frederick Dawson. 6*d*. P.P.

*Pianoforte Accompaniment,* by W. Hickin. 4*s*. Nov.

*Pianoforte Fingering,* by Thomas Knott. 2*s*. 6*d*. net. O.U.P.

*Pianoforte Technique, An Epitome of the Laws of,* by Tobias Matthay. 3*s*. 6*d*. net. O.U.P.

*Rubato, or The Secret of Expression,* by J. Alfred Johnstone. 3*s*. net. Wi.

*Science of Pianoforte Technique, The,* by Thomas Fielden. 8*s*. 6*d*. Mac.

*Teachers' Guide to the Curwen Pianoforte Method,* by Mrs Spencer Curwen. 7*s*. 6*d*. net. Cu.

*Viva Voce: 250 Questions and Answers for Pianoforte Diploma Candidates,* by C. Egerton Lowe. 2*s*. net. Hamm.

## 14. STRINGED INSTRUMENTS

*Art of Violin Bowing, The,* by Paul Stoeving. 3*s*. 6*d*. Ro.

Chamber Music, see *History of Music and Musicians.*

*Encyclopaedia of the Violin, An,* by Alberto Bachmann. 21*s*. Ap.

*Handbook of Violoncello Playing*, by Carl Schroeder. 3*s*. Au.
*Hints to Young Violinists*, by C. Egerton Lowe. 1*s*. 6*d*. Nov.
*Modern Violin Technique*, by Frank Thistleton. 6*s*. Lo.
*Polychordia String Tutor*, by James Brown. In 12 sets. Teachers' parts 2*s*. 6*d*. each; Pupils' parts 6*d*. each. St.
*Viola, The*, by B. Tours. 3*s*. Nov.
*Violin, The*, by E. G. Knocker. 6*d*. P.P.
*Violin, The*, by B. Tours. 3*s*. Nov.
*Violin Playing as I teach it*, by Leopold Auer. 6*s*. Duc.

## 15. LEARNING INSTRUMENTS IN CLASS

Pianoforte: *Piano Class, The first six months in the*, by Florence Axtens. 1*s*. 6*d*. net. Bo.
*Piano Class Teaching*, by J. T. Bavin. 9*s*. 6*d*. Bo.
Strings: *String Instructor*, by J. T. Bavin. In two vols. 1*s*. 6*d*. each. O.U.P.
Wind: *Tutor and directions for organisation of classes*. Oliver Ditson Co. (U.S.A.).

## 16. ORCHESTRA

*Handbook of Orchestration, A*, by Florence Fidler. 4*s*. 6*d*. Keg.
*History of Orchestration*, by Adam Carse. 12*s*. 6*d*. Keg.
*Instrumentation*, by Ebenezer Prout. 3*s*. Nov.
*Instrumentation and Orchestration*, by Hector Berlioz. 11*s*. 6*d*. Nov.
*Instruments of the Orchestra*, by John E. Borland. 1*s*. 6*d*. Nov.
*Modern Instrumentation*, by John Fitzgerald. 3*s*. Wi.
*Orchestra, The*, by Ebenezer Prout. In 2 vols. 7*s*. 6*d*. each. Au.
*Orchestra and how to listen to it, The*, by Montagu-Nathan. 4*s*. 6*d*. Keg.
*Orchestral Technique, The*, by Gordon Jacob. 5*s*. O.U.P.
*Practical Hints on Orchestration*, by Adam Carse. 1*s*. 6*d*. Au.
*School Orchestra, The*, by Adam Carse. 4*s*. Wi.

### 17. CONDUCTING

*Choral Conducting for Women's Institutes*, by Henry Coleman. 1s. O.U.P.

*Conducting School Orchestras*, by Adam Carse. 1s. Au.

*Handbook of Conducting*, by Schercher, translated by M. Calvocoressi. O.U.P.

*Handbook on the Technique of Conducting*, by Adrian C. Boult. 3s. Re.

*Hints to Choral Conductors*, by W. G. Whittaker. 3d. British Federation of Musical Competition Festivals.

*On Conducting*, by Felix Weingartner, translated by Ernest Newman. 2s. 6d. B.H.

### 18. GENERAL

*Acoustics for Musicians*, by Percy Buck. 7s. 6d. net. O.U.P.

*Collected Essays*, by W. H. Hadow. 15s. net. O.U.P.

*Comparison of Poetry and Music*, by W. H. Hadow. 2s. 6d. O.U.P.

*Divisions of Music, The*, by Basil Maine. 2s. 6d. net. O.U.P.

*Foundations of Musical Aesthetics*, by John B. McEwen. 2s. 6d. Keg.

*General Index to Modern Musical Literature in the English Language*, by Eric Blom. 5s. net. Cu.

*Harmonics*, by C. Egerton Lowe. 1s. 6d. Nov.

*Heritage of Music, The*, essays collected and edited by Hubert Foss. 7s. 6d. net. O.U.P.

*Impressions that Remained*, Vols. I and II, by Ethel Smyth. 28s. and 6s. Lo.

*Living Music*, by Herbert Antcliffe. 5s. Wi.

*Margin of Music*, by Edwin Evans. 3s. 6d. O.U.P.

*Music*, by W. H. Hadow. 2s. 6d. W.N.

*Music and Character*, by Thomas Fielden. 6s. N.W.

*Music and Morals*, by H. R. Haweis. 6s. 6d. Lo.

*Music in Public Libraries*, by Lionel McColvin. 7s. 6d. Graf.

*Musical Critic's Holiday, A*, by Ernest Newman. 12s. 6d. Ca.

*Musical Criticism*, by M. Calvocoressi. 6s. 6d. O.U.P.

*Musical Pilgrim's Progress, A,* by J. D. M. Rorke. 4s. 6d.
  O.U.P.
*Musical Taste and how to form it,* by M. Calvocoressi. 2s. 6d.
  O.U.P.
*Musician at Large, A,* by Harvey Grace. 6s. net. O.U.P.
*Musicians and Mummers,* by Herman Klein. 21s. Ca.
*Old Cryes of London,* by J. F. Bridge. 7s. Nov.
*Orpheus,* by W. J. Turner. 2s. 6d. net. Keg.
*Our Favourite Musicians,* by Sydney Grew. 6s. Fou.
*Profession of Music and how to prepare for it, The,* by Annie
  Patterson. 5s. W.G.
*Scope of Music, The,* by Percy Buck. 6s. O.U.P.
*Spirit and Music,* by Ernest H. Hunt. 2s. 6d. Cu.
*Stepchildren of Music,* by Eric Blom. 6s. Fou.
*Style in Musical Art,* by C. H. H. Parry. 12s. 6d. Mac.
*Terpander,* by E. J. Dent. 2s. 6d. net. Keg.
*Up to Now,* by Martin Shaw. 7s. 6d. net. O.U.P.

### 19. Music through Movement

(a) *Infants and Junior Children:*

*Easy Rhythmic Dances for Junior Classes.* 1s. 6d. Nov.
*First Lessons in Rhythmic Movement,* by Winifred E. Houghton.
  4s. And two Supplements, 4s. each. L.S.D.E., 23 Store
  Street, London, W.C. 1.
*Practical Rhythmic Studies for Kindergarten and Junior Schools,* by
  Kathleen Mortimer and E. Gwynne Davies. 5s. net. Pi.
See also *Infants and Junior Children* sections under *Ear Training
  and Musical Appreciation,* and *Song Books.*

(b) *General:*

*Eurhythmics of Jaques-Dalcroze,* with Introduction by Sir M.
  Sadler. 3s. 6d. Co.
*Maypole Dances,* by W. Shaw. 2s. 6d. Cu.
*Music through Games,* by Lorna Stirling. 3s. 6d. net. Ev.
*Rhythm, Music and Education,* by Emile Jaques-Dalcroze,
  translated by Harold Rubenstein. 15s. Cha.
*Rhythmic Movement,* by Emile Jaques-Dalcroze. Vol. I,
  4s. 6d.; Vol. II, 6s. Nov.

## 20. MECHANICALLY REPRODUCED MUSIC

(a) *Gramophone:*

*Columbia History of Music through Ear and Eye,* by Percy Scholes, the musical illustrations being recorded. Vol. I, To the Opening of the Seventeenth Century; Vol. II, To the Death of Bach and Handel; Vol. III, To Beethoven. 28s. each album including text-book and eight records. Col.

*First Book of the Gramophone Record, The,* by Percy Scholes. 4s. 6d. O.U.P.

*Golden Treasury of Recorded Music,* by Alec Robertson. Vol. I, Bach to Beethoven; Vol. II, Wagner; Vol. III, César Franck. 1s. each. Gra.

*Learning to listen by means of the Gramophone,* by Percy Scholes. 3s. net. Gra.

*Music and the Gramophone,* by H. L. Wilson. 7s. 6d. A.U.

*Pathways to Music,* by J. T. Bavin. 2s. 6d. net. Ha.

*Practical Lesson Plans in Musical Appreciation by means of the Gramophone,* by Percy Scholes. 1s. net. O.U.P.

*Two Thousand Years of Music,* compiled and arranged by Dr Curt Sachs, translated by Mark Lubbock, 12 records in album. 36s. Parlo.

(b) *Player Piano:*

*Appreciation of Music, The* (Player Piano), by Percy Scholes. 5s. net. O.U.P.

*Appreciation of Music, The,* by Thomas W. Surette and Daniel Mason. Five vols. 8s. net each. Nov.

*Art of the Player-Piano, The,* by Sydney Grew. 12s. 6d. Keg.

*Player-Piano and its Music, The,* by Ernest Newman. 6s. Ric.

(c) *Wireless:*

*Everybody's Guide to Broadcast Music,* by Percy Scholes, 3s. 6d. net. O.U.P.

## APPENDIX F

# PERIODICALS ON MUSIC

1. *The Musical Times*, edited by Dr Harvey Grace assisted by William McNaught. Issued monthly, price 6*d*., annual subscription 7*s*. 6*d*. post free. Published by Novello & Co. *The Musical Times* was founded in 1844, with the sub-title "The Singing Class Circular", and at first it was devoted specially to the fostering of choral music. The journal now covers a wide field, although it still devotes special attention to choral singing. It includes articles on the aesthetic, historical, and practical sides of music; a comprehensive monthly review of new books and music, gramophone records, and player-piano rolls; notes on broadcasting; a Teachers' Department, in which appear technical and other articles, answers to correspondents, a précis of recent lectures; on the news side, sections devoted to church and organ music, competition festivals, London concerts, notes from the Provinces. *The Musical Times* has its own correspondents in various European centres, and in New York and Toronto.

2. *Musical Opinion and Music Trade Review*. Issued monthly, price 6*d*., annual subscription 7*s*. 6*d*. post free. Founded in 1877. It contains critical articles, reviews of new music and gramophone records, accounts of concerts and recitals in London, the Provinces, and abroad, reviews of activities in the world of amateur opera, and a special section devoted to the interests of organists.

3. *School Music Review*. Issued monthly up to May 1930 when it was withdrawn from publication, price 3*d*., annual volumes 7*s*. 6*d*. Published by Novello & Co. It was edited on its inception in 1892 by W. G. McNaught, and afterwards by William McNaught, and Mabel Chamberlain; it contained articles on all aspects of music teaching, and two or three songs in each number; some back numbers and volumes are still obtainable.

4. *The Music Teacher*, edited by H. S. Gordon. Issued monthly, price 1s., annual subscription 14s. Published by Evans Bros. *The Music Teacher* was founded in 1908 as *The Music Student*; in 1921 it incorporated *The Musician* and changed to its present title in 1922. It contains articles, notes, answers to questions, and reviews of interest to teachers of music.

5. *The Music Student* was first issued in 1915 under the title *Youth and Music*, later altered to *Music and Youth*, and in 1932 to its present title; 6d. monthly, annual subscription 7s. Published by Evans Bros. It contains articles, stories, pictures, and competitions of interest to the young student; it includes a supplement for very young people, originally issued separately until 1928 under the name of *Panpipes*.

6. *The Chesterian*, edited by G. Jean-Aubry. Founded in 1915 and issued eight times a year by J. and W. Chester Ltd. It gives special attention to contemporary music.

7. *The Musical Mirror and Fanfare*, edited by Ralph Hill. Issued monthly, price 6d., annual subscription 7s. 6d. It was founded in 1920 as *The Musical Mirror* and was reorganised in 1932 under its present title. It includes informative and critical articles on a wide range of musical subjects, gramophone notes, a survey of concerts and recitals, reviews of British and foreign music, and a service department for teachers and students.

8. The *Sackbut*, edited by Ursula Greville. Issued quarterly, price 2s. 6d., annual subscription 10s. 8d. post free. Published by Curwen. It was founded in 1920; and contains general articles, dealing largely with contemporary music, by foreign writers as well as British, and accounts of recitals and reviews of gramophone records.

9. *The Gramophone*, edited by Compton Mackenzie and Christopher Stone. Issued monthly, price 1s., annual subscription 14s. post free. Published by Gramophone (Publications) Limited. *The Gramophone* was founded in 1923, and contains, in addition to technical articles and others of general interest, regular reviews of all important gramophone recordings.

10. *British Musician,* edited by Sydney Grew. Issued monthly, price 6*d.*, annual subscription 7*s.* 6*d.* post free. It was founded in 1926, and incorporated *The Musical News* in 1929; it contains general articles on music and musicians, detailed analyses of important works, and critical reviews of gramophone records and player-piano rolls.

11. *The Music Lover,* edited by Edwin Evans assisted by Christian Darnton. Issued weekly, price 2*d.*, annual subscription 10*s.* Published by the British-Continental Press. It was founded in 1931, and contains articles of an informative and educational nature; special attention is given to amateur musicians. Useful weekly features are: a guide to musical events; lists of recommended books, musical plays, music, and musical films; and a news service.

### Music Periodicals Published
### in the United States

(*a*) *General.* The *Musical Quarterly* (founded 1915), published by G. Schirmer of New York; a scholarly periodical with contributions from leading music writers in Europe and America. *Pro Musica* published quarterly in New York; deals largely with modern music. *The New Music Review* (founded 1904) published by H. W. Gray Co. in New York; official journal of the American Guild of Organists. *Diapason* published monthly in Chicago; official journal of the National Association of Organists. *The Music Leader* (founded 1895) published weekly in Chicago. *The Musical Courier* (founded 1880) published by the Musical Courier Co., New York; a weekly musical newspaper. *Musical America* (founded 1898) published by Musical America Co., New York; a weekly musical newspaper. *The Musical Digest* (founded 1921) published monthly in New York; gives summaries of musical events throughout the world. *Musical West* (founded 1923) published in San Francisco; monthly journal dealing with Music and the Dance. *Disques* published monthly in Philadelphia by the R. Royer Smith Co.; deals principally with the gramophone.

*(b) Educational.*

1. *Partly*: *The Étude* (founded 1883) published by Theodore Presser Company, Philadelphia; contains articles of general and pedagogic interest, and musical compositions. *The Musician* (founded 1896) published monthly by Paul Kempe, New York; devoted to the educational interests of music. *Musical Observer* published monthly by the Musical Observer Co., New York. *Singing and Playing* published monthly by the Singing Magazine Co., New York.

2. *Wholly*: *Music Supervisors' Journal* published five times a year in Chicago by the Music Supervisors' National Conference of which it is the official organ; deals with music in the public (elementary) schools of America. *School Music* (founded 1900) edited and published five times a year by P. C. Hayden, Keokuk, Iowa; devoted entirely to the teaching of music in public (elementary) schools. *The School Musician* published monthly in Chicago; the official organ of the National School Band and Orchestra Association. *Music Clubs Magazine* published five times a year in New York; official organ of the National Federation of Music Clubs. *Jacobs' Orchestra Monthly* and *Jacobs' Band Monthly* published at Boston.

## APPENDIX G

## INSTRUMENTS, APPARATUS AND PICTORIAL ILLUSTRATIONS

*(a) Instruments:*

Percussion Instruments for school bands including dulcimers: Bo. & Cu., and W. H. Austin (Worcester) for the Worcestershire Association of Musical Societies.

Special Instruments for School Orchestras: the following supply suitable instruments, and maintain a regular service, providing teachers where required: Murdoch &

Murdoch (London), Rushworth & Dreaper (Liverpool), and Manby Violin School organised by the Metropolitan Academy of Music (London).

(*b*) *Apparatus*:

Crotchet Pointers, pair—stem-up and stem-down for use on blackboard staff: by Mabel Chamberlain. 1*s*. 3*d*. pair. Nov.

Metronomes: (i) table models, with and without bells for marking stressed beat: various prices: all music dealers.
(ii) pocket metronome: on principle of swinging pendulum. 1*s*. We.

Model Keyboards, etc., for Class Teaching of Pianoforte: by J. T. Bavin. Complete 9*s*. 6*d*. Bo.

Modulators, Tonic Sol-fa, by John Curwen, one column (coloured) 4*s*. Seven columns (black) 6*s*. 6*d*. Cu.
——, ——, ——, three columns. 2*s*. 6*d*. We.

(*c*) *Pictorial Illustrations*:

Instruments of the Orchestra by Sight, Sound, and Story: large coloured illustrations of orchestral instruments (musical sounds of the instruments given on two records). 15*s*. Gra.

Portraits of Musicians. Au and Bo.

## APPENDIX H

# ORGANISATIONS

### Which can give outside musical help, and the nature of the help given

1. *British Federation of Musical Competition Festivals* (incorporated, 1921): represents the majority of festivals in England, Scotland, and Northern Ireland and some in the colonies. The affiliated festivals control the Federation

through its Area Councils. The Federation gives advice, when asked, on all the phases of the festival movement: prints special mark sheets, annual series of choral sight-tests, and a *Year Book* (price 1*s*. 3*d*. post free): holds an Annual General Meeting and Conference in different parts of the country: is ready to arrange classes or schools for training conductors: finds conductors for groups: organises an annual Summer School of Chamber Music. Address: The Secretary, 22 Surrey Street, Victoria Embankment, London, W.C. 2.

2. *British Music Society*: founded in 1918 by Dr A. Eagle-field Hull for the furtherance of music: arranges recitals and lectures for schools affiliated to the Society: local branches organise concerts and recitals for members, and in some cases, special concerts for children: Headquarters avail themselves of opportunities to co-operate in musical affairs of international interest: a *Bulletin* is published periodically. Address: The Secretary, 295 Regent Street, London, W. 1.

3. *Carnegie Orchestral Loan Library*: administered by the British Federation of Musical Competition Festivals: for the use of amateur orchestras only. Particulars and catalogue from The Librarian, c/o The National Operatic and Dramatic Association, 85 Eccleston Square, London, S.W. 1.

4. *English Folk Dance Society*: founded in 1911 by Cecil Sharp, and directed by him until his death in 1924. The present Director is Mr Douglas Kennedy, who shares with Dr R. Vaughan Williams and Miss Maud Karpeles the general artistic direction of the Society. The object is to preserve English Folk Dances, Folk Music, and Singing Games, to make them known and to encourage the practice of them in their traditional forms. Cecil Sharp House, the headquarters, was opened in June 1930, and contains the administrative Offices, Library, Museum, and Halls for Dance Meetings, Concerts, Lectures, Performances and Courses of Instruction. Other activities are the publication of literature, including a Journal and News: Holiday Courses in different parts of the country: participation in Inter-national Folk Dance Festivals: and an annual All-England Festival in London. In addition to this central organisation,

there are Branch Societies with independent activities in the suburbs of London, in the Provinces, and in U.S.A. The Society is prepared to recommend courses of study, visiting teachers and adjudicators, instruction books and music, and to give general information concerning English Folk Music and Dance. Address: The Secretary, Cecil Sharp House, 2 Regent's Park Road, London, N.W. 1.

5. *Incorporated Society of Musicians*: established 1882: incorporated 1892: reconstituted 1928: "the main objects of the Society are—The promotion of the Art of Music and the maintenance of the honour and interests of the musical profession". Admission to the Society is restricted to those solely engaged in the practice of music as a profession: all *bona fide* professional musicians are eligible for membership. Local centres are established in the principal towns of the British Isles. The Society includes the following Specialist Sections: Music Masters' Association Section, Music Mistresses' Section, Appointments Board administered by the M.M.A. Section and the Music Mistresses' Section, Solo Performers' Section, and Cinema Organists' Section. Address: The General Secretary, 19 Berners Street, London, W. 1.

6. *Hertfordshire Rural Music School*: formed in association with the Hertfordshire Rural Community Council: its aim is to further the revival of music in English country life by providing a centre from which qualified teachers can reach the villages of the district, and to which village students and village organisations can go for advice and help in musical matters. Address: The Director, 109 Bancroft, Hitchin.

7. *League of Arts*: founded on the day the Great War ended (1918) to arrange music and pageantry for Peace Celebrations: its object is "to bring art and public life into contact": it provides free entertainments by distinguished artists in the Victoria and Albert Museum, and in Hyde Park (in the summer months): it runs a voluntary choir to which members are always welcomed. Address: The Secretary, 12 Berwick Street, London, S.W. 1.

8. *Music Teachers' Association*: founded in 1908 for the improvement of general musical culture: members have the

privilege of attending lectures, using the Reference Library, participating in an Insurance scheme, and of social intercourse with others engaged in similar work: membership is not confined to professional musicians. Address: The Acting Secretary, 295 Regent Street, London, W. 1.

9. *Musical Association, The*: founded in 1874 "For the Investigation and Discussion of Subjects connected with the Art, Science and History of Music": membership is available for "practical and theoretical musicians (professional or amateur) as well as those whose researches have been directed to the science of Acoustics, the history of the art, the construction of instruments, or other kindred subjects": periodical meetings are held, and the *Proceedings*, printed in full, are sent to members. Address: The Secretary, 48 Comeragh Road, West Kensington, London, W. 14.

10. *National Association of Boys' Clubs*: has for one of its main objects the establishment of musical and dramatic activities in Boys' Clubs: gives advice on syllabuses to centres desiring it, and recommends leaders and arranges training classes: Official organ *The Boy*, published quarterly. Address: The General Secretary, 27 Bedford Square, London, W.C. 1.

11. *National Council of Girls' Clubs*: encourages musical activities in its clubs both as a National body and through the Unions and Societies affiliated to it: arranges conferences at which the teaching of music is included as a subject: Festivals, competitions, lectures and concerts are arranged by a large number of its clubs, and some clubs have their own choirs and orchestras. Address: Organising Secretary, 3 Bloomsbury Place, London, W.C. 1.

12. *National Council of Social Service*: administers in conjunction with the National Federation of Women's Institutes a fund to help Music and Drama in the Villages from which grants may be made towards the cost of lectures, courses and short schools intended to help those who produce plays or conduct choral societies or orchestras in country districts. Address: The Secretary, Music and Drama Joint Committee, c/o The National Council of Social Service, 26 Bedford Square, London, W.C. 1.

13. *National Union of School Orchestras, The*: founded 1906 to give advice and aid in the formation and organisation of school orchestras, in order to promote the study and practice of stringed instrumental music along sound educational lines: to provide skilled instructors for classes: to supervise the work of orchestras by annual inspection: to hold conferences and annual festivals at the Crystal Palace: it has established a Violin School, and keeps a Violin Class Teachers' Panel. Address: The Hon. Secretary, St Bride Foundation Institute, Bride Lane, Fleet Street, London, E.C. 4.

14. *Royal Society of Teachers*: established by Parliament 1907, and constituted by Orders in Council 1912 and 1926. The statutory purpose of the Council of this Society is to form and keep a Register of Teachers, and it is the duty and privilege of all teachers (including music teachers) who meet the requirements laid down by the Council to register and thus maintain the standing of their profession. To obtain membership evidence must be furnished of (*a*) a good general education (not necessarily an examination success), (*b*) professional attainment and (*c*) training in teaching or teaching experience. In 1929 the King ordered that the whole body of Registered Teachers should be known as the Royal Society of Teachers, the members of which are now entitled to use the letters M.R.S.T. The list is alphabetical in order, thus expressing the unification of the teaching profession. The fee for registration is a single and final payment of three pounds which may be paid in instalments. Particulars and forms of application from The Secretary, 47 Bedford Square, London, W.C. 1.

15. *Scottish School Music Association*: its object is "to further the interests of musical education in schools and colleges in Scotland", and its members comprise professional musicians engaged in educational institutions recognised by the Scottish Education Department, and teachers qualified to teach music under the Department's regulations: it holds conferences and issues schemes of work: publishes a monthly page in *The Musical Times* copies of which are issued to members. Address: The Hon. Secretary, 142 Craiglea Drive, Edinburgh.

16. *Society of Women Musicians*: founded in 1911 to provide a centre for women musicians and to represent their interests: membership is open to women composers, executants (including performers, teachers, and conductors) and writers on music, and to amateurs: men musicians are also eligible for membership: the Society holds periodical meetings and arranges practices of vocal part music and chamber music: it also possesses the Cobbett Free Lending Library of British Chamber Music, scores from which may be borrowed by members of the public. Address: The Organising Secretary, 74 Grosvenor Street, London, W. 1.

17. *Tonic Sol-fa Association, The*: founded in 1853 to promote a practical knowledge of music, through ear-training and reading notation at sight. It arranges periodical lectures, recitals and discussions, and an Annual Festival at the Crystal Palace which includes a choral concert by a massed choir of children trained on the Tonic Sol-fa method. Address: The Secretary, 82 Ashgrove Road, Goodmayes, Essex.

17. *Workers' Educational Association, The*: founded in 1903: a federation of over 2000 Educational and Workers' Organisations: encourages the formation of classes for the education of adult workers both men and women, in a number of subjects, including music: publishes a periodical, *The Highway*, which deals with a wide range of subjects. For particulars of local branches apply to the General Secretary, 38*a* St George's Road, Victoria, London, S.W. 1.

# APPENDIX I

## SOCIETIES AND COMPANIES

Which publish educational gramophone records and player-piano rolls, and Music and Educational Publishers who have educational departments

1. *International Educational Society*: incorporated under the Board of Trade, 1927: founded in order that students could hear by gramophone the greatest thinkers and teachers

lecture on their own subjects. Lectures of special interest to music teachers include "The Progress of Music" (Dr George Dyson), "How to listen to Music" (Dr Percy Buck), "Great Composers" (Sir Henry Hadow), "The Art of Singing" (H. Plunket Greene), "Tchaikovsky and Chopin" (Dr Markham Lee). A wide range of subjects is covered in the series. The Society also organises a circulating library of gramophone records. The records can be obtained from any gramophone dealer, from the Columbia Graphophone Company, or from the offices of the Society. Address: The Secretary, 26 Buckingham Gate, Westminster, London, S.W. 1.

2. *Columbia Graphophone Company* and *The Gramophone Company* (*H.M.V.*) both publish records specially designed for educational purposes, and a combined educational department is available to give advice to teachers requiring it. Address: The Principal, The Gramophone and Radio in Education, Central Educational Offices, 98 Clerkenwell Road, London, E.C. 1.

3. *Aeolian Company* publish a wide range of player-piano ("Duo-Art" "Pianola") rolls specially designed for educational purposes, edited by Percy A. Scholes, and written by a number of distinguished musicians. Rolls may be purchased through any music dealer. A circulating library is available.

4. Certain music publishers maintain special educational departments which will give advice to teachers on application. These include amongst others: Messrs Augener Ltd., 18 Great Marlborough Street, London, W. 1; Messrs Boosey & Hawkes, Ltd., 295 Regent Street, London, W. 1; Messrs J. B. Cramer & Co., Ltd., 139 New Bond Street, London, W. 1; Messrs J. Curwen & Sons, Ltd., 24 Berners Street, London, W. 1; Messrs Evans Bros., Ltd., Montague House, Russell Square, London, W.C. 1; Messrs Novello & Co., Ltd., 160 Wardour Street, London, W. 1; Oxford University Press, 36 Soho Square, London, W. 1; Messrs A. Weeks & Co., 14 Hanover Street, London, W. 1.

For EU product safety concerns, contact us at Calle de José Abascal, 56–1°,
28003 Madrid, Spain or eugpsr@cambridge.org.

www.ingramcontent.com/pod-product-compliance
Ingram Content Group UK Ltd.
Pitfield, Milton Keynes, MK11 3LW, UK
UKHW020451240426
470322UK00016B/290